Production in the Innovation Economy

Production in the Innovation Economy

Edited by Richard M. Locke and Rachel L. Wellhausen

The MIT Press
Cambridge, Massachusetts
London, England

MIT Press books may be purchased at special quantity discounts for business or sales promotional use. For information, please email special_sales@mitpress.mit.edu.

This book was set in PalatinoLTStd by Toppan Best-set Premedia Limited, Hong Kong. Printed and bound in the United States of America.

Library of Congress Cataloging-in-Publication Data

Production in the innovation economy / edited by Richard M. Locke and Rachel L. Wellhausen.
    pages   cm
Includes bibliographical references and index.
ISBN 978-0-262-01992-7 (hardcover : alk. paper)
1. Manufacturing industries—United States. 2. Manufacturing industries—Technological innovations—United States. I. Locke, Richard M., 1959– II. Wellhausen, Rachel L.
HD9725.P76   2014
338.0973—dc23
2013023697

10 9 8 7 6 5 4 3 2 1

Contents

Richard K. Lester
Japan Steel Industry Professor and Head, Department of Nuclear Science & Engineering

Richard M. Locke
Class of 1922 Professor of Political Science and Management, and Head, Political Science Department; Deputy Dean, Sloan School of Management

Fiona Murray
David Sarnoff Professor of Management Technology, Skolkovo Foundation Associate Professor of Entrepreneurship, and Faculty Director, Trust Center for MIT Entrepreneurship, Sloan School of Management

Paul Osterman
Nanyang Technological University Professor, Professor of Human Resources and Management, and Co-Director, MIT Sloan Institute for Work and Employment Research, Sloan School of Management

Michael J. Piore
David W. Skinner Professor of Political Economy, Emeritus, Departments of Economics/Political Science

John S. Reed
Chairman, MIT Corporation

Elisabeth B. Reynolds
Executive Director, MIT Industrial Performance Center

Donald Rosenfield
Senior Lecturer, Operations Management, Sloan School of Management; Director, Leaders for Global Operations

Sanjay Emani Sarma
Professor of Mechanical Engineering, Director, MIT/SUTD Collaboration Office, Lab for Manufacturing & Productivity, and Director of Digital Learning

Martin Arnold Schmidt
Professor of Electrical Engineering and Associate Provost

Charles G. Sodini
LeBel Professor of Electrical Engineering

Edward Steinfeld
Professor of Political Science, and Co-Director, China Energy Group

ADVISOR
William B. Bonvillian
Director, MIT Washington Office

STAFF
Anita Kafka

PIE COMMISSION RESEARCHERS
Jonté Craighead
Civil and Environmental Engineering

Radu Gogoana
Mechanical Engineering

Jesse D. Jenkins
Technology and Policy Program

Joyce Lawrence
Political Science

Florian Metzler
Technology and Policy Program

Jonas Nahm
Political Science

Hiram M. Samel
Sloan School of Management

Andrew Weaver
Sloan School of Management

Rachel L. Wellhausen
Political Science (currently Assistant Professor, Department of Government, University of Texas at Austin)

Acknowledgments

The works collected in *Production in the Innovation Economy* are the product of countless hours of research undertaken over two years by faculty and graduate students at MIT. Like its companion volume, *Making in America* by Suzanne Berger, this volume emerged from the efforts of the MIT Production in the Innovation Economy (PIE) Commission and its benefactors. We give particular thanks for the support of three MIT alumni, Mark Gorenberg, Diane Greene, and Ray Stata. The Alfred P. Sloan Foundation, Carnegie Corporation of New York, Russell Sage Foundation, and the Ewing Marion Kauffman Foundation have been most generous, as was the Lockheed Martin Corporation in providing an open gift to the PIE Commission. In the course of our research, we interviewed hundreds of people, from multinational corporation CEOs to plant managers of small enterprises, in the United States and abroad. While respecting their wishes to remain anonymous, we thank them all for their insights and time. Neither the donors nor the interviewees bear any responsibility for the findings or recommendations reported herein.

At MIT, the PIE Commission was spread over fourteen departments. Anita Kafka was key to the broader project and in getting this volume to press. We cannot thank her enough for her tireless efforts and humor along the way. Organizing the whole undertaking was also made possible thanks to the help of Maria DiMauro, Paula Kreutzer, and Kathleen Searle in the Department of Political Science and Ronald Hasseltine, Assistant Provost for Research Administration. We thank the PIE "Backbone Group," comprised of faculty and students who met weekly to shape the Commission's research agenda: Jesse Jenkins, Joyce Lawrence, Jonas Nahm, Hiram Samel, Andrew Weaver, and Rachel Wellhausen, as well as the hundreds of firms, large and small, that welcomed us to their offices and factories and shared with us many of the insights we present in this volume.

Finally, we thank Suzanne Berger, who lead the PIE Commission with grace and whose thinking on the problems of innovation and production irrevocably shaped our own. It is a joy and an inspiration to see her explore a factory floor, savor a sandwich at a supermarket deli between interviews, and light up whether learning about massive drilling equipment or rubber production.

1 Introduction

Richard M. Locke and Rachel L. Wellhausen

"To live well, a nation must produce well." This statement, which opened the MIT *Made in America* study in 1989, is as true today as it was when the book was originally published (Dertouzos, Solow, and Lester 1989). In the late 1980s, when *Made in America* was being written, the key challenge facing U.S. manufacturers was a decline in international competitiveness due to comparatively low levels of productivity and quality. More than twenty years later, American manufacturers appear to be as efficient and quality focused as any of their foreign rivals. Yet once again, U.S. companies are suffering a crisis that has led to massive losses in employment and in some cases, the viability of entire sectors. Between December 2007 and June 2009, the U.S. economy lost over two million manufacturing jobs, accounting for 15 percent of the nation's manufacturing workforce. Thousands of firms either filed for bankruptcy or dramatically reduced their operations to the most basic, skeletal activities simply so that they could survive. As unemployment rates and firm closings increased, many in this country wondered what, if anything, could be done to reverse this trend and relaunch economic growth and job creation in the United States.

To address this pressing question, a number of scholars and policy-makers alike embarked on a series of studies aimed at understanding the current state of U.S. manufacturing and whether or not it could be strengthened and once again generate high-paying jobs for millions of Americans. Many of these reports made numerous policy recommendations—ranging from changes in our tax codes and trade rules to reforms of our education system and intellectual property regimes to overhauling our financial system and immigration policies (Helper, Krueger, and Wial 2012; Houseman et al. 2010; Fuchs and Kirchain 2010; Wessner and Wolff 2012; Pisano and Shih 2012). The MIT Production in the Innovation Economy (PIE) Commission, established in 2010 by then–MIT president Susan Hockfield, took a slightly different approach to addressing this issue. Rather than focusing solely or even primarily on manufacturing as a source of job creation, the MIT PIE Commission asked what production capabilities are necessary to maintain, let alone enhance, our economy's ability to innovate. Our premise, informed by the work of our MIT colleague Robert Solow and others, is that employment is tied to economic growth, which in turn is the product of both productivity increases and the development of new products, services, and business models. And enhanced productivity and new products, services, and business models are the result of innovation, broadly defined. Thus, for the MIT PIE Commission, the central focus of our study was on innovation and the relationship between innovation and manufacturing: those productive capabilities on the shop floors of our remaining manufacturing companies as well as in the laboratories and R&D centers developing new products and services that will lead to either new enterprises and industries or revolutionize existing business models. A related question pursued by the MIT PIE Commission focused on how one maintains, let alone enhances, essential productive capabilities in a global economy where leveraging the geographic dispersion of a company's operations generates significant value for its shareholders even if, at times, this may be at the expense of domestic workers.

This book, and its companion volume, *Making in America* by our colleague Suzanne Berger, report the findings of the MIT PIE Commission's two years of research (Berger 2013). Both books grew out of an interdisciplinary research effort at MIT. The research team consisted of some twenty professors from engineering, science, management, and the social sciences as well as pre- and postdoctoral fellows in different fields. The PIE Commission conducted original surveys of established manufacturing firms, innovative start-up companies, and principal investigators engaged in manufacturing-related research. Individual team members also participated in various initiatives such as the federal government's Advanced Manufacturing Partnership as well as other, more regionally focused efforts. In the process of engaging with these other initiatives, we were able to test out our ideas and have found support for our conceptualization of the challenges facing the U.S. economy today.

The team's biggest undertaking was its two-year effort to interview the heads of manufacturing firms in the United States, Germany, Japan, and China. A major push focused on a list of 3,596 predominately small- and medium-sized manufacturing firms in the United States that doubled their revenues between 2004 and 2008—and survived the financial crisis (Berger 2013).[1] In an effort to uncover whether and to what extent such "viable" firms innovate, and what inputs are necessary to their efforts, the team interviewed 107 of these firms in Massachusetts, Ohio, Arizona, and Georgia. In addition, we interviewed top executives at mid-sized and large, well-established companies throughout the country. Regardless of whether we were interviewing owner-managers of family-run small businesses in the Midwest or chief executives and research scientists at some of the country's most successful large enterprises, we heard the same emphasis on the importance of linkages between innovation and production capabilities.

In this book, we focus on innovation as a rationale for why manufacturing still matters to the U.S. economy. We argue that a holistic concept of production is intertwined with the process of innovation. Producing new goods relies on the capability to prototype rapidly, to iterate between designers and shop floor operators, to optimize production processes, to scale up new goods and services, and to do after-market incremental innovation—including the provision of services alongside and sometimes embedded in new goods. Without access to these capabilities, firms, industries, and even national economies cannot take full advantage of their ability to innovate. Thus, an innovation economy such as that in the United States continues to benefit from manufacturing capacity and, what is more, from the maintenance of manufacturing-oriented firms. In some of the great hallmarks of past innovation, such as Bell Labs, the capabilities integrating innovation and production coexisted within large, vertically integrated firms (Gertner 2012). In today's economy, in which corporations have slimmed down to focus on their "core competencies," what were once internal systems are now often provided by external firms, often (but not always) colocated in geographically distinct "ecosystems." Large and small, established and entrepreneurial firms rely on these ecosystems to facilitate the innovation-production connection. Moreover, manufacturing capacities often span national borders. From one point of view, where firms may find manufacturing capabilities is largely irrelevant. However, firms fully capitalize on these external capabilities when they bring skills and know-how learned abroad back to their home operations. Without vibrant local ecosystems, firms are limited in their ability to translate whatever lessons they learned abroad through their interactions with foreign manufacturers to their home-based R&D operations. In other words, even in today's global economy, local capabilities and local ecosystems matter. From a political economic point of view, a government interested in growing manufacturing capacity would do well to strengthen these ecosystems in order to reap benefits from innovation and the production integral to it. Strong local ecosystems can maximize firms' abilities to accomplish the innovation-production tasks that are essential in today's economy.

In the remainder of this chapter, we first discuss why it is that manufacturing might still matter in an advanced economy such as that in the United States. Second, we elaborate on what the connection between innovation and production looks like in practice. Given this connection, we preview the book's arguments about how production ecosystems within and external to firms, and within and across national borders, provide capabilities central to firms' abilities to innovate. We conclude by pondering the policy implications for the key findings of this study.

Why manufacturing still matters

There are two powerful but very different explanations for the decline of manufacturing in the United States. The first, a theory about increasing productivity in manufacturing, presumes that the eventual loss of manufacturing in the United States is "natural." We owe this teleological formulation of natural shifts from an agricultural to a manufacturing and eventually to a service-based economy to Colin Clark, an Australian economist who observed what he called "a wide, simple, and far-reaching generalization" that, alongside economic progress, "the numbers engaged in agriculture tend to decline relative to the numbers in manufacture, which in their turn decline relative to the numbers engaged in services"(Clark 1940, 492).[2] Today, this point usually is applied to the U.S economy to explain the decline in the percentage of workers employed in agriculture and the more recent drop in the manufacturing workforce—22.1 percent in 1980 to 10.2 percent in 2011 (Bureau of Labor Statistics 2012).

However, recent research has given us reason to doubt how much of the tremendous decline in U.S. manufacturing jobs can be attributed to the inevitable growth of productivity in manufacturing (Atkinson, et al. 2012; Houseman et al. 2011; Helper, Krueger, and Wial 2012). Perhaps most important, the idea that industry necessarily shrinks to a very small share of a modern economy does not hold up well when we look abroad. Germany, for example, employs almost 20 percent of its workforce in manufacturing and has a large trade surplus, even with China. Japan has close to 17 percent of its workforce employed in manufacturing. And Italy—another major world exporter nation—has 19 percent of its labor force employed in industrial activities (U.S. Department of Labor 2012). Nor do these international comparisons conflate wage competition with productivity gains: in 2010, total compensation costs per hour in U.S. manufacturing were $34.74 whereas in Germany they averaged $43.76 (U.S. Department of Labor 2011). The argument about productivity gains and the natural evolution of economies is a powerful heuristic but it does not sufficiently explain away concerns that lost manufacturing capacity may matter even in a services-oriented, innovation-based economy.

The second account of why manufacturing may not matter in advanced industrial countries presumes that lost manufacturing is compensated for in other ways, thanks to economic globalization. To the standard theory of comparative advantage, Vernon (1966) and, more recently, Pisano and Shih (2012) add the theory of the product cycle. In the first phases of the production of new products, the complexities of scaling them up from prototypes are still significant, and these complexities require keeping early phases of production close to the R&D engineers. Scaling-up complexities—plus intellectual property protections—constitute barriers that prevent the migration of early activities abroad. But, according to the theory, when production processes become standardized they do migrate to countries with lower-cost factor inputs. As the capabilities of foreign producers improve, the point along the trajectory where key activities migrate abroad moves ever closer to the "core" new product development phases of the product cycle. This explains why U.S. firms might still profitably keep early stages of product development, design, and prototyping in this country but increasingly move full-scale production activities to less expensive and perhaps more capable markets abroad.

However, in our interactions with both large and small manufacturers, we heard over and over again narratives of innovation throughout the product cycle and not only in early product development. In the chapters that follow, different authors document how innovation takes place not merely in the early phases of product development and design but throughout the value chain, including on the shop floor, as products are modified for new applications as well as through repeated interactions with customers. These patterns of innovation and production vary by industry and even by firm. But there does not appear to be a fixed point in the international division of labor where innovation takes place in certain advanced industrial economies and manufacturing activities take place in other emerging markets.

Whereas some scholars assume or argue away the problem of manufacturing in the United States and other advanced economies, there is no doubt that the state of manufacturing has become politically salient. Yet many underestimate the continuing strengths of American manufacturing. The output of U.S. high-tech manufacturing is still the largest in the world and accounted for $390 billion of global value added in high-tech manufacturing in 2010, although the share of this world market has declined from 34 percent in 1998 to 28 percent in 2010. United States medium- and low-tech manufacturing industries (such as rubber, plastic, and metals) have almost held their own during the period from 1995 to 2010, falling by only 1 percent to a global market share of 18 percent. In short, the relative decline of U.S. manufacturing does not mean that manufacturing is no longer part of the U.S. economy. Nevertheless, what role manufacturing continues to play in the U.S. economy and why certain industry segments have continued to thrive whereas others have virtually collapsed is essential to investigate if we are to better understand the possibilities for production in our innovation economy. Such an investigation is crucial to moving beyond stale partisan and academic debates about the future of American manufacturing. Without a clearer theory of firms' production choices and the importance of those production choices to the broader political economy, attempts to solve the problem of U.S. manufacturing through various policy proposals appear haphazard and their impact unclear.

The research conducted through the MIT PIE Commission shifts the focus from manufacturing per se to innovation and illustrates how ongoing connections between innovation and production, throughout the product cycle, are key to our continuing ability to innovate and thus to grow the economy. We have found that manufacturing firms can and do innovate in the production of goods and services for sale, and that their innovation can scale up within traditional, large firms but also across external ecosystems of manufacturers and lead firms. We propose that in the absence of access to manufacturing, firms would not be able to innovate as rapidly or as well as they do. Robust ecosystems that provide inputs necessary for building prototypes, for incrementally improving production processes, and for after-market modifications are key to successfully operationalizing innovation.

Industrial ecosystems and their importance to the U.S. economy

Since Alfred Marshall first described "industrial districts" in his 1890 book *The Principles of Economics*, numerous scholars have written about the virtues of geographically concentrated "clusters," "agglomerations," and "districts" and their dynamic effects on certain local economies (Marshall 1890). More recent scholarship has focused primarily on the experiences of clusters of small- and medium-sized manufacturing firms in southern Germany and northern Italy. These so-called industrial districts have excited the interest of policymakers and scholars alike because they appear to constitute viable yet alternative models of economic success in the advanced industrial economies (Locke 1995). In fact, these networks of small-scale producers—who compete with one another on some dimensions and cooperate together on others—appear to demonstrate that certain kinds of production capabilities can not only survive but also thrive in a world of rapid technical innovation and fierce international competition. Industrial districts' success is based on the close ties that firms develop with other actors in their local ecosystems, including suppliers, customers, competitors, regional innovation centers, and local vocational education institutes. Dense networks permit local producers to respond more flexibly to shifting consumer markets and continually innovate their products as well as their production capabilities. In short, being embedded in local ecosystems facilitates the frequent iterations and mutual learning between production and innovation that underlie the success of local firms. Similar arguments have been advanced by scholars focused on the U.S. economy. In *The Rise of the Creative Class*, Richard Florida argues that dynamic entrepreneurial economies rely on local concentrations of not simply human capital and financial capital but also on networks of institutions that facilitate the circulation of innovative ideas and people throughout entrepreneurial clusters (Florida 2002). More recently, Enrico Moretti has argued that agglomeration economies are key to explaining differential patterns of growth and employment in the U.S. economy (Moretti 2012).

The MIT PIE Commission research focused neither on industrial districts in Europe nor on clusters of small- and medium-sized firms in the United States. But one of the key findings of this research project is the importance of local ecosystems and their role in providing firms with complementary resources and capabilities that they could not (or no longer) maintain on their own. By ecosystem we do

not mean simply the geographic proximity of R&D labs and manufacturing plants but also the existence of a critical mass of other
firms—competitors, suppliers, financial intermediaries, lead customers—as well as skilled laborers and the schools that produce them.
Together these different actors form a local ecosystem that promotes
rapid prototyping of new products and processes as well as the
support needed to move innovative ideas into the marketplace. As the
various chapters in this book illustrate, the existence of these ecosystems is important not just for traditional "Main Street" firms in the
industrial heartland but also for entrepreneurial start-ups like those
emerging from MIT. The different types of support provided by industrial ecosystems are also important at different stages of firm development, from the original conceptualization of new products and
services, to the start-up period, and finally into the scale-up phase of
efforts to commercialize these innovations for a larger market. Moreover, as chapter 6 by Jonas Nahm and Edward S. Steinfeld illustrates,
industrial ecosystems are important not just in the United States but
also in China and Germany. The German renewable energy firms
described by these authors depend not just on the manufacturing
capabilities of their Chinese partners but also on their own domestic
ecosystems. Without the skill formation and productive capabilities
maintained by German companies at home, they would be unable to
engage in the multidirectional learning and next-generation product
designs described in that chapter. And these firm-level capabilities
were developed not by the firms themselves but rather are a by-
product of the rich industrial ecosystem that continues to exist in
Germany, in which local industrial firms continue to benefit from the
common pool resources created through the Fraunhofer Institutes and
the vocational training system.

   This book includes many approaches to understanding the link
between innovation and production: a focus on skills and start-ups, an
international perspective, analysis of existing and proposed firm strategies, and a review of exciting emerging technologies that advance our
ability to manufacture. In chapters 2 and 3, Paul Osterman and Andrew
Weaver address three questions: What skills do manufacturing firms
need? Are these skills in shortage in the sense that they are not readily
available in the labor market? If so, what kinds of policies focused
on skill formation and job matching might be appropriate and useful?
To answer these questions, Osterman and Weaver undertook a large
and multifaceted data collection project. They interviewed firms

throughout the country, particularly in areas where manufacturing and training linkages have been strong, in order to understand best practices in the area. They also visited community colleges, high schools, and other labor market institutions. Moreover, the authors conducted a nationally representative survey of manufacturing establishments, asking factual questions concerning hiring, the skills required of workers, and to what extent the firm interacts with other firms or intermediaries to address skills concerns. Chapter 2 details the survey and interview results, concluding that skill demands have risen but only modestly and at a pace that make most jobs accessible to most people. Although three out of four manufacturing establishments can find the workforce they desire, a significant minority—including some of the most highly innovative firms—are experiencing difficulties hiring workers with the appropriate mix of skills they need. In chapter 3, Weaver and Osterman spell out the policy implications of these findings. In particular, they focus on improving "intermediaries," which are institutions in the labor market that can help match employer needs and training. They advocate improvements in community colleges as an important, established set of intermediaries.

In chapter 4, Elisabeth B. Reynolds, Hiram M. Samel, and Joyce Lawrence discuss findings that emerge from another large-scale and multi-method research effort. The authors focus on two related questions: first, what factors facilitate or hinder entrepreneurial start-up efforts to scale up and develop commercially viable products; and second, what are the implications of these scale-up strategies for the U.S. innovation system? Concern over the failure of so many start-ups to grow into robust and independent firms has led to broad concern about the loss of downstream benefits of American innovative capacity. The authors choose to analyze a critical case—spin-offs in the Cambridge, Massachusetts, area and particularly those coming from MIT labs. If even these privileged and well-placed firms struggle to scale up their operations, what might we extrapolate for less privileged entrepreneurial ventures located throughout our economy? At least for this sample of firms, at the early stages of development venture capital is available, skilled labor markets are thick, and suppliers are plentiful. Yet once these firms reach what the authors call an "inflection band," they face a critical stage of growth in which a significant new influx of capital is needed to reach commercial scale. In many cases, strategic partners—including foreign governments— provide the necessary capital and, at the same time, acquire the start-up or pull it overseas. Capital shortage at the stage of the scale-up process is what the authors identify as the critical juncture where innovations developed in the United States are lost; this hinders the generation of significant downstream activities such as manufacturing. Moreover, when start-ups are pulled overseas by foreign investors or incorporated into large firms that have acquired them, the robust networks of small, local suppliers that start-ups rely on and support are also made more vulnerable.

In chapter 5, Richard K. Lester also explores innovation in the energy sector and focuses on the need for government intervention to overcome the significant scale-up problems associated with developing more sustainable sources of energy in the United States. Lester compels his readers to consider the very serious and increasingly pressing challenges generated by climate change and the role carbon-based energy sources play in these challenges. In order to reduce our dependence on nonrenewable fossil fuels, massive investments in energy innovation and infrastructure are necessary. But because of the enormous capital requirements and financial risk involved in bringing these new technologies to the market, let alone rebuilding the country's infrastructure to accommodate them, private firms are unwilling, or perhaps unable, to do it on their own. As a result, government must step in to encourage and support investments at all stages of the energy sector innovation process. The U.S. government could intervene in many different ways, ranging from providing tax credits and subsidies to encouraging private investment in particular technologies to pricing carbon to even entering into partnerships with private actors to fund or conduct research, development, and demonstration activities. Whatever specific roles the government chooses to (or is politically able to) pursue, the key message of this chapter is that some extra-firm interventions and investments are needed if the United States is going to promote a more sustainable energy system within a relatively short amount of time. In many ways, the issues raised by Lester's chapter—investing in innovation, managing risk, acquiring needed capital, navigating competing regulatory systems, and competing with what appear to be better financed, larger-scale rivals—encapsulate the challenges facing other firms in other sectors in this country. At the same time, energy supply and costs are key to the viability of all other sectors analyzed in this research project. Lester's chapter documents the major challenges facing the energy sector and innovation within this sector and reminds us that the failure to address these challenges could prove disastrous to not only our economy but our social and political systems as well.

Chapters 6 and 7 move the focus of analysis to connections between advanced economy innovators and overseas firms, particularly in China. To what extent is this movement abroad a "zero-sum game," in which the United States loses and China wins? Jonas Nahm, Edward S. Steinfeld, and Florian Metzler present strong arguments that in cross-border partnerships, learning and innovation flow both ways. Whereas Chinese firms gain access to innovations from abroad, their innovative manufacturing practices, especially in rolling out complex products, also provide their non-Chinese partners an opportunity to learn and improve their own product offerings. Nahm and Steinfeld use rich interview and case study evidence to make these arguments against the backdrop of the wind and solar industries, two emerging industries with different manufacturing characteristics in which Chinese firms have nevertheless gained great proficiency. In particular, Chinese firms are able to scale up new innovations through advanced manufacturing techniques, drawing on skills and resources not found in the United States. In contrast to some other authors in this book, Nahm and Steinfeld downplay the importance of colocation between original innovation and the manufacturing process. Their argument implies that a stable set of arrangements could exist in which cross-border transactions become the norm, assuaging the worry that offshoring inevitably leads to the total loss of innovative capacity in the United States. At the same time, however, their case studies of German manufacturers show that the ability of German companies to benefit from the learning they gain through their interactions with Chinese manufacturers is dependent on the continuing existence of their own manufacturing and innovative capabilities—capabilities that are provided by the German industrial ecosystem. In chapter 7, Metzler and Steinfeld turn to the civilian nuclear industry in China to demonstrate how Western firms bring specific technologies and managerial skills to large projects, but local resources are necessary to build out something as complex as a nuclear power plant. Western and Chinese firms thus find that their skills are in many cases complementary rather than inherently competitive. Nevertheless, the build-up of large infrastructure projects in countries outside the United States does mean that U.S. firms nurture local suppliers abroad rather than at home. This, however, does not mean that the United States is losing out because once again, lead firms could (theoretically) learn from the actions of their Chinese partners. Whether or not these U.S. firms are able to translate the lessons gained through their interactions with Chinese manufacturers into new innovative capabilities remains an open question, especially given the weakness of industrial ecosystems in the United States.

Donald B. Rosenfield's chapter turns the question of offshoring on its head, looking systematically at the conditions under which firms should keep manufacturing jobs onshore notwithstanding relatively high labor costs in the United States. Chapter 8 draws on a series of interviews with large, innovative firms in the United States. Rosenfield finds that onshoring is important when transportation costs are high and when responsiveness to customers is key to competitive advantage. Interestingly, Rosenfield goes on to make the case for product variety as a measure of innovation. If product variety is strategically important to the firm's activities, it too provides a key reason to onshore. Rosenfield models manufacturing and supply chain costs to corroborate this argument. If product variety is critical to a firm's production strategy—as it is to so many firms—this is an as-yet little recognized factor that incentivizes firms to stay in the United States.

In the final chapter, Olivier L. de Weck and Darci Reed lay out a detailed conception of advanced manufacturing. In their approach, advanced manufacturing differs in several key ways from the linear traditional manufacturing model that moves from raw materials, to fabrication, to parts assembly, to finished products. At each stage of this process, new technologies are generating change. Materials design and the creation of synthetic materials facilitate new inputs into the process; continuous manufacturing enables variation in production strategies; integrated recycling processes have knock-on effects on the environmental impact of production; and the bundling of services with final products creates new, integrated solutions rather than the finished products of old. Using a survey of practitioners around the country as well as contemporary scholarly literature, de Weck and Reed identify seven cutting-edge fields relevant to advanced manufacturing: materials and nanotechnology, additive and precision manufacturing, pharmaceuticals and biomanufacturing, robotics and automation adaptability, green and sustainable manufacturing, supply chain design, and advanced electronics. Such technologies can change the kinds of products produced, and they may also allow less reliance on capital-intensive tooling and enhance the flexibility of manufacturing processes.

Production in the innovation economy: Policy implications

The chapters in this book highlight the link between innovation and production from the point of view of the innovator, the worker, the firm, the industry, and the manufacturing system. Building on interdisciplinary work across political science, management, engineering, and science, the authors apply qualitative and quantitative approaches to questions key to the future of a country's innovative capacity. From an American point of view, there is reason to believe that it would be beneficial to maintain production ecosystems in the United States so that firms have the opportunity to link production and innovation within U.S. borders. Without that, firms that need geographic proximity to innovate—and that is many of them—will have to look elsewhere and move innovation in the process. The link with local geography is not unconditional: as some of the chapters in this book document, many firms have engaged in cross-border partnerships that may allow gains to accrue to actors in both home countries. Yet access to ecosystems at home may indeed be a constraint on the long-term success of cross-border partnerships. U.S. policy would therefore do well to nurture the components of ecosystems and their inputs, such as capital access for small- and medium-sized enterprises, human capital investment in manufacturing-related technologies, and deeper commitments to labor-market intermediaries and community colleges. One advantage the United States has is in its innovative capacity in manufacturing technologies themselves. With advances in additive manufacturing, nanotechnology, and biomanufacturing, among others, the input of creative and novel ways to produce goods (and services) is present within our borders. Whether or not the other inputs that build ecosystems are present is less certain. In the current political climate, "industrial policy" has become taboo in the United States. But promoting targeted investments into infrastructure that support industrial ecosystems—regardless of whether it is financial or energy or educational or R&D-related infrastructure—is key to maintaining the innovation economy in the United States.

Notes

1. See chapter 4, Berger, *Making in America*. Data as described in S. Tracy Jr., Accelerating Job Creation: The Promise of High-Impact Companies, Corporate Research Board LLC, for Small Business Administration Contract no. SBAHQ-10-M-44 (2010).

2. As quoted in Berger, *Making in America;* C. Clark, *The Conditions of Economic Progress* (London: Macmillan, 1940), 492.

References

Atkinson, Robert D., Luke A. Stewart, Scott M. Andes, and Stephen J. Ezell. 2012. "Worse Than the Great Depression: What Experts Are Missing about American Manufacturing Decline." *Information Technology and Innovation Foundation* (March).

Berger, Suzanne. 2013. *Making in America*. Cambridge, MA: MIT Press.

Bureau of Labor Statistics. "International Comparisons of Annual Labor Force Statistics, Adjusted to U.S. Concepts, 1970–2011, Table 7." http://www.bls.gov/fls/flscomparelf .htm.

Clark, Colin. 1940. *The Conditions of Economic Progress*. London: Macmillan.

Dertouzos, Michael L., Richard K. Lester, and Robert M. Solow. 1989. *Made in America: Regaining the Productive Edge*. Cambridge, MA: MIT Press.

Florida, Richard. 2002. *The Rise of the Creative Class and How It's Transforming Work, Leisure, Community, and Everyday Life*. New York: Basic Books.

Fuchs, Erica R. H., and Randolph E. Kirchain. 2010. "Design for Location? The Impact of Manufacturing Offshore on Technology Competitiveness in the Optoelectronics Industry." *Management Science* 56 (12):2323–2349.

Gertner, Jon. 2012. *The Idea Factory: Bell Labs and the Great Age of American Innovation*. New York: Penguin Press.

Helper, Susan, Timothy Krueger, and Howard Wial. 2012. *Locating American Manufacturing: Trends in the Geography of Production*. Washington, DC: Brookings Institution.

Houseman, Susan, Christopher Kurz, Paul Lengermann, and Benjamin Mandel. 2010. *Offshoring and the State of American Manufacturing*. Kalamazoo, MI: W. E. Upjohn Institute.

Houseman, Susan, Christopher Kurz, Paul Lengermann, and Benjamin Mandel. 2011. "Offshoring Bias in U.S. Manufacturing." *Journal of Economic Perspectives* 25 (2):111–132.

Locke, Richard M. 1995. *Remaking the Italian Economy*. New York: Cornell University Press.

Marshall, Alfred. 1890. *The Principles of Economics*. London: Macmillan.

Moretti, Enrico. 2012. *The New Geography of Jobs*. New York: Houghton Mifflin Harcourt Publishing.

National Science Board. 2012. *Science and Engineering Indicators 2012.*, 6–22. Arlington, VA: National Science Foundation.

Pisano, Gary P., and Willy C. Shih. 2012. *Producing Prosperity: Why America Needs a Manufacturing Renaissance*. Cambridge, MA: Harvard Business School Press.

President's Council of Advisors on Science and Technology. 2012. "Report to the President on Capturing Domestic Competitive Advantage in Advanced Manufacturing."

Tracy, Spencer. Jr. 2010. "Accelerating Job Creation: The Promise of High-Impact Companies." Corporate Research Board LLC, for Small Business Administration Contract no. SBAHQ-10-M-44.

Vernon, Raymond. 1966. "International Investment and International Trade in the Product Cycle." *Quarterly Journal of Economics* 80 (2):190–207.

Wessner, Charles W., and Alan Wm. Wolff, eds. 2012. *Rising to the Challenge: U.S. Innovation Policy for the Global Economy*. Washington, DC: National Academies Press.

2   Skills and Skill Gaps in Manufacturing

Paul Osterman and Andrew Weaver

Production workers are at the core of the manufacturing work force, just as they have always been. In 2011 blue collar jobs accounted for over 40 percent of all manufacturing employment. Without these employees products would simply not get out the door. But the importance of these jobs extends beyond this obvious point. A great deal of research, not to mention the experience of leading firms, demonstrates that the skills, ideas, and commitment of blue collar workers are central to obtaining the levels of quality and productivity needed to succeed in today's hypercompetitive economy. Furthermore, these production jobs have long been the path to middle-class lives for people with relatively modest levels of education. Consider that in 2011 a U.S. manufacturing production worker with just a high school degree earned $17.29 an hour and equivalent employees in all other industries earned $15.87 (Lemieux 2006).[1] The goal of this chapter is to understand the nature of production jobs and to shed light on some puzzles and controversies that have arisen regarding them. In chapter 3 we take up policy solutions to the challenges that we identify.

The two main puzzles on which we focus in this chapter turn on issues regarding skill. There is a great deal of uncertainty regarding just what capacities firms are looking for in their production workforces. What mix of hard skills—math, reading, writing, computers—is needed, and how important are capacities such as the ability to work in teams or to solve unexpected problems? There is a great deal of speculation, as well as several well-respected research efforts, but a comprehensive study of the manufacturing sector per se has yet to be undertaken. The second puzzle concerns whether manufacturing firms are able to find what they need. Numerous reports of shortages coexist with other reports of unemployed people lining up for jobs when they are announced. Firms complain that they cannot find the workers they want, but the main signal that economists look at—wages—has remained flat in the face of supposedly rising demand and limited supply. Just what is going on? Are there shortages, and, if so, in what kind of firms and for what skills?

To answer these questions we base much of this chapter on two sources of data: an original nationally representative survey of 885 American manufacturers that we conducted in 2012 and a wide-ranging set of face-to-face interviews with manufacturing firms in a variety of regions around the country. See appendix 2.1.[2] The details of the survey and the interviews are provided in the appendixes to this chapter. We believe that they provide a unique and valuable insight into the workforce issues confronting American manufacturers.

Two key features of our survey are important to understand up front. First, the survey was directed to establishments and not to firms. This is not a meaningful distinction for a firm that has only one location, but consider, at the other extreme, General Motors. If GM happened to be in our sample we would have interviewed a plant and not the corporate headquarters. We adopted this approach because we believed that the respondent, typically the plant manager, would be far more knowledgeable about the issues that concern us than would someone buried in corporate headquarters. For many questions we asked about the establishment and not the firm as a whole. However, when it came to questions about skill, shortages, and hiring practices, we built on previous research we have conducted and focused on what we termed *core workers,* who were defined as the occupational groups most central to production (Osterman 1994, 2000). We targeted this group because it would not be sensible to ask a question about hiring or skills and expect any reasonable answer to apply to blue collar, administrative, or managerial employees in the aggregate.

To preview our results, we find that there is widespread demand for basic hard skills such as reading, writing, math, and computers, but that the demand for more advanced levels of these skills is modest. Interpersonal skills such as the ability to work in teams and to get along with colleagues are quite important, whereas demand for problem-solving abilities and initiative is somewhat less so. When it comes to the skill shortage debate we focus on long-term vacancies, and our results indicate that the majority of manufacturers do not face significant obstacles in accessing skilled production workers. At the same time, we do find persistent long-term vacancies among a subset of manufacturing establishments. The most consistent predictors of these extended vacancies are demands for advanced math and reading skills. Low wages and frequent product innovation are also contributing factors.

General characteristics of the manufacturing workforce

Before discussing some of the specific issues regarding skill require-ments and skill gaps, it is helpful to describe some of the basic charac-teristics of the U.S. manufacturing workforce.

From a demographic point of view, contrary to some conventional wisdom, the manufacturing workforce is not consistently older than the rest of the workforce across all age categories. That said, about 17 percent is approaching retirement. This will prove important when it comes to thinking about hiring needs. In addition, the percentage of the youngest workers trails that of other industries. See table 2.1 for comparisons.

The manufacturing workforce contains a variety of occupational categories. Not surprisingly the largest occupational group is produc-tion workers, followed by managers, engineers, and scientists. Note that the U.S. Census Current Population Survey (CPS) data do not distinguish skill levels within each group (table 2.2).

With regard to education, we are interested in both the level and the rate of change. In other words, what are the education levels of the manufacturing workforce compared to workers in other industries, and how does the rate of change in education levels compare to the rest of the economy?

We use data for twenty-five- to thirty-year-olds to answer these ques-tions because these are new hires and, as such, best capture trends in skill and education that represent the future of the industry. Comparing

Table 2.1
Age Distribution, Manufacturing, and the Rest, 2010–2011 (Percentage)

	Manufacturing	Not Manufacturing
25–34	23.3	29.7
35–54	59.1	53.2
55+	17.5	19.9

Source: Authors calculations based on Current Population Survey, Merged Outgoing Rotation Group (CPS ORG) data. See http://data.nber.org/morg/annual.

Table 2.2
Occupational Distribution, Manufacturing (Percentge)

	2000–2001	2010–2011
Management, business, financial	13.9	16.0
Computer, math, life, physical, social sciences	4.7	4.8
Architecture and engineering	6.9	8.1
Production, installation, repair	47.6	42.5
Other	26.8	28.4

Source: Authors calculations based on CPS ORG data.

Table 2.3
Education Distribution, Manufacturing Mechanics, Installation/Repair/Production Workers, Ages 25–34 (Percentage)

	2000–2001	2010–2011
High school dropout	14.0	12.7
High school graduate	37.3	32.3
Some college	17.2	16.7
AA degree	8.0	8.7
College degree or more	23.4	29.4

Note: "Some college" can be anything from one course in a community college to all courses except graduation from a four-year college.

Source: Authors' calculations based on CPS ORG data.

the education distribution for manufacturing workers for 2010–2011, it is clear that the manufacturing workforce is less well educated than is the workforce in the rest of the economy (table 2.3). At the same time, we can also see that there is indeed some evidence that the education level of the manufacturing workforce is increasing more rapidly than the average for nonmanufacturing industries (see table 2.4).

Skills and shortages

The national discussion regarding the manufacturing workforce has centered on two questions: (1) what are the skills that production workers need to help manufacturers thrive and (2) do sufficient numbers of employees possess these skills to meet employers' needs? In this section we will review the state of knowledge and the open questions regarding each of these issues. This will set the stage for the findings that flow from the national survey and our fieldwork.

Table 2.4
All Nonmanufacturing Distribution, All Occupations, Ages 25–34 (Percentage)

	2000–2001	2010–2011
High school dropout	9.7	8.3
High school graduate	25.9	23.2
Some college	20.0	18.0
AA degree	9.1	10.9
College degree or more	34.3	39.3

Source: Authors' calculations based on CPS ORG data.

Skills

Historically, manufacturing was a sector in which unskilled but strong and hardworking people could earn a decent living. Of course, there have always been higher level blue collar craft and repair jobs, but the bulk of employees could do well with basic skills and a strong work ethic. Today there is a general perception, which extends well beyond manufacturing, that the diffusion of information technology as well as organizational innovations such as quality programs and self-managed teams has raised the bar for what is expected of employees. In manufacturing this view is reinforced by perception that unskilled work has moved overseas and that what remains in the United States are sophisticated, highly automated factories and production sites. In this view individuals who do not meet the new, higher expectations will be trapped in lower paying service work (Dietz and Orr 2006).

This said, there is uncertainty about what the actual skills are that employees need. Most of the discussion about skill requirements relies on educational attainment, but education is a noisy proxy for concrete skills. In addition, there is a fundamental identification problem associated with using education as a proxy of skills. If we observe that, say, the education level of a group of incumbent workers in a given occupation is rising, does this reflect an increase in the skill demands of the job, or is it a reflection of an increase in the educational level of the available workforce due to any number of possible reasons—such as the consumption value of education or an educational "arms race"—that are unrelated to actual job requirements?

In short, when it comes to understanding skills we want to know what skills are needed, whether skill requirements are accelerating, and what we can say about the existence and characteristics of any mismatch between the supply of and demand for skills. Our survey results provide some of the first detailed evidence on these questions with regard to manufacturing establishments.

The current state of understanding regarding skill requirements, leaving aside the research that uses education as proxy for skill, is fairly thin. Representative of the view that skill demands are high and accelerating is recent work by David Autor, Frank Levy, and Richard Murnane (ALM) that examines the impact of the diffusion of information technology on skill requirements (Autor, Levy, and Murnane 2003). This work centers on the distinction between routine and nonroutine skills. The argument is that computers increasingly perform routine tasks that can be programmed, hence substituting for human labor that previously did this work. The research points to a variety of jobs that are nonroutine (i.e., not programmable), both at the high end (managers, brain surgeons) and the low end (hotel room cleaners, home health aides). ALM find that from 1960 to 1998 the share of work in the economy that was nonroutine interactive and nonroutine analytical rose and the share that was nonroutine manual, routine manual, and routine cognitive fell.[3] In general they find these trends occurred across all industries. They also find that much of the shift takes place within education groups. In addition, the pattern is largely due to the adoption of computers and not to other forms of capital investments. However, the data are not presented in a way that enables one to determine the percentage of work that the authors believe fall into each category.

This set of findings points to a shift in the demand for skill and contributes a new model to explain this shift. Although it is clear that the computerization processes that ALM describe have altered the labor market, what is less clear is the magnitude of the shifts and whether this transformation is the type of discontinuous change that would drive gaps between the supply and demand for skills.

Other researchers have examined skill changes and found them to be either modest or manageable with current workforce capabilities. Michael Handel finds a steady growth in skill demands but not any evidence of acceleration in recent decades. For example, Handel concludes that "overall, it seems that rather basic levels of math, corresponding to two years of ordinary high school instruction, are sufficient for most jobs"(Handel 2010).

In their book *Teaching the New Basic Skills*, Richard J. Murnane and Frank Levy provide a case study of hiring at Honda Motors in Ohio in the early 1990s (Murnane and Levy 1996). Honda hired only one in ten applicants, but the hard skill demands were very low. The company used only simple math tests—at a high school level or less—in its screening process, and it did not even use past manufacturing experience as a selection criterion. Ultimately Honda was more concerned about attitude, ability to work in teams, and flexibility than previously acquired hard skills.

Roberto Fernandez studied these issues in the context of a technological change in a food processing factory (Fernandez 2001). The factory totally redesigned its production process in order to implement continuous processing and control systems. Fernandez collected numerous direct measures of skill changes, and these do show generally increased skill demands in the new jobs, although the increases are not radical. However, and this is very important, the firm kept its old workforce and retrained them despite the fact that the average education level at the plant was below twelfth grade. The fact that existing workers could be successfully retrained to use modern production technologies casts some doubt on the existence of the skill shortage problem.

As is apparent, there has been a substantial amount of research on the trajectory of skill demands in manufacturing but these investigations have not converged on a consistent story. Our survey is intended to bring clarity to this debate as well as address the question, described in the next section, of whether skill demands have accelerated and moved jobs out of the reach of many Americans.

Mismatch and shortage?

Has the demand for skill increased in a way that has outrun what today's blue collar workforce can deliver? Have jobs suddenly become so demanding that most candidates for production jobs are not qualified? In short, is there a skill shortage facing America's manufacturing firms? Here too there is considerable uncertainty and controversy.

A great deal of concern has been expressed about a skills shortage in manufacturing. In 2005, the National Association of Manufacturers endorsed a study by Deloitte that asserted "today's skill shortages are extremely broad and deep . . . impacting more than 80 percent of the companies surveyed. . . . [S]kill shortages are having a widespread impact on manufacturers' abilities to achieve production levels, increase productivity, and meet customer demands" (Deloitte and The Manufacturing Institute 2005). In 2011 another NAM/Deloitte report indicated that 74 percent of the firms surveyed said that shortages or skill deficiencies in skilled production workers "harmed their ability to expand operations or improve productivity" (Deloitte and The Manufacturing Institute 2011).

Numerous newspaper articles reporting from different parts of the country have echoed these worries as they quote firms complaining about difficulties in hiring. One typical headline from Indiana reports that "hundreds of manufacturing jobs go unfilled," and in another story the mayor of Chicago states that six hundred aircraft maintenance positions are going begging (Kavilanz 2012; Emanuel 2011).

The widespread nature of these complaints commands attention, and in fact these concerns were echoed in some, though far from the majority, of our own interviews with firms. This said, there are several stumbling blocks in the way of believing that shortages are in fact a major problem. First, with unemployment at high levels it is hard to believe that potential employees cannot be found. This observation is given additional weight by the success of manufacturing in ramping up production in the past two years. From October 2010 to October 2012, U.S. employment of manufacturing production workers grew by 4.0 percent, and overall manufacturing employment grew by 3.5 percent. Total private sector employment grew by 3.7 percent over this time period (BLS Current Employment Survey).[4] If labor shortages were a major obstacle, then it seems unlikely that manufacturing employment growth would keep pace with overall employment growth.

More worrisome to the shortage argument is the fact that manufacturing wages have not risen disproportionately for more highly skilled or educated production workers. Simple supply and demand economics implies that when a factor is in short supply, its price will rise. It is well understood that there are frictions in the labor market that slow adjustments and that these frictions are due to factors such as the lack of homogeneity of the "product," barriers to mobility, and the institutional characteristics of the labor market. That said, it is hard to believe that wages will not rise over a reasonable period of time if shortages represent a serious obstacle to profitability. We can look at a variety of datasets to get a handle on manufacturing wage trends. In the Bureau of Labor Statistics (BLS) Current Employment Survey, average hourly wages in the manufacturing sector rose by 6.9 percent from 2008 to 2011, as compared to 6.7 percent for average hourly wages across all private sector industries. Thus, overall manufacturing wages do not appear to have spiked.

Of course, one might worry that aggregate manufacturing wage data are too crude and do not distinguish among levels of skill. To address

Table 2.5
Average Hourly Wages by Selected Manufacturing Occupations

	2008	2011	Percent Change
Production occupations	$15.87	$16.74	5.5
Machinists	18.17	19.51	7.4
Industrial engineering technicians	22.89	24.42	6.7
Mechanical engineering technicians	23.74	24.92	5.0
Industrial engineers	35.47	37.56	5.9

Source: BLS Occupational Employment Statistics.

these concerns, we can examine the BLS Occupational Employment Statistics (OES) and the Census's CPS. Using the OES, we can compare wages from several detailed occupations within manufacturing. Although the OES is not well suited to comparisons over time for many occupations (particularly fast-changing information technology positions), the manufacturing positions we have chosen are relatively well defined and have not undergone radical redefinitions in recent years. Table 2.5 contains the change in average hourly wages for overall production workers and machinists compared to three higher skill categories of employees: industrial engineers, industrial engineering technicians, and mechanical engineering technicians. These three occupations represent the types of higher paid, higher skill workers that are often thought to be in short supply.

We can see from these data that wage growth in the higher skilled occupations does not appear to be any more rapid on average than that among the less skilled job categories.

CPS data can also shed light on manufacturing wage trends. Figure 2.1 shows the wage premium for workers who hold an associate's degree (AA) from a community college, expressed as a ratio of wages for degree holders compared to high school graduates. The wage premia are presented for manufacturing workers and nonmanufacturing workers.

We can see from the chart that although there is year-to-year variation in the return to an AA, the manufacturing wage premium has not been rising relative to the nonmanufacturing premium. If anything, the manufacturing premium has shown a relative decline in recent years.

These wage data, along with the successful expansion of manufacturing output and hiring, raise questions about the shortage argument. Spot shortages might arise from time to time in any market, but this is

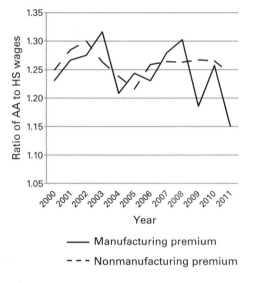

Figure 2.1
Community college wage premium by industry sector. *Source:* Current Population Survey, May ORG.

to be expected. The serious question is whether in general manufacturing is facing a hiring crisis. Although our initial analysis provides grounds for healthy skepticism, given the widespread complaints—including those we turned up in some of our fieldwork—it is not prudent to simply dismiss the shortage argument out of hand. We will use our own survey results to explore this issue more carefully and will in fact identify specific circumstances in which shortages are a real concern.

Survey evidence

Given the broad uncertainty regarding what skills manufacturers require, a substantial portion of our survey was devoted to this topic. Our overall approach was to ask very specific questions about the activities and capabilities required of core employees. Our view is that by being as concrete as possible we are able to move beyond the broad generalities that characterize much of the popular discussion.

We did, nevertheless, ask a few opinion questions about the trajectory of skill change. Of the respondents, 7.1 percent said that skill requirements had increased a great deal in the past five years, and 34.4

percent said that they had increased somewhat. The remainder indicated that there had been no change (48.2 percent) or that requirements had declined (10.1 percent). These data add additional support to the view that although skill demands have gradually increased over time, the perspective that we are in a period of sudden discontinuous new demands is something of an exaggeration. A more concrete question aimed at understanding the skill-related challenges facing firms was how many weeks it takes a new hire to attain an acceptable level of proficiency. This is a complicated question because the reply is a function of the skills demanded in the job and the nature of the hiring process. However, the question does provide some insight into the challenges facing managers. In response, the median establishment reported that a new hire was up to speed in three months, and less than 10 percent of establishments reported that it takes more than six months. On the whole, these time periods seem manageable.

All this said, it is important to drill down beyond generalizations to examine skills in a more concrete way. In the discussion that follows, the data represent yes-no answers to questions that took the form of asking, "does the core job require . . .?" The questions were grouped into six categories: reading skills, writing skills, mathematical skills, computer skills, interpersonal skills, and problem-solving skills. Multiple questions were asked for each category.

We began by asking about basic skills and then turned to more advanced job requirements. For reading we defined basic skills as the ability to read basic manuals, we defined writing as the capacity to write short notes, and for math it was the ability to add, subtract, multiply, divide, and handle fractions. We asked an additional question regarding the frequency of computer use. Table 2.6 shows the results.

Table 2.6
Basic Skill Demands (Percentage)

Establishments requiring basic reading for core jobs	76
Establishments requiring basic writing for core jobs	61
Establishments requiring basic math for core jobs	74
Establishments requiring basic reading, writing, and math skills for core jobs	43
Establishments reporting that usage of computers at least several times a week is part of the core job	63

Source: PIE Manufacturing Survey.

These results certainly do suggest that basic skills are important in most firms, but one can also read them to suggest that there is a large segment of employers that do not require the full range of basic reading, writing, and math skills, or regular computer usage. It would indeed be surprising if these employers were facing difficulties in recruiting, but we will hold off on this question until we explore the demand for more advanced skills.

As noted, we measured six bundles of more advanced skills: reading, writing, mathematics, computer skills, interpersonal skills, and problem solving or initiative. Within each of these, depending on the group, we asked between two and five specific questions. For example, for computer skills one of the questions was whether the job required the ability to use computer-aided design or computer-aided manufacturing programs, and for the math questions one item was whether the job required probability or statistics. For interpersonal skills, one of the questions was whether it is important to be able to work effectively in teams, and for the set of initiative questions one item was whether the employee needed to be able to initiate new tasks without guidance from management. A full list of all the skill questions and the distribution of answers is provided in appendix 2.2.

In table 2.7 we show for each of the advanced hard-skill bundles the percentage of establishments that requires at least one additional advanced skill, as well as the percentage that requires two or more.

These data on advanced skills contain a number of interesting results. First, although demand for reading and math is comparable at the basic level, reading is in greater demand among advanced skills. Advanced math and computer skills are both very important, but fewer than half of manufacturing establishments require at least

Table 2.7
Establishments Requiring Advanced Skills by Number of Additional Skills Required (Percentage)

	At Least One Additional Skill	Two or More Additional Skills
Advanced reading	53	25
Advanced writing	22	4
Advanced math	38	12
Advanced computer	42	23

Source: PIE Manufacturing Survey.

one advanced skill in these skill bundles. With regard to the 38 percent of establishments that do require advanced math skills, it should be kept in mind that the level of additional math that is expected (beyond the basic skills described previously) is in reality not out of reach. In breaking down this bundle, 32 percent of respondents said that employees should be able to use algebra, geometry, or trigonometry, whereas for statistics and probability the figure was 14 percent, and for calculus it was 7 percent.

Another point that comes out of the data presented in table 2.7 is that requirements for advanced skills are often limited to particular advanced skills. As we can see by the reductions in the percentages requiring two or more skills, it is not the case that establishments that require one advanced skill in, say, math, are equally likely to require multiple advanced skills in that same area. This would imply that firms have very specific needs for certain advanced skills. These specific needs may be more amenable to training than would broad-based requirements for competency across many advanced skills.

Table 2.8 presents the results for two characteristics that are often referred to as "soft skills": cooperation and teamwork. Here the message is clear: the typical manufacturing firm places substantial weight on these behavioral traits, which in turn suggests that the widespread discussion about the importance of soft skills has a strong basis in reality.

We also asked about two additional bundles of skills that fall somewhere between hard skills and soft interpersonal skills. The first bundle is the ability of employees to operate on their own and to show initiative. The second bundle is the ability to spot and to address quality problems. These questions and the fraction of establishments that indicated that the capacities are very important are shown in table 2.9.

It is striking that well under half of the surveyed establishments feel it is very important for their core workers to display the self-starting

Table 2.8
Interpersonal Skill Demands (Percentage)

	Percent Responding "Very Important"
Cooperation with other employees: very important	81
Ability to work in teams: very important	65

Source: PIE Manufacturing Survey.

Table 2.9
Demand for Problem Solving and Initiative (Percentage)

	Percent Responding "Very Important"
Ability to initiate new tasks without guidance	35
Ability to independently organize one's time	46
Ability to critically evaluate options	36
Ability to solve unfamiliar problems	39
Ability to evaluate the quality of output	71
Ability to take action if quality is unacceptable	76

Source: PIE Manufacturing Survey.

or initiative traits described in table 2.9. Although the percentage totals obviously rise if we include respondents who indicated that these characteristics are "somewhat important," these results nevertheless imply real limitations on reinforcement of personal initiative that is often thought to be at the heart of developing an advanced manufacturing system.

A final skill question that we asked was directed toward the ability to learn new skills. When asked about the importance of the ability to learn new skills, 50 percent of respondents replied that this capacity is very important for their core employees. An additional 39 percent indicated that it is moderately important.

It is possible to read the overall thrust of these patterns from several perspectives. First, in general it is clear that, as many people have observed, we are well past the era in which a strong back is the primary capacity needed for manufacturing work. The majority of manufacturing establishments require basic reading and mathematics, and many go beyond this in their expectations. The second way of reading these data is to observe that the range of skills that are required, both at the basic and advanced levels, would seem to be well within the reach of a strong high school graduate and, without question, a holder of a community college degree or certificate. These data do not support the idea of across-the-board skill demands that are unattainable for potential production workers with high-school or sub-baccalaureate training.

The final observation points to the importance of moving beyond a discussion of the central tendency in these results and instead observing that there is diversity in skill demands across establishments. Of particular interest are establishments that have relatively high skill requirements for their core employees. For example, consider the following bundle of skill needs: establishments whose employees use computers at least several times a week, who require that their employees have some level of math beyond the basics, and who require that their employees be able to read more than basic instruction manuals. The needs and experiences of this particular subset are likely to diverge from the average. In our survey data, only 21 percent of establishments fit this description. Although these establishments are not typical, they are likely to be the ones with the most advanced technology that may be at most risk of having difficulty finding appropriate employees— though, again, it is important to emphasize that even in this situation the skills are well within the reach of community college graduates. In our subsequent discussion of skill shortages we will more rigorously characterize the distribution of skill demands and relate it to labor market issues.

Vacancies

Much of the discussion concerning the manufacturing workforce has centered on whether firms are facing significant difficulties obtaining an appropriate workforce. One interpretation of this discussion, and one that may be significant, is that these concerns are forward looking and point to the problems that firms will confront as the baby boom wave retires. Related to this are concerns regarding attracting young people into the manufacturing field. While these worries about the future will be addressed in chapter 3, the issue we take up here is whether firms today are having problems identifying and hiring the employees they need.

We asked employers the general question of whether in the past two years it had become more difficult to recruit core employees, and 41 percent indicated that it had. Just what "difficult" means is, of course, in the eye of the beholder. A more objective measure is the time it takes to identify an appropriate candidate. The median time was four weeks, and more than 90 percent of establishments reported that they were able to identify a candidate in twelve weeks or less. Once a candidate is identified, establishments seem to have little difficulty in actually hiring the person, with the average acceptance rate being 86 percent and the median 95 percent.

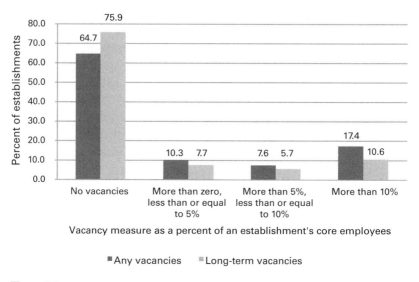

Figure 2.2
Vacancies. *Source:* PIE Manufacturing Survey.

To understand where the problem with hiring might lie and what the characteristics are of firms that face challenges, we asked two questions about vacancies. First, we asked about the number of current vacancies, and second, about the number of long-term vacancies in which jobs remained unfilled for three months or more. The distribution of the replies is shown in figure 2.2.

Similar to the survey responses on skills, these data show some clear, broad patterns and at the same time display diversity. The strong majority of manufacturing establishments simply do not have a problem recruiting the employees that they need, and this should be no surprise given the current state of the job market and wage data trends. Sixty-five percent of establishments report that they have no vacancies whatsoever, and 76 percent report that they do not have any long-term vacancies. There is, however, a subset of establishments that report problems in the form of extended vacancies. Overall, 24 percent of establishments report some level of long-term vacancy, and 16 percent report higher levels of long-term vacancies equal to or greater than 5 percent of their core employee workforces. There is no way of knowing if these are the firms whose complaints we hear in the public discussion because it is actually in the interest of all employers, regardless of their situation, to beat the drums for more investments in producing a manufacturing workforce. However, we will pay special attention to these establishments with extended vacancies because we have a general concern with any significant labor market frictions that might harm workers and hold back economic growth.

Are vacancies a problem for the establishments that are experiencing them? In general, the answer concerning long-term vacancies is that for a subset of establishments they are a moderate problem. When we asked the entire sample whether "lack of access to skilled workers is a major obstacle to increasing financial success," 16.1 percent reported that this was a major obstacle. Notably, this percentage is lower than the percentages reporting that weak demand, taxes, or regulation were major barriers to financial success. Again, however, the central tendency is misleading. Among those establishments who reported no long-term vacancies, only 10.6 percent reported that access to a skilled workforce is an obstacle to their success. Among establishments with some long-term vacancies, the response increased to a strikingly high 33 percent. Among establishments with 5 percent or more long-term vacancies, it was 41 percent.

Explaining vacancies

What distinguishes establishments that are suffering from long-term vacancies from others? This question is important for several reasons. First, some might argue that these firms should simply be left to struggle through their problems, and in general it is reasonable to argue against intervening to help companies deal with every difficulty they face. This, after all, is the essence of a market-driven system. However, if the firms that have difficulty attracting the workforce they need are in some ways "advanced" or "cutting edge" then we might be more worried because, in some sense, they represent the future and a case can be made for nurturing them.

What can we say about the characteristics of establishments that report the existence of long-term vacancies that they cannot fill? In answering this question we focus on three sets of variables that relate to three different categories of explanations: (1) the general characteristics and human resources policies of the establishment, (2) the skill requirements of the establishment, and (3) the competitive strategy of the establishment. In examining these we distinguish among establishments with no long-term vacancies, those whose percentage of long-term vacancies are in the upper third of the distribution of all

Table 2.10
Establishment Characteristics and Vacancies

	No Long-Term Vacancies	In the Upper Third of the Distribution of Establishments with Any Long-Term Vacancies	Report that Obtaining a Skilled Workforce Is a Major Obstacle to Financial Success
Mean number of total employees	.65	.37	.60
Mean hourly wage	$16.56	$18.62	$17.79
Prefer to promote (obtain skills) from within (Percent)	62	49	50

establishments with any long-term vacancies, and those establishments who report that obtaining skilled workers is major obstacle to their financial success. There is considerable overlap between the last two groups but it is worth distinguishing between them because the upper-third cutoff is potentially arbitrary.

Table 2.10 examines establishment size, wage levels, and the firm's policy regarding training internally versus hiring in the external market. Smaller organizations typically have less well-developed human resource functions. In addition, on average they pay less than do larger establishments and may offer less secure employment. Finally, they may have fewer contacts in their communities that aid in attracting employees. We also present data on wage levels because these clearly have an impact on the relative ease of recruitment and hiring. Finally, some employers seek to hire the skills they need on the external market whereas others hire "trainable" people and then develop them internally. We asked respondents to characterize their organization's philosophy along this dimension, and it is reasonable to expect that these alternative approaches may be correlated with challenges in attracting the workforce that the establishment seeks.

The establishments with long-term vacancies are smaller, are more reliant on the external labor market, and pay more. There is, of course, a paradox here: the establishments having difficulty seemingly want more skilled employees yet appear to rely less on internal resources in obtaining them. A partial resolution to this paradox is establishment size: smaller establishments often operate on tighter margins and have more limited internal systems for skill development.

The wage pattern is a reminder that we are examining correlations. We saw previously in the national data that in the aggregate manufacturers have not disproportionately raised wages for production workers. At the same time, it makes sense that the subset of manufacturing establishments that are having difficulty recruiting have raised wages somewhat. From table 2.10 we do not yet have a sense of whether the correlation between long-term vacancies and higher wages will remain positive once we take into account other factors, such as the relative levels of skills demanded. We will explore this in the following in a multivariate regression framework.

Table 2.11 examines the relationship between skill and long-term vacancies. A reasonable expectation is that establishments that seek relatively high skills or scarce skills are those that experience vacancies. The results in table 2.11 provide general support for this expectation, but, perhaps more important, it helps us distinguish the kinds of skill demands that pose challenges.

The central message of these patterns seems clear: establishments that experience difficulties with long-term vacancies are those that seek a skill that is unique in their area, and are also those that seek employees with reasonably advanced levels of math and computer skills. For establishments in the upper third of the distribution of long-term vacancies, advanced reading requirements are also associated with higher levels of long-term vacancies. In general, most of the interpersonal or problem solving–initiative skills do not vary consistently with vacancies. We will further explore these relationships in a multivariate framework.

One feature of the foregoing discussion is that it is done on a variable-by-variable basis. It is important to understand the patterns when the variables are considered simultaneously; that is, it is important to execute a more sophisticated statistical model. We have employed models with two different dependent variables: long-term vacancies as a percentage of core employment and a binary indicator variable for establishments that report high levels of long-term vacancies (defined as greater than 5 percent of core employees). We use a standard regression model with the first dependent variable and a logistic regression model with the second. As explanatory variables we use indicators for establishment size, an indicator for low wages, a measure of the firm's preference for internal hiring and promotion, several measures of the competitive strategy of the establishment, indicators for increasing and decreasing production, and a range of measures of the skill demands of the establishment. We also control for industry using industry-fixed effects based on disaggregated two-digit industry (NAICS) codes. A summary of the results is shown in table 2.12, and the full results are shown in appendix 2.3.

Table 2.11
Skill Demand and Vacancies

	No Long-Term Vacancies	In the Upper Third of the Distribution of Establishments with Any Long-Term Vacancies	Report that Obtaining a Skilled Workforce Is a Major Obstacle to Financial Success
Job requires unique specialized skills not used by other firms in the area (percent)	23	43	39
Mean number of additional math skills employees require	.45	.83	.88
Mean number of additional computer skills employees require	.69	1.25	1.26
Mean number of additional reading skills employees require	.80	1.16	.82
Mean number of additional writing skills employees require	0.27	0.2	.17
Percent indicating ability to learn new skills is a very important core job capacity	49	51	54
Percent indicating ability to cooperate with other employees is a very important core job capacity	82	76	86
Percent indicating ability to work in teams is a very important core job capacity	64	59	70
Percent indicating that the ability to evaluate the quality of output is very important	70	72	72

Table 2.11
(continued)

	No Long-Term Vacancies	In the Upper Third of the Distribution of Establishments with Any Long-Term Vacancies	Report that Obtaining a Skilled Workforce Is a Major Obstacle to Financial Success
Percent indicating that the ability to take appropriate action if quality is unacceptable is very important	75	82	75
Percent indicating ability to solve unfamiliar problems is very important	38	60	53
Percent indicating ability to initiate new tasks without guidance is very important	36	37	43
Percent indicating ability to independently organize one's time is very important	46	63	50
Percent indicating ability to critically evaluate options is very important	37	33	41

The most consistent finding from this exercise is that there is a strong relationship between certain skill measures and long-term vacancies. In our first model, establishments that require a unique skill not readily found in their region have higher percentages of long-term vacancies. Likewise, establishments that demand advanced math and reading skills experience higher levels of long-term vacancies. In the model measuring the presence or absence of any levels of long-term vacancies above 5 percent of core workers, the indicator for advanced math remains significant at the 95 percent level, and the indicator for advanced reading is significant at the 90 percent level. Although advanced computer skills are not significant predictors of long-term vacancies in these models, if a measure of the number of advanced

Table 2.12
Results of OLS and Logit Models of Long-Term Vacancies

	Dependent Variable	
Independent Variables	Long-Term Vacancy (Percent)	Long-Term Vacancy Indicator
Advanced reading	.012*	.049
	(.006)	(.027)
Advanced math	.017*	.065*
	(.007)	(.027)
Advanced computer	.007	.025
	(.006)	(.027)
Advanced writing	-.003	.007
	(.008)	(.029)
Unique skill demand	.016*	.038
	(.007)	.026
Ability to learn unfamiliar tasks	-.005	.015
	(.006)	(.025)
Cooperation is important	-.001	-.007
	(.009)	(.035)
Work in teams is important	.005	-.011
	(.007)	(.029)
Low wage indicator	.150**	.102
	(.034)	(.112)
Frequent product innovation	.014*	.064
	(.007)	(.028)
Preference for internal promotion	-.003	-.025
	(.006)	(.024)
Number of observations	698	696
R^2 / Pseudo R^2	.110	.133

Note: Results for logit/indicator model are marginal effects.
* = significant at 5 percent level;
** = significant at 1 percent level.
Source: Author's calculations based on PIE Manufacturing Survey. See text for details.

computer skills required is used, then these skill demands become significant as well (results not shown). In both models, establishments in the ten to nineteen employee size category have a greater chance of experiencing high levels of long-term vacancies than larger establishments (the effect is significant at the 95 percent level in the logit model and at the 90 percent level in the base model). In the first model, an indicator for low wages relative to other area employers is a highly significant predictor of percentage vacancies. A measure indicating that an establishment frequently engages in product innovation also has a significant positive relationship with long-term vacancy levels in both specifications, although other innovation and quality variables are not significant. In neither specification are soft skills, such as cooperation or ability to work in teams, a factor.

As a final topic, we asked the establishments why they thought that they were experiencing difficulties in recruiting core employees. We offered a series of possible explanations, asked the respondents to indicate which played any role, and then asked them which were the first and second most important explanations for the long-term vacancies. The results are shown in table 2.13 for establishments with 5 percent or more core vacancies. The patterns are fundamentally similar for establishments that experience any level of core vacancies.

The explanations are grouped into four categories: skills, character, aspects of the firm, and insufficient labor supply (in the questionnaire the items were randomly spaced and not clustered). These results are interesting for what they do and do not show. First, it is clear that skill concerns are very important. Second, it is apparent that so-called character issues are much less so. Despite all the rhetoric about failed drug tests and bad character, these factors are listed infrequently as the top reason for recruiting problems. What is also interesting is when the respondents simply listed concerns without ranking them, 35 percent of those reporting long-term vacancies did cite drug tests and 59 percent cited character (skills continued to dominate with 89 percent citing a lack of specific skills). One interpretation, albeit speculative, is that character concerns are easy instinctive responses, but when respondents are forced to rank issues and consider which problems are truly pressing, they fade in importance. In any case, these patterns support the earlier analysis of long-term vacancies: for the minority of establishments that have this problem, skill issues loom large.

Table 2.13
Two Most Important Reasons for Significant Long-Term Vacancies (Percentage)

	First Most Important Reason	Second Most Important Reason
Candidates lack sufficient general skills (reading, math, etc.).	8.48	5.9
Candidates lack sufficient specific skills for your industry.	41.4	17.8
Candidates fail drug test.	1.9	4.7
Candidates have poor attitude or character.	2.4	21.5
Poor social or interpersonal skills	2.0	1.6
Wages not attractive to qualified candidates	10.7	5.9
Insufficient resources for recruiting	8.4	5.9
Working conditions are difficult (hot, dirty, etc.).	1.5	3.5
Too few candidates apply.	5.5	13.1

Columns do not add up to 100 percent because of the "other" category.

Conclusion

Understanding what skills modern manufacturers demand and whether shortages of these skills among production workers hold back economic growth have been contentious topics of debate in recent years. We have sought through our research to shed light on these subjects by gathering new empirical data that capture skill requirements through very concrete and specific questions. In terms of skills, math and reading stand out as the most widespread requirements, but it is important to recall that for the majority of establishments the level of skills demanded is quite basic. Computer skills are also important, although they are not as consistently prominent in our data. Some soft skills, such as cooperation and teamwork, are also widely sought by employers.

Our results indicate that for the majority of manufacturers, no significant barriers exist to accessing the skilled workers they demand. However, it is at the same time worth noting that for a minority of manufacturing establishments—about 16 percent of our sample—long-term vacancies among core production workers are at levels that are potentially troubling. For these employers, demand for advanced math and reading skills appears to be the most significant predictor of long-term vacancies. Although they may be important in other contexts, soft skills and character issues do not appear to play a large role in skill shortages as measured by long-term vacancies. In addition to core hard skills, our data also suggest that low wages and frequent product innovation may contribute in certain cases to higher levels of extended vacancies.

Appendix 2.1

As part of this research effort, an original national survey was administered to manufacturing establishments. In addition, we conducted numerous in-person interviews with manufacturers, community colleges, trade associations, and other relevant parties in various geographic locations.

Survey methodology

Starting in October 2012, the survey was mailed out to 2,700 manufacturing establishments with at least ten employees. Manufacturing establishments were randomly selected from Dun & Bradstreet's database. The random sample was drawn on a stratified basis to make it representative of the frequency of different establishment sizes by employment level based on 2010 data from the U.S. Bureau of the Census's County Business Patterns survey. The sample was also trimmed to exclude SIC codes for the baking, printing, and publishing industries (which are sometimes included in the broad manufacturing category).[5]

The survey administrators called each firm in the sample to identify the individual who would be the most appropriate respondent. As an incentive and as compensation for response time, a $10 bill was included with each survey packet. The target respondents were either plant managers or human resources staff with knowledge of operations. The survey specifically asked respondents to answer questions about "core" workers. These were defined as the workers who were most critical to the production process. Examples of a core worker include manufacturing associate, fabricator, assembler, production technician, and process operator.

The response window for the survey was closed on January 3, 2013. By the end of the response period, 885 establishments completed and returned the survey, 427 establishments declined to participate, 1,230 did not respond, 126 establishments were determined to be ineligible for the survey, and 32 surveys were returned due to incorrect addresses. Eleven of the 885 completed surveys contained missing or zero responses for the total number of core workers and were not included in the analysis. Excluding the ineligible establishments, the incorrect addresses, and the surveys with incomplete core worker totals, the total response rate was 34.5 percent. Reasons for deeming an establishment ineligible include that the establishment did not actually engage in manufacturing; the establishment only carried out manufacturing activities outside of the United States; or the establishment said that it had less than the cutoff level of ten employees for survey participation.

The actual employment size breakdown and the regional breakdown of respondents compared to the target levels from County Business Patterns is as shown in table A2.1a and A2.1b.

Table A2.1a
Employment Size Breakdown: Sample versus County Business Patterns

Establishment	Percent of Total Employment for Establishments ≥ 10 Employees	
	Target	Respondent
1–9 employees	0	4.1
10–19 employees	6.2	10.8
20–99 employees	26.9	33.8
100–249 employees	22.9	22
250–499 employees	15.9	15.6
500+ employees	28.1	13.8

Source: PIE Manufacturing Survey and County Business Patterns (2010).

Table A2.1b
Regional Breakdown: Sample v. County Business Patterns

Census Region	Dun & Bradstreet Percent	Respondent Percent
Northeast	20.4	22.1
Midwest	39.0	42.1
South	20.4	16.8
West	20.2	19.0

Source: PIE Manufacturing Survey and Dun & Bradstreet.

Although the responding establishments roughly track the targets, small establishments are overrepresented and large establishments are underrepresented among the actual respondents. In statistical analyses we employ establishment size weights to correct for these deviations.

From a geographic perspective, the percentage of actual respondents from the Northeast and the West Census regions are not significantly different than the percentages of establishments in these regions in the original Dun & Bradstreet sample (see table A2.1b). However, establishments located in the Midwest are somewhat overrepresented, and establishments in the South are somewhat underrepresented. We have not adopted weights to address these deviations because they are relatively small in magnitude and most of our arguments do not rest on regional differences. When appropriate, we control for region or breakout regional results.

We conducted a slightly more formal bias analysis using size, geographic, and industry data. We used a linear probability model to regress an indicator for completing the survey on indicators for the various establishment size categories, indicators for geographic region, and indicators for two-digit SIC codes.[6] The results are consistent with the previous discussion. The largest size categories of establishments were significantly less likely to respond. As noted, we have corrected for this via weights. Establishments in the South were 5 percent less likely to respond than their New England counterparts. Other geographic differences were insignificant. Out of the twenty two-digit industry SIC codes, only two were significant at the 5 percent level.

In-person interview methodology

We conducted on-site interviews of manufacturers, educational institution staff, and trade association staff in a variety of locations in order to ground our analysis and flesh out our hypotheses. In North Carolina, from January 9 to January13, 2012, we interviewed people from six firms, two universities, three community colleges, and two industry associations in the biopharma-biomanufacturing industry. The interviews were semistructured and were oriented toward discussion of skill requirements for production workers and the challenges (or lack thereof) in hiring skilled workers. In Ohio, we conducted similar interviews focusing on the metal-working firms located in the state's northeast region. During the week of October 23, 2012, we interviewed people from seven firms and one community college, with a subsequent follow-up interview with individuals from a second community college via phone. In Rochester, we targeted the region's optics manufacturers and conducted interviews with people from six firms, two community colleges, and two trade associations. In Michigan we visited McComb Community College in October 2012, and in Springfield we visited the Regional Employment Board as well as several employers and community colleges in November 2012.

Appendix 2.2: Skill demands

Table A2.2
Skill Question Responses

	Percent Answering Yes or Selecting Option
Does the job require reading:	
Basic instruction manuals	75.9
Complex technical documents or manuals	39.2
Any document that is longer than five pages	35.2
Articles in trade journals, magazines, newspapers	10.7
Does the job require:	
Preparing bills, invoices, etc.	18.1
Writing short notes, memos, reports, or requests	61.2
Writing anything at least one page long or longer	21.8
Writing anything at least five pages long or longer	4.5
What is the frequency of computer use:	
Everyday	50.6
A few times per week	12.2
Less often	11.1
Never	26.1
Does this job require (applies only to establishments that do not report "never" requiring computer use):	
Use of word processing software	38.3
Use of spreadsheet or database software	60.5
Computer-aided design (CAD) or computer-aided manufacturing (CAM) skills?	39.3
Use of other engineering or manufacturing software	40.0
Ability to write computer programs	25.6
Performing Internet searches and/or using the World Wide Web to gather information or seek solutions	45.2

Table A2.2
(continued)

	Percent Answering Yes or Selecting Option
Does this job require mathematical operations involving:	
Addition and subtraction	94.5
Multiplication and division	85.9
Fractions, decimals, or percentages	78.0
Using algebra, geometry, or trigonometry	31.8
Probability or statistics	14.1
Calculus or other advanced mathematics	7.3
How important is cooperation with other employees:	
Very important	81.1
Moderately important	18.2
Not very important	0.5
Not at all important	0.0
Not applicable	0.2
How important is the ability to work in teams:	
Very important	64.6
Moderately important	26.7
Not very important	7.6
Not at all important	0.2
Not applicable	0.9
How important is the ability to solve unfamiliar problems:	
Very important	39.1
Moderately important	44.0
Not very important	14.3
Not at all important	1.9
Not applicable	0.8
How important is the ability to learn new skills:	
Very important	50.1
Moderately important	39.2
Not very important	9.5
Not at all important	1.0
Not applicable	0.2
How important is the ability to initiate new tasks without guidance from management:	
Very important	35.0
Moderately important	45.8

Table A2.2
(continued)

	Percent Answering Yes or Selecting Option
Not very important	16.9
Not at all important	1.5
Not applicable	0.9
How important is the ability to independently organize time or prioritize tasks:	
Very important	46.0
Moderately important	38.2
Not very important	13.4
Not at all important	1.7
Not applicable	0.7
How important is the ability to critically evaluate different options:	
Very important	35.9
Moderately important	38.6
Not very important	19.9
Not at all important	4.4
Not applicable	1.2
How important is the ability to evaluate quality of output:	
Very important	70.6
Moderately important	25.1
Not very important	3.5
Not at all important	0.3
Not applicable	0.5
How important is the ability to take appropriate action if quality is not acceptable:	
Very important	76.2
Moderately important	21.4
Not very important	1.8
Not at all important	0.3
Not applicable	0.3

Source: PIE Manufacturing Survey.

Appendix 2.3: Regression tables

Table A2.3 contains the complete regression results for the two models referred to in the text. The first column contains results from an ordinary least squares regression with long-term vacancies as a percentage of core workers as the dependent variable. The second column contains a logit model with an indicator for the presence of high levels of long-term vacancies (> 5 percent of core workers) as the dependent variable. Both models include industry-fixed effects based on two-digit NAICS codes. We also conducted the analyses using three-digit fixed effects (not shown). The results were very similar, although advanced math skills become significant only at the 10 percent level due to collinearity between specific industries and demands for math skills.

Table A2.3
Complete Results of OLS and Logit Models of Long-Term Vacancies

Independent Variables	Dependent Variable	
	Long-Term Vacancy (Percent)	Long-Term Vacancy Indicator
Advanced reading	.012*	.049
	(.006)	(.027)
Advanced math	.017*	.065*
	(.007)	(.027)
Advanced computer	.007	.025
	(.006)	(.027)
Advanced writing	-.003	.007
	(.008)	(.029)
Unique skill demand	.016*	.038
	(.007)	.026
Ability to learn unfamiliar tasks	-.005	.015
	(.006)	(.025)
Cooperation is important	-.001	-.007
	(.009)	(.035)
Work in teams is important	.005	-.011
	(.007)	(.029)
Low wage indicator	.150**	.102
	(.034)	(.112)
Frequent product innovation	.014*	.064*
	(.007)	(.028)
Preference for internal promotion	-.003	-.025
	(.006)	(.024)

Table A2.3
(continued)

Independent Variables	Dependent Variable	
	Long-Term Vacancy (Percent)	Long-Term Vacancy Indicator
10–19 employees	.033	.200*
	(.018)	(.100)
20–99 employees	.004	.119
	(.017)	(.099)
100–249 employees	-.010	.026
	(.017)	(.103)
250–499 employees	-.006	.093
	(.018)	(.101)
500+ employees	-.012	.044
	(.018)	(.104)
Production has increased over last five years	.003	.001
	(.008)	(.033)
Production has decreased over last five years	-.002	-.053
	(.009)	(.038)
Currently provide formal training to core employees	-.006	-.023
	(.006)	(.026)
Ability to evaluate quality of output is very important	-.004	-.011
	(.008)	(.031)
Ability to take appropriate action if quality is not acceptable is very important	.014	.043
	(.008)	(.035)
Number of points respondent allocated to the importance of new products out of 100	-.0003*	-.001*
	(.0001)	(.0007)
Number of points respondent allocated to the importance of quality out of 100	.0001	.0002
	(.0002)	(.001)
NAICS two-digit industry fixed effects	X	X
Number of observations	698	696
	.110	.133

Note: Results for logit/indicator model are marginal effects.
* = significant at 5 percent level;
** = significant at 1 percent level.
Source: Author's calculations based on PIE Manufacturing Survey. See text for details.

Notes

1. These figures come from our calculations using the Census Outgoing Rotation Group data. These data are also used in some of the tables presented in the chapter. The wage data that follow are taken from the Outgoing Rotation Groups (ORGs) (i.e., the Current Population Surveys [CPSs] of April and August) in which wage data are collected for that point in time. These wage data are considered to be more accurate than the wages calculated from the March CPS, which asks about earnings over the prior year and for which the wage has to be calculated by dividing annual earnings by annual hours worked, both of which are recalled with some error. In the ORG data we eliminated allocated wages as well as wages that are reported below $1 an hour in 1979 dollars. See Thomas Lemieux, "Increasing Residual Wage Inequality: Compositional Effects, Noisy Data, or Rising Demand for Skill?" *American Economic Review* 96, no. 3 (June 2006): 461–498, for a discussion of processing these data.

2. Subsequent to writing this chapter, more replies were received and hence future publications will have a modestly higher sample size.

3. In their empirical implementation of this idea ALM use the 1977 and 1991 *Dictionary of Occupational Titles*, which provides (imperfect) data on the skill content of occupations. There are many serious criticisms of these data but for the purposes of their research there was nothing better available. They append occupational skill measures to Census data for several years ending in 1998.

4. BLS Current Employment Survey. Current Employment Survey, Series CES3000000006, CES3000000001, and CES0500000001.

5. The Standard Industrial Classification (SIC) codes that were excluded from the survey sample are:

2051 (bread, cake, and related products)
2759. (commercial printing, n.e.c.)
2711. (newspaper publishing and printing) 2721. (periodicals publishing and printing)
2731. (book publishing and printing)
2732. (book printing)
2741. (misc. publishing)

6. We conducted this bias analysis with SIC rather than NAICS codes because for the nonrespondents in the sample only SIC codes were available.

References

Autor, David H., Frank Levy, and Richard J. Murnane. 2003. "The Skill Content of Recent Technological Change: An Empirical Exploration." *Quarterly Journal of Economics* 118 (4): 1279–1333.

Deloitte and The Manufacturing Institute. 2005. "2005 Skills Gap Report: A Survey of the American Manufacturing Workforce." http://www.themanufacturinginstitute.org/~/media/738F5D310119448DBB03DF30045084EF/2005_Skills_Gap_Report.pdf.

Deloitte and The Manufacturing Institute. 2011. "Boiling Point: The Skills Gap in U.S. Manufacturing." http://www.themanufacturinginstitute.org/~/media/A07730B2A798437D98501E798C2E13AA.ashx.

Dietz, Richard, and James Orr. 2006. "A Leaner, More Skilled U.S. Manufacturing Work-force." *Federal Reserve Bank of New York Current Issues in Economics and Finance* 12 (2): 1–7.

Emanuel, Rahm. 2011. "Chicago's Plan to Match Education with Jobs." *Wall Street Journal*, December 19.

Fernandez, Roberto. 2001. Skill-Biased Technical Change and Wage Inequality: Evidence from a Plant Retooling. *American Journal of Sociology* 107 (2): 273–320.

Handel, Michael. 2010. "What Do People Do at Work? A Profile of U.S. Jobs from the Survey of Workplace Skills, Technology, and Management Practices." Northeastern University Working Paper.

Kavilanz, Parija. 2012. "Northeast Indiana: Hundreds of Factory Jobs Go Unfilled." *CNN Money* (August 8). http://money.cnn.com/2012/08/08/smallbusiness/Indiana-manufacturing-jobs/index.htm.

Lemieux, Thomas. 2006. "Increasing Residual Wage Inequality: Compositional Effects, Noisy Data, or Rising Demand for Skill?" *American Economic Review* 96 (3): 461–498.

Murnane, Richard J., and Frank Levy. 1996. *Teaching the New Basic Skills: Principles for Educating Children to Thrive in a Changing Economy*. New York: Free Press.

Osterman, Paul. 1994. "How Common Is Workplace Transformation and How Can We Explain Who Adopts It?" Evidence from a National Survey. *Industrial & Labor Relations Review* 47 (2): 173–188.

Osterman, Paul. 2000. "Work Organization in an Era of Restructuring: Trends in Diffusion and Impacts on Employee Welfare." *Industrial & Labor Relations Review* 53 (2): 179–196.

3 The New Skill Production System: Policy Challenges and Solutions in Manufacturing Labor Markets

Andrew Weaver and Paul Osterman

In chapter 2 we reviewed a wide range of issues touching on the nature of work in manufacturing and the challenges that firms face in obtaining the workforce that they need. That chapter drew on a nationally representative survey we conducted of manufacturers, a survey that focused heavily on skill and hiring issues as well as the human resource practices of establishments. Even if there were no problems, it is important to understand the skills that employees will need in the future so that educational and training institutions can better prepare young people and adults looking to obtain manufacturing employment. That said, the national dialogue goes beyond this and has centered on a widespread perception of shortfalls in labor supply and skill gaps among available employees. The analysis in chapter 2 provided a more skeptical and nuanced view of these issues but also identified some concerns. The goal of this chapter is to draw on our fieldwork and data analysis (both of which were described in more detail in chapter 2) to suggest constructive policy responses to these concerns.

We showed in chapter 2 that the concern regarding a shortfall of appropriately skilled workers is not a general issue affecting all manufacturing but nonetheless is a real problem in specific circumstances. About 16 percent of establishments have a significant number of long-term vacancies, and about a quarter have some difficulties obtaining the workforce they require. The firms that are experiencing higher levels of difficulties tend to be smaller, to have demands for skills that are unique in their geographic area, to require relatively more advanced math and reading skills, and to engage in more frequent product innovation. These firms often find themselves cut off from a supply of trained labor that used to flow out of large firms in their region and from local institutions that could help address their needs. Larger firms that have lower levels of internal training and promotion also experience long-term vacancies, although the vacancies represent a smaller and more manageable percentage of their production workforces. The forthcoming wave of retirements will exacerbate these challenges. In this chapter we propose a number of specific policies that address problems relating to the development and employment of a skilled workforce in the U.S. manufacturing sector. We will also provide an overarching rationale why these particular policies are likely to pass the cost-benefit test.

For manufacturers to ensure access to the workforce they need, all parties involved in the system must commit themselves to a set of actions that move them beyond where they are now. It is very important to be clear about the double-edged character of this message. We will argue for an active public policy response to the needs of firms, and we will also describe steps aimed at improving the performance of educational institutions.

At the heart of our public policy recommendations is an analysis of how a new skill production system has emerged in the United States. In order to ensure that this system meets the skill demands of manufacturers, it is essential to strengthen labor market intermediaries, improve the performance of community colleges and high schools, and reduce the risks associated with manufacturing employment in order to stimulate the flow of young people into the field. To make these steps effective, employers for their part need to commit to work with local schools, be willing to engage with other firms in their area on labor market issues, increase the level of training that they offer to their employees, and rethink a wage policy that has suppressed starting wages to the point where they often compare unfavorably to less skilled service sector employment.

The analysis we present here is based on extensive fieldwork and interviews with firms, public officials, and school systems across the country, and also on a large representative survey of manufacturing establishments that offers the most detailed available evidence on workforce issues and relationships with educational institutions, especially community colleges. (See appendix 2.1 in chapter 2 for details.)

Background

The system by which the United States produces a skilled workforce has changed dramatically since the 1970s and 1980s. This is particularly true for the manufacturing sector. During this time period, American manufacturing shifted from a regime in which skills were produced in a context of larger plants, long job tenure, thick internal labor markets, and internal corporate training to a context of smaller establishments, shorter job tenure, reduced job ladders, and external training conducted by various institutions and intermediaries.

The average size of manufacturing establishments has declined significantly over time and the number of very large plants located in the United States has fallen precipitously (Henly and Sanchez 2009; Holmes 2011). This decline in size has changed the economics of internal company training. Smaller establishments realize fewer economies of scale in training and consequently have more difficulty in providing both formal and informal training.

Another critical factor that has shaped changes in training and skill development in manufacturing is the rise in uncertainty and volatility in employment. In an environment of higher turnover and less job security, firms have less time to recoup their internal training investments, whereas workers are more cautious about up-front investments in new skills (e.g., financing apprenticeship training via lower initial wages).

American communities, industries, and workers are in the process of adapting to this new world. A new skill production system is emerging that relies heavily on training provided by external actors such as community colleges or job training programs. It is not uncommon for multiple companies to work with local two-year colleges, nonprofit training providers, and government agencies to design and implement training for incumbent and potential workers. The financing for this training comes from myriad sources, including firms, colleges, government at all levels, foundations, and workers themselves. In some areas of the country, this system is very advanced and has been in place for many years. In other regions the new system remains stunted and has thus far failed to fill the gaps left by the dissolution of the old training regime.

The key observation about this new training regime from a public policy standpoint is that it vastly increases the number of independent actors who must collaborate to produce a skilled workforce. Because the new system has so many moving parts, it is much more subject to market failures than the old system. The first problem is one of coordination. Individual actors respond to different incentives and are free to pursue their own objectives and strategies. If the actors all pursue conflicting strategies, the new system will fail to efficiently produce skilled workers. The second problem relates to the level of investment (or effort). No one actor in the new regime can completely internalize the benefits of contributing to an efficient skill production system. This is a classic public goods externality that will lead to underinvestment in skill production by key actors in the system. To use a metaphor: the first problem is to get everyone rowing in the same direction (coordination), and the second is to get everyone rowing with compatible strength and intensity (public goods production).

The principle that underlies all of the policy recommendations we offer in this chapter is that these recommendations are specifically designed to remedy one or both of the two market failures that disproportionately characterize the operation of the new skill training regime. Furthermore, these policies are likely to be ones in which benefits exceed costs because they apply not only to places that have failed to develop a viable new external training system. Even in the areas where this new system is more advanced, it requires much more maintenance than the old system. It is like a garden that requires constant tending lest one key element in the environment deteriorate. Unlike an internal corporate training system in which training incentives are more aligned by default, the new system contains the constant possibility that wedges will emerge among the needs of employers, the content of training curricula, and the goals of students. Thus the recommendations we make in this chapter are as relevant for regions with advanced external training as they are for areas that lag in this regard.

Making connections

A core explanation of why some firms face challenges in obtaining skilled workers is that they lack effective connections to an ecosystem of what might be termed *skill suppliers.* The consequence is a recurrent pattern of poaching employees from one another or else engaging in suboptimal work organization and production because of labor supply issues.

The best example of an effective ecosystem is perhaps the German dual apprenticeship system. As is well known in Germany, employer associations, unions, and the government work together to establish a national curriculum in vocational skill training, and a majority of German youth spend the latter part of their high school years in a mixture of classroom and on-the-job apprenticeship training. All observers agree that the training is high quality and that the skills that it produces are an important source of German competitive advantage. It is notable in this regard that when German firms, accustomed to being deeply embedded in a well-developed skill-providing environment, come to the United States, they often seek to replicate the German environment as much as possible given local constraints (Furmans 2012).

Having said this, it is not realistic to attempt to replicate the German model here. The United States lacks strong employer associations and strong unions. In addition, there exists no national consensus that would enable such a uniform system, not least because no consensus exists that such a system is even desirable. Nevertheless, as we will describe shortly, the United States is not without resources, and the community college system is an important source of potentially high-quality skill training. However, there remains a significant issue of how to better connect firms to each other and to educational institutions in order to stimulate the supply of skilled labor. We believe that there is a central role to be played by labor market intermediaries and that encouraging and diffusing the intermediary model would be a very positive step forward.

In general terms, a labor market intermediary is an entity or organization that connects labor market actors to each other. In addition, the intermediary may undertake activities, ranging from collecting information to fundraising to policy advocacy, that are public goods and hence are not likely to be undertaken by any given organization operating on its own. Intermediaries are the glue that holds a disaggregated skill system together; they enable the type of feedback that overcomes coordination failures. As we will see shortly, intermediaries can range from employer trade associations to local government employer boards to private nonprofits devoted to economic growth or job creation.

It is instructive to examine what happens in the absence of intermediaries. As an example, we interviewed a wire cage manufacturer that had succeeded in securing high-margin aerospace contracts. This firm, however, had great difficulty hiring skilled production workers. Although the firm is located in a large metropolitan labor market with a substantial number of different types of educational institutions, it is not part of a cluster, and it does not have the size to draw the attention of regional community colleges.

The consequence of the firm's isolation was an inability to hire, which, when combined with a fear that internal training would lead to poaching by other firms, created a labor force crisis. The best solution for this employer would be to make common cause with firms in other area manufacturing industries that need somewhat similar skilled production workers. Together, these firms might have the combined aggregate demand to justify the creation of a targeted community college training program. The problem was that there was no institution or mechanism that could bring this about. Addressing this challenge is the reason that intermediaries need to be diffused, strengthened, and supported.

In our fieldwork we identified several best practice examples of intermediaries. What is striking about these cases is that although they share a good deal in common in terms of activities and impact, they differ in their organizational form and the auspices under which they are organized.

An employer-driven intermediary: Rochester, New York

Rochester, New York, is home to one of the premier optics clusters in the world. Kodak, Bausch and Lomb, and Xerox were all founded in Rochester, and during much of the twentieth century they, along with other optics and photonics firms such as Corning, were the regional employment leaders. At its height in the early 1980s, Kodak employed more than sixty thousand workers in Rochester. In the early 1960s, Kodak worked with Monroe Community College (MCC) to create a two-year associates program to produce optics technicians. The program provided training in physics and engineering topics related to optics, and it prepared individuals to perform jobs such as the operation of sophisticated lens grinding and polishing equipment. For decades, Kodak essentially underwrote the program, filling its classes with Kodak apprentices. There were spillover benefits as well. In addition to the students following a career path at big employers such as Kodak, some of the graduates of the program went on to lead innovative small optics companies in the area. However, because of industry shifts and poor business decisions, Kodak's fortunes declined. Employment fell consistently during the 1990s, and today the company employs only a little more than five thousand workers in Rochester. As Kodak experienced these shocks, it pulled back from the relationship with MCC and the apprenticeship program. By the mid-2000s, the program had only a handful of students, and MCC was considering shutting it down. The University of Rochester had already closed its optics manufacturing center, despite the fact that the program had launched a number of successful optics companies. The irony was that, despite Kodak's decline, the Rochester optics cluster was actually doing well. Many small firms had grown up over the years and were thriving. These include companies that produce lenses for 3D movies, components for the semiconductor lithography process, and sophisticated glass grinding and polishing equipment. These firms wanted to hire skilled optics technicians, and they were alarmed at the decline of the MCC program and the possibility that the program would be permanently shuttered. However, no individual firm had enough capital or volume of hires to be a "market maker" for the MCC program. Furthermore, individual firms had idiosyncratic needs. Building the curriculum too closely around any one of these firms would have excluded others. Ultimately, the firms were not able to speak clearly with one voice, to aggregate their demand, or to provide coherent feedback to the community college system. Lack of coordination rather than lack of market demand was on the verge of killing a key element of Rochester's skill production system.

The outcome of this story points to one type of solution to coordination failures in skill production systems. Around the time that MCC was thinking about closing the optics program, a dynamic individual took over the leadership of an industry group called the Rochester Regional Photonics Cluster (RRPC). This individual realized that unless the small- and medium-sized enterprises that now characterize Rochester's optics industry joined together, the industry would lose an important element in the skill production system, one that could not easily be replaced. The RRPC joined together with an energetic leader of one of the local optics firms and convinced MCC to give the program another chance. A new advisory board composed of leaders of small- and medium-sized optics firms was established. The RRPC and executives from small optics firms also began working with local high schools to ensure a flow of students into the new program. Over the years, high school guidance counselors had lost knowledge of viable optics careers as the locus of the industry shifted from visible corporate giants such as Kodak to small specialty firms such as Optimax or OptiPro. RRPC also helped convince Corning to make a $500,000 donation to the program for new facilities and equipment. One of the small firms, Sydor Optics, followed this with an additional $250,000 donation. In short, various firms in the area had demand for MCC graduates, interest in the program, and even willingness to donate funds, but they lacked coordination. What was required was an intermediary—in this case the RRPC—that could overcome the disaggregation of the various actors.[1]

A workforce board intermediary: Springfield, Massachusetts

Springfield, Massachusetts, is a region with a long and rich history of manufacturing, particularly in the machine tool industry. In 2011 the region was home to forty-two precision manufacturing firms with just under four thousand employees (Regional Employment Board of Hampden County 2012). Up until recently the smaller firms in the area were able to obtain a skilled workforce by taking advantage of the apprenticeship training provided by larger companies such as Lennox and United Technology as well as the Springfield Armory. In the past, a sufficient number of employees who received this training went to work at smaller manufacturers due to a preference for a smaller environment or the hope of eventually striking out on their own. The firms we interviewed all reported that although this system worked well for some time, it eroded as the larger firms cut back on internal training and also became, in the words of our interviewees, "design and assembly" operations with less emphasis on actual production. The consequence, much as in the Rochester case, was a shortfall in skilled labor.

For a period of time this shortfall was addressed via a training institution established by the local chapter of the National Tooling and Machining Association (NTMA). The training school was funded by a grant from the U.S. Department of Labor, and when that grant was not renewed, firms found themselves at sea. For reasons laid out previously very few firms were willing or able to mount their own internal training and instead, according to our interviews, reverted to what was termed the "standard" behavior of trying to steal recruits from each other.

Faced with this situation the NTMA approached the Hampden County Regional Employment Board (REB). The REB is a public intermediary and is mandated by federal job training legislation to represent firms, government, and educational institutions in the operation of the Workforce Investment Act of 1998. The actual performance of these REBs is very uneven across the country, with many acting as mere funding conduits with little proactive behavior (Barnow and King 2003). The Hampden County REB had a quite different attitude. In 2005 it began the complex process of connecting firms to local educational institutions and of encouraging these institutions to build up their offerings in relevant curriculum tracks. Just as the firms were disconnected from the educational institutions, the schools themselves were passive in their relationships with employers. In some schools individual staff members in particular departments had relationships with firms, but schoolwide commitments and connections were weak. REB staff met with all NTMA member firms as well as with five vocational-tech high schools and two community colleges. These meetings were aimed at collecting data about needs of firms and the curriculum, actual and potential, in the schools. The result of this process was a memorandum of understanding crafted by the REB and signed by all of the firms and schools. REB staff personally traveled to all firms and schools to get the signatures on the memorandum of understanding to ensure commitment.

As a result of this process the Springfield REB has built a substantial set of programs and activities aimed at meeting workforce needs in the precision manufacturing sector. One set of actions involve data collection: surveys of firms on hiring needs and data collection on enrollment in high school and community-college manufacturing programs. Until the board undertook these, there was no information available on the balance, or lack thereof, between supply and demand of relevant skills. The board has also connected employers directly to schools in order to improve curriculum and to assist in job placements. This has taken the form of encouraging meetings and also of creating a more formal process that strengthened school advisory councils and placed employers as the chairs. In addition, the board organized a training program for supervisors in member firms, funded and managed a dislocated worker training program in machining skills, and organized career fairs and firm visits in order to increase the interest of high school students in manufacturing careers. Due to the actions of the REB, manufacturing firms in the region are now organized, cooperative with each other, and proactive in their stance toward schools and their own workforce needs. The REB has thus helped solve a fundamental coordination problem in the Springfield skill production system.

A community nonprofit intermediary: Cincinnati, Ohio

Partners for a Competitive Workforce is an intermediary that was initiated by the Greater Cincinnati Foundation in 2008 and is, as of 2013, housed and managed by the Cincinnati United Way. It is supported locally by various funders and nationally by the National Fund for Workforce Solutions. The organization works on labor supply issues in a tristate area of southwest Ohio, northern Kentucky, and southeast Indiana. Manufacturing is one of several industry foci, along with health care, construction, IT, and finance.

The organization supports manufacturing curriculum and certifications at local community colleges, as well as at other sites such as community-based organizations. Partners has arranged for local firms to promise a modest hourly pay supplement for new hires and incumbent workers who obtain these certificates. Second, Partners has worked with several firms to start internal apprenticeship programs and has provided subsidies to the firms that have launched these. Finally, just as is true in Springfield and Rochester, Partners is working with local schools on career exploration programs aimed at increasing the flow of young people interested in manufacturing careers.

Despite these successes, Partners does face challenges that reflect the issues confronting manufacturing workforce development throughout the country. Starting wages in local manufacturing establishments are low and fairly stagnant, and this fact, along with the sometimes negative image of manufacturing, discourages new entrants to the workforce. Employers become engaged in activities of Partners only when they themselves feel under immediate pressure, and, as a consequence, it is hard work to develop forward-looking proactive programs. Asked whether they could double their activities if their budget were magically increased, Partners staff expressed doubt largely because of the difficulty of obtaining broad employer engagement.

With these examples in mind we can see that there is no single model of an effective intermediary, and they vary by auspices as well as by sources of support. Indeed there are more models than we have described here (Hunt 2012). What all effective intermediaries do have in common is that they solve problems involving coordination or public goods production. However, the market will not automatically produce intermediaries that solve these market failures. As a result, there is a role for public policy in terms of either launching the intermediary or providing at least some of the necessary resources, or both.

Intermediaries typically do not directly provide training but rather connect employers to the educational institutions in their regions. For this process to be effective there need to be institutions whose curricula and educational capacities can meet the requirements of local manufacturers. In other words, in order to create a viable skill production system, communities not only need mechanisms that can overcome the market failures that characterize the new skill training regime but they also need the raw material of the skill production system: high-quality and flexible educational institutions. Community colleges are one of the best examples of these necessary institutions, and it to these that we now turn.

Community colleges

Community colleges have emerged as one of the most central institutions for training the new manufacturing workforce. They are, of course, not the only institutions devoted to developing skills. In parts of the country technical high schools remain strong, and in some communities nonprofits and community-based organizations directly provide training. However, community colleges tend to be the dominant players in the design and delivery of industry-focused, high-skill training for several reasons. First, community colleges have much greater scale and resources than nonprofit training providers or other training institutions. Second, community colleges often have a culture of openness to multiple stakeholders. Many community colleges strive to include employers in their course designs and to solicit employer feedback concerning the quality of their graduates' training. At the same time, community colleges take seriously the demands and concerns of local officials and parents. This institutional openness means that individuals and organizations that seek to adapt worker training for a new economic environment are frequently able to interact with the community college system in a way that is not possible with, for example, the local high school system.

There are over 1,100 U.S. community colleges that enroll over seven million students in credit-bearing courses (National Center for Education Statistics 2008).[2] Among students who are enrolled for credit, most are in degree programs, but a substantial minority seeks certificates. We are not sure how many students are enrolled in noncredit community college courses, on topics ranging from the directly vocational to the recreational, because not all states keep data on these enrollments. However, experts agree that the numbers are close to those in credit courses. Hence, roughly twelve million people are enrolled in U.S. community colleges (Osterman 2011).

In two-year degree programs over half of enrollment is in occupational fields, and virtually all certificate programs, either of the credit or the noncredit variety, are occupational (Bailey et al. 2004). Returns to community college education, either for obtaining a two-year degree or for earning a shorter certificate in a specific field, are substantial. For AA degrees, the returns range from 13 to 38 percent, depending on the population in question and the field of study.[3] The research on the rates of return to community college certificates is thinner but still leads to impressive conclusions. According to a recent report by the Center on Education and the Workforce, 12 percent of adults hold certificates, and the rates of return to certificate holders are as high as 20 percent for high school graduates. In these data, individuals who hold certificates in metalworking earn about the median among all certificate holders (Carnevale, Rose, and Hanson 2012).

To get an idea of the role played by community colleges it is helpful to take a look at best-practice cases. In choosing these cases, we focus not simply on individual community colleges but rather on community colleges that have effective institutional relationships that extend beyond the walls of the community college itself. Specifically, we highlight McComb Community College in Michigan and its relationship with the federal Advanced Technical Education (ATE) program, as well as the BioNetwork in North Carolina.

McComb is a community college located just north of Detroit. Over the years, the college has been hit hard by the shocks that have affected Detroit's auto industry. The number of apprentices from Chrysler taking courses at McComb declined from one thousand to ninety since the early 2000s. The college has demonstrated its flexibility in filling niches in the skill gap system by shifting its focus to producing more workers for small- and medium-sized enterprises. McComb has also continued to bring knowledge of advanced technical processes into the region. Through the federal ATE program, McComb learned about a high-tech auto curriculum in California and now partners with California institutions to implement it.

The ATE program is important not only for McComb but also for other community colleges seeking to improve their relationships with manufacturing firms. It began in 1992 and supports manufacturing curriculum development in more than thirty community college–based centers throughout the country. We interviewed centers in Michigan, South Carolina, and Connecticut. It was clear from these interviews that the program is effective in improving the quality of curriculum materials in area community colleges. In addition, by using ATE support, schools are able to experiment with new delivery methods such as providing internships during the academic year and summer break. McComb is effectively using the program to adapt to changing needs and gaps in the region's skill production system. More extensive assessments of the program also support its efficacy (Lloyd 2013).

The Research Triangle Park (RTP) area in Durham, North Carolina, is home to a world-class biopharma cluster. Unlike some other biotech and pharmaceutical clusters, however, RTP combines a substantial amount of manufacturing alongside cutting edge research. It is in this context that the story of North Carolina's BioNetwork is instructive. BioNetwork is a program that links North Carolina's community colleges by providing shared biotech workforce training services. As the director of the BioNetwork noted, BioNetwork exists because there are fifty-eight community colleges in North Carolina that "need it but cannot individually support it." In 2011, the BioNetwork trained more than 4,300 students in short classes. More than 80 percent of these students were incumbent industry workers. In many cases, the training is branded by the local community college and delivered by one of Bio-Network's contract instructors. BioNetwork also conducted outreach to thousands of middle and high school students regarding the bio-pharma industry and potential career paths. Ultimately, BioNetwork is an "efficiency enhancing measure" that "saves duplication and provides resources to smaller colleges."

One of the BioNetwork's latest initiatives is a mobile unit—essentially a big recreational vehicle—that contains lab equipment and fume hoods for biotech skill training. By deploying this unit, BioNetwork can serve North Carolina firms on-site without disrupting production. The net result is that North Carolina's community colleges and their associated institutions—such as BioNetwork—are able to fill a wider range of gaps in the new disaggregated skill production system than in states that lack such a diverse group of flexible institutions.[4]

Challenges facing community colleges: Findings from the survey

The rates of return to achieving a community college degree or certificate are high but the community college system as a whole faces significant challenges (Belfield and Bailey 2011, 46). The community colleges are themselves subject to coordination failures. There often exists no coherent community college "system." In fact that the use of the term *system* is misleading in that community colleges are governed at the state, not national, level. Moreover, within some states community colleges are often fairly autonomous within their own funding districts. The fact that one innovative or responsive community college exists in a given region is no guarantee that the other community colleges that serve the region will have high-quality or complementary offerings. In addition to inconsistency, community colleges suffer from very high student dropout rates, a challenge that concerns all community college programs, not just those in manufacturing (Integrated Postsecondary Education Data System).[5]

Despite the importance of community colleges, there has been little data on the relationship between manufacturing firms and community colleges. The MIT Production in the Innovation Economy (PIE) manufacturing survey of nearly nine hundred nationally representative manufacturing establishments includes a rich set of questions on this relationship in order to determine the nature of the role that community colleges are currently playing with regard to the training of manufacturing production workers (the survey is described in detail in chapter 2).

The coverage areas of community colleges are quite substantial. Eighty-eight percent of establishments in our survey reported that a community college served their area. However, actual contact between community colleges and manufacturers is somewhat less extensive. Among manufacturing establishments that had a community college in their area only 49 percent reported that they had had discussions with the community college regarding training or hiring core production employees. When we ask about an actual relationship the numbers fall further. Among the 49 percent reporting some type of contact, 43 percent report that they have had a community college deliver training for experienced core employees, and 18 percent report that they have had training delivered for new hires or potential recruits.

The net result of the survey is that only 21 percent of all establishments have ever had a community college deliver training to core production employees. Thus, although community colleges are regarded as critical institutions for the training of highly skilled workers, a substantial majority of U.S. manufacturers do not rely on community colleges for training.

The picture improves when we ask whether the establishments that do use community colleges are satisfied. Eighty-nine percent report that the community college was very or somewhat helpful. Thus manufacturing establishments that actually work with community colleges are overwhelmingly satisfied with the quality of services that they receive. Another way of approaching these issues is to focus on the opinion of manufacturing establishments about community college–trained workers as opposed to opinions about the institutions themselves. Of those establishments with direct experience of community college applicants, 81 percent reported that they feel the general academic skills of community college applicants for core production positions were either good or very good, and 50 percent felt the same way about job-specific skills. Of course these findings must be set against the fact that 37 percent of respondents with a community college in their area said that they had no community college–trained applicants.

Responses about the quality of communication between firms and community colleges were concerning. Overall, 57 percent of respondents did not believe that the local community college did a good job of communicating with industry employers. This result points to the importance of the types of intermediaries discussed previously.

We can gain further insight into the dynamics of community college training by analyzing the relationship between the incidence of this training and establishment size. The probability that a manufacturing establishment will use a community college to train its employees rises substantially with the total size of the entity. Among establishments with fewer than fifty employees, only 14 percent have arranged for community college training. This compares with 44 percent of establishments with 100 to 499 employees and 59 percent of establishments with five hundred or more employees. Thus, any given small establishment is much less likely to access one of the key resources in the new skill production system: community colleges. To the extent that we have seen a decline in the average size of establishments over the past few decades, and to the extent that manufacturers have reduced the level of internal training they once provided, these results indicate that over time there may be a class of smaller manufacturing employers who will face significant challenges in accessing the new skill production system.

Taken as a whole, these results are very consistent with the themes that characterize the new skill production system. Employers tend to be favorably impressed with community colleges, particularly with regard to the general skills that these institutions impart. They have somewhat more reservations about the quality of job-specific skills, but half of manufacturing establishments still rate these skills as good or very good. What is more striking is the fact that many employers do not have relationships with their local community college, and many do not receive any community college applicants for positions in their plants. These results point to the possibility that certain segments of the manufacturing industry experience information or coordination failures with regard to their participation in the skill production system. This possibility is reinforced by the fact that questions regarding communication elicited significantly more negative responses than questions regarding skills or quality. Ultimately, the challenges of managing a disaggregated skill production system may be even more important than the particular content of the training curriculum.

High schools

A great deal of energy at the national level has been directed toward school reform, and it probably fair to say that more attention has been paid to the lower grades than to high schools. Nonetheless high schools certainly merit attention. The quality of high school education and graduation rates include far broader challenges than issues concerning manufacturing, but they are relevant because many of the young people at risk are potential candidates to enter into manufacturing careers.

One of the findings of our research is that, even in areas with strong community college systems such as North Carolina and Ohio, there are many employers who are looking for workers with a skill level that is below that of a two-year college graduate but above that of a typical high school graduate. In some cases, community college certificate programs may fill this need, but in other cases it may be much more economical—and effective—to involve high schools in producing the required skills.

A broader discussion of the role of high school career and technical education is complicated by the need to take seriously the argument that, as the dismal average earnings of high school–only employees shows, postsecondary education should be encouraged whenever possible. This concern is given heightened resonance by the fear that telling some students that they should stop their education with vocational high school training harkens back to a social class (and race)–based era of tracking and stratification.

These concerns are valid but need to be weighed against several other considerations. First, there exist some high-quality vocational and technical high schools providing levels of training that rival community college certificate programs and perhaps some community college degree programs. An example of such a school is Greater Lowell Technical High School (GLT) in Tyngsboro, Massachusetts. GLT is a large vocational-technical high school with a strong record of placing students into jobs. Firms from as far away as Rhode Island regularly approach GLT placement staff often bypassing other closer vocational schools. Part of GLT's success relates to top-quality facilities and advanced curricula. For example, according to GLT staff, the auto tech curriculum that GLT uses in its full-sized auto garage is the same as the curriculum used in Southern New Hampshire University. Part of the school's success is also attributable to the general advantages of the Massachusetts vocational high school system, which involves significantly more time spent in applied learning on the job than other states' systems.

The biggest part of GLT's success, however, is due to its personalized approach to learning. Rather than just focusing on the skills of a given career, GLT goes out of its way to counsel students, track their progress, and offer them opportunities for leadership and management. The school runs a special preparatory camp for underprepared students before entering ninth grade. Students are required to commit to spending a certain amount of time with mentors and guidance counselors, and this time is tracked. Most important, when the various programs in the school engage in any sort of production work, GLT seeks to have students manage the project. For example, in recent school renovations, computer-aided drafting (CAD) students were responsible for soliciting specifications and drawing up plans. Likewise, students manage the on-campus restaurant. GLT has a variety of programs serving area manufacturers, including machining, metal fabrication, CAD, and electronics. The combination of high-quality applied learning and person-centered leadership development has enabled GLT to serve the skill needs of area employers and to put at-risk youth on viable career tracks.[6]

Unfortunately, most communities do not boast high-quality vocational-technical high schools. The larger point we wish to make is that the type of training required to produce highly skilled production workers does not have to take place in rarefied and expensive four-year college settings. Other options, ranging from community college degrees and certificates to high school programs to high-quality job-training programs, all merit consideration. One effective example of how to accomplish this is the early college high school model in which high school students take community college–level courses during part of the week and earn college credit in doing so. Evaluations of this model suggest that it substantially increases graduation rates among at-risk students and also increases postsecondary attendance as well as skills acquisition (Le and Frankfort 2011; American Institutes for Research and SRI International 2009). Other school districts have experimented with somewhat different models that link high schools and community colleges, and that include an element of skills training (Baker 2012).

Although high schools deserve more attention than they have received as part of the manufacturing workforce training system, as institutions high schools often exemplify the challenges facing disaggregated skill production systems. In our interviews, it was notable that many employers said they had no contact with local school administrators, and others said that their attempts at making contacts had gone unanswered. Thus one positive goal is to find ways to create a feedback loop between metropolitan school systems and local employers. In Rochester, an intermediary serving the local optics industry has helped to create such a feedback loop by working with local science teachers to develop early college optics programs and optics laboratories.[7]

Another initiative that attempts to overcome the isolation of high schools with respect to industry-relevant curriculum development is Project Lead the Way (PLTW), an organization that provides science, technology, engineering, and mathematics (STEM) curricula to high schools and middle schools. PLTW is in nearly five thousand schools nationwide and has a rigorous project-oriented approach that has shown promising results. Evaluations suggest that students in PLTW programs have shown better test performance, better attendance, more interest in college, and more willingness to take STEM subjects in college than comparable students (Tai 2012).

There is clearly a balance to be maintained here. School systems are responsible for general education, and it would be a mistake to tie the incentives of schools too closely to an overly specific agenda or the idiosyncratic needs of particular companies. However, by the same token, general education that leads to neither college nor a job is problematic.

Priming the pump: The manufacturing workforce

Many employers believe that they simply cannot convince people to work for them, and national associations echo these worries. When firms express concern about their difficulties in attracting the work-force and skills that they require, they often point to the reluctance of young people and their parents to consider manufacturing as a career. With remarkable consistency, employers say that manufacturing has acquired a "bad rap." They state that today's youth mistakenly believe that manufacturing jobs are hot, dirty, and dangerous. Alternatively, if the work environment is in fact physically challenging, one hears that the work ethic of today's youth has declined. It is also commonly asserted that parents and high school guidance counselors irrationally steer students away from viable careers as skilled production workers.

One issue concerning the flow of employees is the frequently heard concern that too few students are enrolled in STEM courses and that math capacities are declining. Perhaps surprisingly, research shows that there has been no decline in STEM education, and in fact there has been an increase (Carnevale, Smith, and Melton 2011).[8] When it comes to math skills, the National Assessment of Educational Progress found in its most recent (2008) long-term trend assessment that the math achievement scores of nine- and thirteen-year-olds have improved since 2004 and the scores of seventeen-year-olds have held steady (Rampey, Dion, and Donahue 2009).

Our survey also gives reason to doubt that an inadequate flow of workers is the central issue. In our data only a quarter of the establish-ments experienced long-term vacancies that they could not fill, and only 16 percent experienced high levels of these vacancies. In addition, in response to a question about what the primary reason for long-term vacancies was, only 5 percent of respondents selected "too few candi-dates apply."

In light of this evidence, these employer complaints lack a certain face validity. In today's environment of high unemployment and scare jobs, why would people turn away from firms that do offer opportuni-ties? Notwithstanding what we regard as strong reasons to be skeptical of these complaints, we have come to believe, based on our fieldwork and the evidence from our survey, that there is some truth to them in certain situations. We base this conclusion not simply on firms express-ing their concerns, of which we also heard many, but also on observed actions or lack of actions by employers and young people. As examples, consider some of the high-quality manufacturing vocational training programs that we examined: the mechatronics program at McComb Community College and the advanced technology education programs in South Carolina and Connecticut. In these programs, students receive strong training in modern manufacturing skills, and in both cases the graduates of the program consistently obtain good jobs. Yet in both cases there are empty seats. Additional evidence of a problem of too few applicants is the time that managers in the firms we interviewed spent visiting schools, holding career fairs, hosting tours, and engaging in other actions aimed at attracting students. Time is money, and unless these firms actually faced challenges, it is not plausible that they would invest so much in these activities.

All of this forces us to return to the core issue: why is the supply of labor to these jobs sometimes restricted? Why are some students, their parents, and their school counselors not as enthusiastic about manufacturing employment as one might expect? A reasonable hypothesis is that the reluctance is a reflection of the poor employment prospects and risk in the industry. Consider that between 2000 and 2010 manufacturing employment fell by one-third (Bureau of Labor Statistics). Given this fact, it is entirely understandable that students and their parents would be leery of a mechatronics training program, even if it had the potential to lead to a relatively high-paying job. Furthermore, although many manufacturing jobs have the potential to end up at a decent rate of pay, many start at low rates in the $12 to $15 per-hour range. When students look at the fact that some level of job tenure is required to become fully productive (and hence move into the $20+ per-hour range), and the fact that the job they are training for may not exist in five years, the payoff to attending a two-year community college manufacturing program—or even obtaining a nine-month certificate—becomes somewhat unclear. The risks facing new entrants in the field are very real and cannot be mitigated by any single employer. There are, however, public policies that can alter the calculations that may bias young people away from manufacturing careers. A potential package might include part-time unemployment insurance (so-called short work) and improved training for dislocated workers.

The core challenge is to find ways to cushion the consequences of volatility and job loss. The idea behind part-time unemployment insurance is that a firm can choose to reduce hours and engage in work-sharing instead of laying people off. For those employees whose earnings are reduced because they are now part-time, the unemployment insurance system will pick up the difference. This option has long been available to states in America, and currently twenty-three have adopted it, but it has not been taken up aggressively nor publicized to employers. This is unfortunate because in a careful study of those states that have adopted the program, Katharine Abraham and Susan House-man show that the short-work option succeeded in reducing manu-facturing unemployment (Abraham and Houseman 2012). Recent legislation extending the payroll tax cut included several steps aimed at encouraging and subsidizing states to adopt or expand the program (Abraham and Furman 2012).[9] One of the attractive features of short-work policies is that they have the potential to subtly influence firm training and hiring decisions. By lengthening average job tenure, these policies can lengthen the time period over which firms can recoup training investments, thus potentially incentivizing greater levels of training. In addition, longer job tenure lowers the risk of paying higher wages up-front because there is more assurance that a given employee will be around long enough to gain the specific skills necessary to attain full productivity.

Short work can ease the burden associated with temporary layoffs and can delay permanent layoffs. But fundamentally it is a response to cyclical volatility and not a solution to the risks associated with long-run, or secular, shifts in labor demand. Workers with a substantial amount of tenure (three years or more) suffer earnings losses on the order of 20 percent after losing their jobs if they are lucky enough to obtain new work, and many do not even manage this (von Wachter 2010). In contrast to widespread skepticism, however, there is some evidence that for many dislocated workers—particularly those who take technical courses—retraining can raise earnings (Brookings Insti-tution).[10] Enabling dislocated workers, many of whom are not eligible for Pell grants, to access substantial amounts of training in community colleges and other appropriate settings, would be a positive step forward. It is important that the quantity of training truly be substantial and that any reforms move us beyond the short-term training and job-search assistance that characterizes most current efforts (Brookings Institution).[11]

Taken together, the combination of short work and retraining opportunities should ease some of the concern young people, parents, and school counselors feel about the prospects of entering an uncer-tain and volatile industry. The key point is that to the extent we want individuals to make investments in the skill sets demanded by volatile industries in a context of rapid technical change and globalization, we should design institutions that reduce some of the individual risk entailed in these investment decisions. Having said this, short work and retraining are only partial, and in some instances short-run, solutions to the inherent insecurity of manufacturing. Other approaches, such as wage insurance, are probably not feasible and so improving the health of the overall manufacturing sector is likely the best long-run solution.

The potential for certification standards to improve labor supply

Concern about skill shortages in manufacturing has heightened interest in a national program of skill credentials. The core idea is to develop a system of nationally recognized, stackable, modular skill certifications that students obtain and that employers use in their hiring and promotion practices. Certification systems typically involve identifying particular skills or packages of skills that are demanded by employers. The systems specify a training curriculum and a testing procedure that will indicate mastery of the skills in question. Examples of target skills could be particular types of metalworking skills or more general safety or quality skills. President Obama endorsed the concept in a speech at Northern Virginia Community College, and the broad-based nature of the effort is apparent in the impressive range of foundations, employer associations, and nonprofits that have involved themselves in developing and supporting standards (White House Office of the Press Secretary 2011).[12] Given this depth of support, it is important to think carefully about the contributions of the credentials effort to solving the broader challenges presented here.

Efforts to establish a skills credentials system are not new. In 1992, the Department of Labor established twenty-two pilot credentials programs, and in 1994, the Goals 2000: Educate America Act created the National Skills Standards Board with the mandate to develop and market standards across a wide spectrum of industries. The skill standards movement resonates for several reasons. First, it parallels the effort to improve K–12 education via standards, and because there is wide agreement among education experts that standards represent a fruitful strategy, it is an easy step to apply that notion to other arenas. Second, other nations, notably Germany, have had a great deal of success in developing a high-quality manufacturing labor force via a complex system of which standards are a central component.

Our assessment of the certification movement is that there are reasons to hope that the project can improve the quality of the manufacturing workforce, but, at the same time, it is important not to oversell the effort as the centerpiece of an overall workforce strategy.

Certifications can be helpful but have to be seen as just one component of a much more comprehensive strategy.

The main challenge to the effectiveness of certification is low employer use of the system. Because the system is voluntary, the incentive to use the system at the individual firm level must be strong. However, there are several reasons why many manufacturers will likely opt out. First, it is not the case that the U.S. has no existing system of skill credentials on which employers can rely. The alternative to a new credentialing system is clearly not the absence of anything, but instead is the system of community college AA degrees and certifications that is already in place throughout the country. As we saw in our earlier discussion of community colleges, there is a substantial rate of return to both certificates and AA degrees. This fact implies these existing credentials are valued by employers and are thus useful in judging the quality of potential workers. In addition, this system may provide opportunities for customization and tailoring of skill training that a uniform national system cannot.

A second reason some employers may opt out relates to one of the system's potential benefits: mobility. Some employers may be concerned that promoting a credentialing system will make workers more footloose and deprive firms of returns on human capital investments in those workers.

It is hard to know in principle just what the employer take-up rate is likely to be, but the experience of the effort in the 1990s does provide some clues. Evaluations by Mathematica found very spotty use, and a Government Accounting Office review of the initiatives noted that advocates could provide no evidence of benefits to employers. These assessments are not entirely fair because the efforts were pilot programs and lacked the broad-based support that we see now, but the results are at least cautionary.

The results of our survey suggest that concerns about employer take-up are realistic. Only 7.3 percent of establishments responded affirmatively to the question, "Do you use any formal industry skill credentials system, such as those provided by industry associations or national testing services, for hiring core employees?"

Set against these concerns, advocates of new skill certification systems might argue that it is worth pursuing a system with stronger incentives or coercive aspects for three reasons. First, they might say that a national system of credentials would permit much greater geographic mobility of labor and hence a more efficient labor market than currently exists. As an example, in the absence of a national skill certification system, would an employer in Texas know what to make of a community college certificate obtained in Michigan by a job applicant? Second, advocates might point to the very uneven quality of community colleges. They could view a certification system as a tool for upgrading the quality of manufacturing education. Third, proponents might note that even a region with a well-functioning community college system might still exhibit a poor skill-production system for certain industries due to coordination and communication failures. Certifications could theoretically assist in overcoming these challenges.

When it comes to worries about mobility, the evidence does not suggest that this is a serious source of concern. To begin with, a strong credentials system does not necessarily bring with it high mobility. German manufacturing workers tend to have much longer tenure than American workers despite the fact that there is a strong German credentialing system. Perhaps more to the point, there is no strong evidence that U.S. credentials lead to mobility. A useful comparison is between manufacturing workers and construction workers, an occupation with a strong, well-developed, and nationally recognized credentialing system. This comparison also roughly controls for education and occupational strata. Despite the fact that construction credentials might theoretically enable more mobility, between 2011 and 2012 the percentage of construction and manufacturing employees who moved between counties was essentially identical (U.S. Census Bureau 2012).[13]

Credentials can be very helpful in encouraging educational institutions to concentrate on and improve their training efforts in manufacturing skills. The credentialing movement gives advocates of greater community college involvement a tool that schools can focus on and a standard against which to judge their progress. By pushing for national certifications and putting the prestige and funding of many impressive organizations behind the effort, the certification movement does indeed have the potential to highlight the needs of manufacturing and strengthen the offerings of our educational institutions.

Note that in this context certifications have the potential to do more than just enable an under-resourced community college to implement a higher quality curriculum. Even in cases when the community college has substantial resources and curriculum development expertise, it may not receive consistent signals from the employer community. As we saw with the example of the Rochester optics industry, disorganization or changes in industry structure may lead to coordination failures in the skill production system. Certificates can theoretically provide a useful coordinating signal in this situation.

As long as we are realistic about what can and cannot be expected from this initiative, improving certifications is a step that can support the broader strategies aimed at improving the labor supply to America's manufacturing firms.

The employer side of the bargain

Just as prices are the result of the intersection of supply and demand, employment outcomes are the result not only of the supply-side measures discussed previously but also of the demand-side measures that firms take when they recruit, hire, and train workers. Employers must also take action to address the challenges of obtaining a skilled workforce. This is particularly the case in the new disaggregated skill production system. Employers must be more active and outward facing than ever before. The steps employers need to take include upgrading their human resource policies and working cooperatively with their fellow employers and with schools in their regions to address workforce issues.

Firms are under considerable competitive pressure. But it is also important to recognize that although on average manufacturing labor represents only about 15 percent of costs, it appears to bear a disproportionate share of cutbacks (McKinsey and Company 2012, 117). The severity of cutbacks since the new millennium raises the possibility that in pursuit of other strategic goals, firms are actually creating some of the problems that are cited in the skill-gap debate. Two issues are particularly concerning. The first is that many firms have limited the training they provide their employees, which is particularly ironic given the concern about skill shortages. When we asked firms in our survey about their training policy, only 22 percent reported that they had increased their investment in formal training during the previous five years. Second, starting wages are quite low, and, as we demonstrated in chapter 2, manufacturing wages have stagnated. As noted previously, it is not hard to understand why young people are reluctant to enter manufacturing when they consider the risks involved and weigh these against starting wages that are often comparable to wages in service sector industries that show no signs of sectoral decline.

Many of the firms we interviewed have made significant commitments to working with their local educational institutions in terms of giving them advice and, in at some cases, providing modern equipment that the schools can use to prepare students. However, some of the labor market intermediaries we interviewed—particularly those located in more distressed labor markets—reported how hard they found it to get the attention of employers and involve them in solving the labor market challenges that they face. To the extent that employers wish to increase the flow of skilled workers over current levels, commitment to working with partners in the new skill production system needs to become more widespread.

Conclusion: Meeting the workforce needs of U.S. manufacturers

Although skill shortages in the manufacturing sector are not the broad-based problem that is sometimes claimed, our survey evidence indicates that there is a subset of firms that experience real difficulties in accessing skilled workers. To the extent there are challenges, we believe many of these are related to the transformation of the American skill production system. The new system, which is quite developed in some areas and in rough transition in others, replaces the old system of internal corporate training and internal labor markets that characterized larger manufacturing plants in past decades. This new system is characterized by the use of external actors such as community colleges to train workers. Because of its disaggregated nature it is susceptible to a variety of coordination and public goods market failures, and, even when it operates well, it needs a much higher level of maintenance and attention to ensure good labor market outcomes.

The keys to the successful operation of the new system are effective intermediaries and high-quality, flexible educational institutions. We have described a number of examples of these. Ultimately, our survey results indicate that connecting the relevant players—firms, community colleges, and other training resources—may be a more critical task than improving the quality of, say, the training programs offered by a local community college. Thus although there are a number of initiatives aimed at elevating the quality of individual institutions, we would argue that a significant portion of the dollars devoted to addressing manufacturing workforce issues should be directed toward facilitating the creation and operation of intermediaries, or networks of community colleges, and toward overcoming coordination failures more generally. It is important to note that offering financial incentives to individual institutions, or holding competitions with prizes for the development of manufacturing training programs, will be unlikely to address any fundamental underlying problems in skill production for manufacturing. Unless these initiatives contain intermediary or other mechanisms to address coordination and communication failures, they will likely fail in the communities that need them most and succeed only in the areas where they were really unnecessary.

Because the education and career choices of individual students and workers form a key part of the national skill gap debate, we also examine various supply-side barriers that are often claimed to reduce the flow of skilled workers into manufacturing. We argue that to the extent there is any reservation about manufacturing careers on the part of students, parents, and guidance counselors, such reservations are likely rational responses to volatility and sectoral decline in manufacturing. Because workforce investment in the type of engineering and high-tech production skills that characterize modern manufacturing is socially desirable, we propose that public policy, via tools such as short work and a more developed training system for dislocated workers, should shift some of the risk that comes from investing in industry-specific skills away from individuals.

We also assess the potential for national skill certification systems to address manufacturing labor supply challenges. We conclude that these systems are unlikely to improve labor mobility but that they have modest potential to improve the manufacturing-related operations of community colleges and to address communication failures between educational institutions and employers.

Finally, we note that employers have a more active, outward-facing role to play in the new skill production system. Firms must work closely with educational institutions, intermediaries, government actors, and other players to secure the skills that they require to thrive now and in the future.

Ultimately, if firms and policymakers focus attention on all of the components of the new skill production system, and continually seek to strengthen the linkages and communication among the various actors, then there is no reason why the U.S. system cannot produce the skilled workers that manufacturers of all sizes and stripes demand.

Notes

1. Information based on interviews with staff at Rochester optics firms, community college officials, and trade association representatives during the week of October 22, 2012.

2. For the number of community colleges see http://www.aacc.nche.edu/AboutCC/Pages/default.aspx. Among community colleges, 17 percent have enrollment of at least ten thousand and 12 percent have enrollment of five hundred or below. Twenty-three percent of community colleges are in California. See National Center for Education Statistics, "Community Colleges: Special Supplement to the Condition of Education," 033 (2008): 3.

3. The first widely noted research on rates of return to community college credentials reported positive results, and more recent research has updated these findings and controlled for a large range of personal and family variables. The rates of return range from 13 percent for men who obtain an AA degree to a remarkable 38.9 percent for women. In general the results are more robust for women across all specifications, but for both genders the overall positive message is clear for those who manage to obtain a credential.

4. Information based on interviews with staff from North Carolina biomanufacturing firms, community college officials, and trade association representatives, January 9–13, 2012.

5. The federal government collects data on graduation rates via its Integrated Postsecondary Education Data System, and according to the most recent figures only 27.0 percent of public community college students who entered in 2008 had obtained a degree or certificate within 150 percent of the expected time, that is, by 2011. These outcomes are more than a little discouraging. The problem with these data is that they only refer to full-time students whereas we saw that a strong majority of students attend part-time. Many observers would point out that they are also somewhat unfair. Given the substantial fraction of part-time students, focusing on a three-year completion rate may be too stringent. The Department of Education does not collect outcomes for a longer enrollment period; however, a recent effort, executed by Jobs for the Future as part of the Lumina Foundation Achieving the Dream initiative, did collect detailed outcome data from six states for a six-year period since enrollment. In these data, at best only four out of ten students reach their goals within six years of enrolling, and in most of the states the results are even worse (even assuming that the story for transfer students has a uniformly happy ending).

6. Information from interviews with Greater Lowell Technical High School staff on February 7, 2013.

7. Information based on interviews with staff at Rochester optics firms, community college officials, and trade association representatives during the week of October 22, 2012.

8. Carnevale et al. find that although STEM shortages may exist, their cause is diversion of STEM-trained workers into high-paying non-STEM fields rather than stagnant supply of STEM-trained workers. In fact, they find that the number of workers with high-level STEM skills has increased by 60 percent since 1980.

9. As described in a White House blog (http://www.whitehouse.gov/blog/2012/06/18/reforming-unemployment-insurance-protect-jobs-and-incomes-american-workers), "In states that already have a permanent work sharing program in place, the new law provides temporary Federal reimbursement for the benefits paid to workers under the state program. In states that do not, it offers a temporary Federal work sharing program to bridge the gap until the state can create a permanent program. Finally, states that create a new program or wish to expand an existing one will have access to $100 million in Federal implementation grants to help them jump-start program participation."

10. This research is based on evidence from retraining dislocated workers in community colleges in Washington State. As such it is obviously more limited than one would want but still suggestive. See Louis S. Jacobson, Robert J. LaLonde, and Daniel G. Sullivan, "Policies to Reduce High-Tenured Displaced Workers' Earnings Losses Through Retraining," The Hamilton Project (Washington, DC: Brookings Institution, November 2011).

11. For example, a recent proposal put forward by the Hamilton Project (a Brookings Institution initiative) is that employees who earned $50,000 at a lost job be eligible for a training account of up to $30,000 to be allocated on a regular basis as long as the individual is in training.

12. The White House, Office of the Press Secretary, "President Obama and Skills for America's Future Partners Announce Initiatives Critical to Improving Manufacturing Workforce" (June 8, 2011). Among the organizations involved are the Aspen Institute, ACT, Gates Foundation, Lumina Foundation, the Joyce Foundation, the National Association of Manufacturers, the Society of Manufacturing Engineers, the American Welding Society, and the National Institute of Metalworking Skills.

13. From 2011 to 2012, 3.8 percent of construction workers moved out of their county of residence, and for manufacturing workers the figure was 3.4 percent (U.S. Census Bureau 2012).

References

Abraham, Katharine, and Jason Furman. White House Blog. 2012. (June 18). http://www.whitehouse.gov/blog/2012/06/18/reforming-unemployment-insurance-protect-jobs-and-incomes-american-workers.

Abraham, Katharine G., and Susan N. Houseman. 2012. "Short-Time Compensation as a Tool to Mitigate Job Loss? Evidence on the U.S. Experience during the Recent Recession," Upjohn Institute Working Paper no. 12–181.

American Institutes for Research and SRI International. 2009. Six Years and Counting: the ECHSI Matures. Seattle, WA: Gates Foundation.

Bailey, Thomas, Timothy Leinbach, Marc Scott, Mariana Alfonso, Gregory Kienzl, and Benjamin Kennedy. 2004. "The Characteristics of Occupational Students in Postsecondary Education," CCRC Brief no. 21 (August).

Baker, Al. 2012. "At Technology High School, Goal Isn't to Finish in Four Years." New York Times (October 21).

Barnow, Bert and Christopher King. 2003. The Workforce Investment Act in Eight States: Overview of Findings from a Field Network Study. Baltimore: Institute for Policy Studies, Johns Hopkins University (July).

Belfield, Clive R., and Thomas Bailey. 2011. The Benefits of Attending Community College: A Review of the Evidence. Community College Review 39 (1): 46–68.

Bureau of Labor Statistics, Current Employment Statistics.

Carnevale, Anthony P., Nicole Smith, and Michelle Melton. 2011. STEM. Washington, DC: Georgetown Center on Education and the Workforce. http://www9.georgetown.edu/grad/gppi/hpi/cew/pdfs/stem-complete.pdf.

Carnevale, Anthony, Stephen Rose, and Andrew Hanson. 2012. *Certificates: Gateway to Gainful Employment and College Degrees.* Washington, DC: Georgetown University, Center for Education and the Workforce (June).

Furmans, Vanessa. 2012. Germany's New Export: Jobs Training. *Wall Street Journal* (June 13).

Henly, Samuel E., and Juan M. Sanchez. 2009. The U.S. Establishment-Size Distribution: Secular Changes and Sectoral Decomposition. *Economic Quarterly* 95 (4): 419–454.

Holmes, Thomas J. 2011. "The Case of the Disappearing Large Employer Manufacturing Plants: Not Much of a Mystery After All." *Federal Reserve Bank of Minneapolis Economic Policy Paper* 11 (4).

Hunt, Heather. 2012. "The Manufacturing Solutions Center and the Hosiery and Furniture Industries in the Catawba Valley." Chapel Hill: University of North Carolina Planning Department (April).

Le, Cecilia, and Jill Frankfort. 2011. "Accelerating College Readiness: Lessons from North Carolina's Innovator Early Colleges." Boston: Jobs for the Future (March). http://www.jff.org/sites/default/files/Accelerating_College_032011.pdf.

Lloyd, Maggie. 2013. "Review of the NSF's Advanced Technological Education (ATE) Program: ATE's Role in Advanced Manufacturing Education and Training" Washington, DC: MIT Washington Office (February).

McKinsey and Company. 2012. "Manufacturing the Future: The Next Era of Global Growth and Innovation." New York: McKinsey Global Institute (November).

Osterman, Paul. 2011. Community Colleges: Promise, Performance, and Policy. In *Reinventing Higher Education: The Promise of Innovation*, ed. Ben Wildavsky, Andrew P. Kelly, and Kevin Carey. Cambridge, MA: Harvard Education Press.

Rampey, Bobby D., Gloria S. Dion, and Patricia L. Donahue. 2009. *The Nation's Report Card: Trends in Academic Progress in Reading and Mathematics 2008.* Washington, DC: National Center for Education Statistics. http://nces.ed.gov/nationsreportcard/pubs/main2008/2009479.asp.

Regional Employment Board of Hampden County. 2012. "Precision Manufacturing Regional Alliance Project, Workforce Development Report." Springfield, MA.

Tai, Robert H. 2012. "An Examination of the Research Literature on Project Lead the Way." Mimeo. University of Virginia (November).

U.S. Census Bureau. "Current Population Survey, 2012: Annual Social and Economic Supplement." Table 4.

von Wachter, Till. 2010. "Responding to Long-term Unemployment. Testimony before the Subcommittee on Income Security and Family Support of the Committee on Ways and Means (June 10). http://www.columbia.edu/~vw2112/testimony_waysandmeans_Till_von_Wachter_10June2010_final.pdf.

4 Learning by Building: Complementary Assets and the Migration of Capabilities in U.S. Innovative Firms

Elisabeth B. Reynolds, Hiram M. Samel, and Joyce Lawrence

As policymakers in the United States debate how the economy can regain its vitality following the Great Recession, many see innovation as the key to prosperity. The United States excels in product, service, and business model innovation, particularly when this innovation leverages technological advances. The United States is also one of the leading countries for venture capital financing, which supports the creation of many innovative start-up companies every year.[1] Although innovation by young firms is common today, it represents a relatively new economic model. Large vertically integrated firms with centralized R&D were once the primary drivers of innovation in the United States. However, since the 1980s, we have seen smaller, entrepreneurial firms within innovation ecosystems develop into a large source of innovative activity (Lerner 2012). This shift from large firms that moved ideas to products within the boundaries of the firm to a model of smaller, entrepreneurial firms working in conjunction with multiple external innovators and partners to generate new inventions and technologies has become a vital source of innovation and economic growth for the country.

Given the critical role young firms play in the country's innovation engine, it is important to understand the process and pathways by which they scale their innovations and technologies. The decisions start-up firms make early on will have consequences for how and where the firms grow, if at all, in the future. Unlike large, vertically integrated firms, these smaller, entrepreneurial firms often seek out specialized complementary assets, such as distribution or manufacturing capabilities, to help them avoid sunk investments at the early stages of growth (Gans and Stern 2003; Teece 1986). The need for complementary assets pushes these firms to look outside their boundaries to external actors in order to find the critical inputs they need to scale. Young firms that scale novel technology often manage loosely codified knowledge that requires significant iteration to bring a product to market. This iterative activity, which generates significant new capabilities, often occurs across firm boundaries. With whom and how does this activity occur? Does it matter? We argue the nature of this iterative activity, when most of the knowledge is at the technological frontier, is critical to the innovation process and has important implications for national innovation capabilities.

There is an extensive strategy and innovation literature that examines how young firms choose to profit from their innovations.[2] There is also an equally large economic geography literature that explores the role agglomeration and external economies play in enabling such activity.[3] Although these works address overlapping issues, they differ in their unit of analysis, with strategy focusing on the firm and economic geography on industry clusters. There is very little scholarly work that seeks to connect firm-level decisions with long-term national competitiveness outcomes. This research brings together analysis of firm scale-up strategies with a broader perspective on innovation and economic growth, and identifies potential unintended consequences for the American innovation system.

Our research explores how innovative young firms develop and scale their novel technologies, and the critical factors that shape that process. What are the implications of firm scale-up strategies for the U.S. innovation "ecosystem" and for American economic growth more generally? Much has been written recently about weaknesses in the U.S. innovation ecosystem, whether from the point of view of the loss of capabilities in the "industrial commons" (Pisano and Shih 2009, 2012) or regarding the limitations of the financing model for these small, entrepreneurial firms (Lerner 2012). Building on existing theories of innovation strategy, our interviews offer empirical examples of how firm-level decisions highlight weaknesses in the present American innovation model. In particular, our research demonstrates how advanced capabilities developed over long periods of time are pulled offshore, endangering future economic activity and innovative capacity in the United States. We examine the early stages of scale-up for a sample of highly innovative firms that are just entering or soon to be entering the commercialization environment (Gans and Stern 2003).

Our work contributes to the literature on commercializing innovation in two ways. First, we combine existing frameworks with a more nuanced understanding of product development stages. We emphasize how the search for complementary assets for complex technologies in production industries often occurs at a time when knowledge is loosely codified. Second, we extend this work into the area of economic geography by examining the consequences of firms' innovation strategies for the larger innovation ecosystem. The market for ideas as described in Gans and Stern (2003) influences firm strategy, but it also has the potential to alter future capacity for innovation across regions. Although we acknowledge the robust local availability of inputs for early stage innovation that other scholars have noted (Delgado, Porter, and Stern 2012; Moretti 2012), we find evidence that foreign actors play a larger role at later stages of development. This trend challenges the conventional wisdom that the United States can maintain a sustainable cycle of innovation.

We tracked firms' growth trajectories using a sample of 150 production-related start-up firms that licensed their core technology from MIT from 1997 to 2008. In order to understand the choices the firms made along these trajectories, we conducted in-depth interviews with senior managers of a subset of these firms. Because these firms' innovations are often at the technological frontier, they generally need highly complex, advanced manufacturing capabilities that require more time and capital to scale up than nonproduction (e.g., software) firms. These firms provide an important test of the U.S. innovation ecosystem's ability to support the scaling-up of firms producing innovative technologies.

Using this critical case methodology, we find that the United States provides fertile ground as firms prepare to enter the commercialization environment, iterating prototypes, developing pilot production facilities, and in some cases entering into commercial production. Start-up firms in our sample are able to find the skills, financing, and general resources they need to advance through the exploratory stages of technology development: basic R&D, applied R&D, and early market demonstration.[4] However, when these firms need to take the significant leap into larger-scaled processes to prepare for commercial production, the need for additional capital coupled with the search for production capabilities or lead customers willing to be early adopters pulls many firms to move production abroad.

This move comes at a critical stage in which much of the firm's technology and related manufacturing processes are not yet codified or fully modularized. Firms are developing capabilities through multiple iterative steps in the technology's development over extended periods of time. We term this process *learning by building*. Tacit knowledge is still critical to the development process. Tacit knowledge, as opposed to codified knowledge, requires proximity and face-to-face interactions, which makes knowledge "sticky" and thus less mobile and harder to communicate over distances (Gertler 2003). Although this stickiness has historically protected work from being offshored easily, in our interviews we find firms are now willing—or required— to move advanced technology and manufacturing processes before they are fully codified. This movement, which often entails the temporary relocation of key personnel with whom the tacit knowledge resides, leads to the migration of key skills, capability generation, and knowledge development outside of the country. We argue that the migration of these capabilities has two consequences: one, expected returns to public investment in innovation may not be realized in terms of economic growth, and two, the movement offshore of vital capabilities may put at risk the future capacity to innovate in the United States.

Each firm's decision to move technology development and related production processes abroad is based on rational criteria, at least within the realm of the economic incentives available to them in the current innovation ecosystem. However, the collective shift of these innovative firms' productive activities offshore at this critical stage of their technological and economic growth represents a loss for the country as a whole in the knowledge, skills, and capability generation that come with this next stage of scaling. Public resources are often invested in university research and early start-up firms in order to foster greater innovation. Those resources are successfully encouraging new generations of innovative, entrepreneurial firms. We suggest, however, that it is not enough to start firms in the United States; we must also pay attention to how to grow them in the United States. Although creating incentives for individual firms to manufacture in the United States has a long history that has produced mixed outcomes at best, we do believe there is a public interest in finding ways, when appropriate, to help firms to scale production in this country. Although it is not realistic to keep all production in the United States, the innovation ecosystem depends on continued demand for the skills and capabilities required for the new and emerging industries represented by our sample of firms.

Profiting from innovation strategies in entrepreneurial firms

Young entrepreneurial firms, especially those that focus on technological innovation, have a distinct set of characteristics that regularly place their long-term survival in jeopardy. In addition to the significant uncertainty that surrounds any early stage technology, new firms require capital to offset negative cash flow in starting their enterprises. They must be sensitive to protecting their intellectual property from possible imitators, including fellow start-ups that seek first-mover advantage and/or industry incumbents that seek to defend their market positions. Many scholars have studied the strategies innovative entrepreneurial firms use to address the unique circumstances that they face. In particular, there has been extensive research on the factors that determine whether new innovative companies will compete or cooperate with incumbent firms. With limited resources, young firms must decide whether to invest in upstream activities such as materials development or downstream ones such as marketing and distribution.

Young firms engaged in manufacturing may face additional constraints including longer innovation cycle times, higher capital needs, and highly complex technology. Ultimately, they must decide whether to make their own product inside the firm or contract part or all of the manufacturing externally. In other words, young firms constantly face a series of critical decisions as they move from idea to prototype to commercial production and finally to distribution.

Complementary assets

An extensive literature in entrepreneurial strategy and the economics of innovation seeks to understand how firms profit from innovation. Teece (1986) identifies two key factors that influence entrepreneurial firms' decisions to compete or cooperate with existing firms: technology appropriability (ease of imitation) and ownership of complementary assets in production, distribution, and marketing. Following Teece's seminal work, many scholars have built on this framework to understand how young firms profit from innovation. Focusing on young technology firms, Gans and Stern (2003) note that many of the complementary assets sought by firms are owned by incumbents who have incentives to expropriate the inventors' technology. This represents a paradox for entrepreneurs who need to disclose extensive product details to receive the highest valuation for their technology but

fear disclosing too much information to large firms who are both potential partners and potential competitors. In an environment in which
young firms are better at development, but incumbents control complementary assets, young firms may be better off cooperating than
competing with the incumbents. To that end, young firms may seek
complementary assets during the exploration (discovery) and exploitation (production) phases of their development.[5] They must differentiate
between assets that might be generic and thus substitutable, and those
that are specific and offer competitive advantages (Chesbrough, Birkinshaw, and Teubal 2006). In either case, they must decide whether
investing in assets such as production facilities or marketing and distribution networks on their own risks duplicating assets held by others,
leading to the inefficient use of scarce resources and potentially unrea-
sonable sunk costs (Gans and Stern 2003).

Financing and the emergence of new sources of complementary assets

A critical factor in determining whether start-up firms invest in new
assets is their access to capital. Technology entrepreneurs most often
raise funds for their firms from providers of high-risk capital—primarily independent venture capital (VC) and/or corporate venture capital
(CVC) firms. Although VC funds are well established as the major
source of entrepreneurial finance, they are shaped by particular dynamics inherent to their business, for example, the composition and the
objectives of investors that potentially limit long-term investments in
young firms. Boom and bust cycles are another challenge that leads to
the underfunding of novel technologies (Lerner 2012). This uncertainty,
well beyond the control of young firms, may affect young firms' ability
to raise capital for large fixed-cost projects. Moreover, the increasing
specialization of venture firms, which leads them to focus only on
certain stages of a firm's development, forces founders to constantly
maintain an eye on the next round of financing, unsure if current or
future investors will accept their investment plans.

Interestingly, multinational corporations are taking an increasingly
active role in funding new firms through CVC subsidiaries. Intel and
General Electric are well known examples of historic corporate venture
investors. The National Venture Capital Association reports that 2011
was the largest year for total CVC investments since the dot-com

bubble of the late 1990s (National Venture Capital Association 2012). This trend is important because, unlike traditional VCs, CVCs have extensive resources including a supply chain and manufacturing network to help entrepreneurial firms commercialize a technology without investing in fixed assets. As complementary assets have become increasingly global and with the emergence of a secondary market for trading of intellectual property rights, young start-up firms are increasingly attractive to multinational CVCs as partners. Together, these trends increase the likelihood that an upstream or downstream complementary asset holder will place more value on young technology firms.

In addition to CVC partners, national governments in emerging economies have begun to make available complementary assets to innovative American start-up firms (Chesbrough, Birkinshaw, and Teubal 2006). In an effort to seed the development of new technologies and advanced manufacturing capabilities in their country or region, foreign governments are providing direct capital for development as well as indirect capital in the form of plant, equipment, and workforce training. Singapore's aggressive efforts in biotechnology, Russia's efforts in nanotechnology, and China's initiatives in clean energy are salient examples of this trend.

Ultimately, where firms find complementary assets has implications for future economic activity. Whether the means are acquisition, investment, alliance, or just strategic choice, the (re)location of complementary assets overseas may be costly to the U.S. economy and the start-up firm. As Teubal and Avnimelech (2003) show, globalization has favored the acquisition of local start-ups by foreign firms, thereby truncating the R&D leverage of downstream production and any associated economic growth.

Complementary assets are an essential ingredient for the growth strategies of many young entrepreneurial firms. In an effort to access new technologies and build capabilities, U.S. start-up firms are turning to multinational firms and foreign governments that are playing an increasingly important role in providing complementary assets. Such partnerships, although important to the growth of the individual entrepreneurial firm, may shift investments and capability building abroad, away from the national and local economy of the firm, with potentially negative consequences for future innovation and economic growth.

Research methods and data collection

The MIT Technology Licensing Office sample

In order to understand firm decision making related to production in innovative start-up companies, we examine the population of firms founded on technology licensed from the MIT Technology Licensing Office between 1997 and 2008. The MIT Technology Licensing Office's (TLO) mission is focused on bringing inventions from MIT laboratories into the economy, and in this activity, it has been among the most successful bridging agents linking U.S. university research and private industry (Di Gregorio and Shane 2003).[6] In 2011, for example, the TLO registered 694 invention disclosures, filed 305 patents, had 199 U.S. patents issued, and facilitated the start-up of 16 firms (with a minimum of $500,000 in initial capital).

Although MIT TLO firms are not a representative sample of national technology start-ups, they offer the distinct advantage of being among the most likely advanced technology start-ups to succeed (Di Gregorio and Shane 2003). These firms consistently seek to commercialize products at the technological frontier and are well connected to academia and the venture capital industry. Given the historic role of MIT and Boston in successfully commercializing new ideas (Massachusetts is continually ranked among one of the top innovation hubs in the country), we consider this to be a "critical case."[7] We would expect that firms within our sample should be among those start-up firms most likely to succeed at scaling up. Conversely, if firms in our sample, which enjoy extensive local resources, encounter significant challenges in reaching scale, we can only imagine how start-ups not located in the Boston-Cambridge ecosystem and not affiliated with an elite innovation-focused university might fare.

The 1997 to 2008 time frame allows us to look at firms five to fifteen years after their founding. During this period, 189 firms started with technology licensed from MIT patents. We focused only on firms that were engaged in some form of production. We eliminated twenty-nine software firms and ten firms for which we could not locate any recent data from further investigation, leaving a sample of 150 production-oriented firms.[8]

By looking at firms that are between five and fifteen years old, we cover the stages from company formation to prototype to pilot facilities and, in some cases, commercial production. For the older firms, many will have entered into a mass production stage in which a product is commercially produced and brought to market.

Methodology

For this study, we gathered historical data on financing, ownership, and operating status for all of the firms in our dataset in order to better understand the growth trajectories of these firms. In addition to data provided by the TLO, we used online databases from VentureXpert, Lexis-Nexis, and Compustat to build a longitudinal database. Using semistructured interviews with a subset of these firms, we developed a more in-depth understanding of how firms choose strategies to scale up by tracing the pathways from innovation to production. Together these methods enable us to understand how young technology firms make decisions about how to commercialize their innovations and move from R&D toward production.

As seen in table 4.1, of the 150 production companies, 59 percent are still active as independent firms, another 21 percent were acquired, and 20 percent have closed. This survival rate is 150 percent higher than what Hall and Woodward find in their national study of venture-backed start-up firms (Hall and Woodward 2010). Firms in the biopharmaceutical and medical device industries make up 60 percent of our

Table 4.1
MIT TLO Companies 1997–2008

Industry	Number of Firms Started	Percent of Total	Percent Receiving Venture Capital*	Percent Operating^	Percent Closed	Percent Merged
Advanced materials and energy	15	10	33	73	27	0
Biopharma	58	39	59	55	26	19
Medical devices	31	21	52	65	3	32
Robotics	5	3	0	60	20	20
Semiconductors and electronics	26	17	85	62	19	19
Other	15	10	33	47	27	27
All production companies	150	100	55	59	20	21

*Reported by VentureXpert.
^As of June 2012.

sample, semiconductor and electronics firms constitute an additional 17 percent, and advanced materials another 10 percent. Geographically, 63 percent of the sample firms are headquartered in Massachusetts, 15 percent in California, and the rest are spread across the country. Three percent of the firms in our sample are based overseas. The vast majority of firms had little or no revenue. As noted previously, fifteen firms had revenue of over $5 million in 2011. Of these firms, three had sales over $100 million, and only one had sales over $1 billion.

Innovation ecosystem during the exploration phase

Using the VentureXpert database, we identified 82 (of the 150 production) start-ups in our sample as having received VC and/or CVC capital. These eighty-two firms raised a total of $4.7 billion, of which 71 percent came from venture capital and 12 percent from corporate investors.[9] Some firms have raised significant capital: thirty-three firms raised over $50 million and of these, fourteen firms raised over $100 million in investments, which suggests a strong market belief in the technology they are developing. Fifty-seven percent of the firms in our sample were still raising capital after their fifth year.[10] Of these firms, 39 percent were still raising funds after the seventh year, and fifteen firms, or 17 percent of the sample, were able to raise high-risk capital after ten years.

Almost half of the eighty-two venture-backed firms received a financial investment from at least one corporate investor in addition to venture capital. Although strategic corporate investors represented only 8 percent of total funds raised by biopharmaceutical firms (of $1.7 billion), they represented triple that amount, or 21 percent of total investment ($1.1 billion), in semiconductor firms. Another way to raise significant funds for firms seeking to scale up is to sell shares to the public through an initial public offering. Only nine firms of the eighty-two in our sample followed this path. Of these nine, eight were in the biopharma or medical device industries (the exception was a battery manufacturer). On the whole, the data demonstrate that these young start-up firms have had little trouble raising significant amounts of capital during the exploration stage of their technology development even when this phase has taken place over an extended period of time.

For our interviews, we chose only firms in the sample that had demonstrated an ability to reach scale, starting with the fifteen firms with over $5 million in revenue.[11] Given that firms must signal continued progress to potential investors even before they have the possibility of generating significant revenue, we also looked for firms that had received in excess of $50 million in high-risk capital as a proxy for continued market potential. This added another eleven firms to our potential interviews. From this set of twenty-six firms, we conducted a total of seventeen interviews.[12] Not surprisingly, these highly innovative firms are predominantly located in high-skill, technology-leading regions in the United States. Of the seventeen firms in which we conducted interviews, seven firms were based in Boston, nine in the San Francisco–Silicon Valley region, and one firm was in Berlin, Germany.

Thick labor markets and network nodes

Rapid access to diverse talent is the critical input for these young entrepreneurial firms, particularly in the early stages of growth. It is at this point that iterations between lab and production are taking place, road blocks in developing the technology may appear, and new strategic directions might evolve based on what can and cannot be done with the technology. "High intellect" talent, as described by one semiconductor executive, is essential at this stage. One firm estimated that salary for these highly skilled employees represented 70 percent of its budget. Firms locate in or close to labor markets where they can find diverse yet specialized sets of skills.

The ability to hire quickly is important. One firm, which needed equipment engineers, process engineers, device engineers, and a microelectromechanical systems device team, hired twenty-five people almost overnight. This need to draw from a diverse set of skills and to hire a workforce in a relatively short period of time drives these firms to locate near educational institutions with strong track records for graduating well-trained engineers or in regions with reservoirs of engineering talent from previous rounds of industrial creation. This was true for all five of the semiconductor companies we interviewed on both the East and West Coasts. The situation was similar with the biopharmaceutical firms we interviewed in Boston as well.

The importance of connecting start-up firms to networks of capital, human resources, potential strategic partners, and early adopters and customers has been studied extensively in the literature on entrepreneurship.[13] In the small, innovative firms we studied we usually found that there was at least one individual playing a critical role in the initial formation of the firm as well as in connecting the firm to resources, talent, and partners. These unique individuals, who have deep industry knowledge and experience as well as strong local networks, are especially important at three points in the firm's development: firm formation, testing market viability, and integrating novel technology into existing systems.

In several cases, a venture capitalist saw the potential for a new technology and pooled the intellectual property (IP) from different universities, assembled the initial team, and formed a firm. The individuals acted in these cases as visionaries who understood the potential for a particular type of technology and assembled the right IP and team to help build a firm. In one medical device company case, this involved assembling IP from five different universities and funding a team that would ultimately build a billion-dollar firm.

This unique individual might be a person who is intimately connected to a particular industry and who can make important introductions to potential funders or partners. Within each of the industries we studied there are several critical people who had worked in a particular industry for years, participated in building several firms, and had achieved great respect in both the national industry and regional innovation networks. These individuals guide firms as they test the market viability of their technology and help to identify the most appropriate capital providers. In one case, this key actor arranged to have a major potential customer from Asia come to MIT to see the prototype. Based on the potential customer's enthusiasm for the product, the team went forward, created the firm, and began hiring a team and raising money.

In the early stages of scale-up, as a firm decides how to integrate its technology into incumbent systems, seasoned industry executives who have deep knowledge of the prevailing industry production architecture can be key agents, as they understand how new technology can be incorporated and are familiar with specific facilities that are best suited for introducing new technology. For one set of firms, these individuals were retired production executives of large integrated petrochemical firms who understood which plants had the managerial and technical abilities to successfully integrate a new technology. They also could bring in experienced production engineers on an as-needed basis to ensure that the technology could be inserted into existing larger production lines, without the sort of disruptions that have scuttled other previous projects.

Our sample firms' abilities to access networks through these individuals appeared integral to their success. Although not limited necessarily by distance, these networks are often enhanced by proximity and encourage firms to locate in places where there are dense networks within their specific industry.

Thick supplier markets

Although these firms draw on a deep and specialized talent pool, they are also drawing on a range of suppliers for certain products, services, and skills. The firms in our sample are engaged in complex engineering and manufacturing. One medical device firm that has successfully scaled production has a product with ten thousand components, and three hundred suppliers of custom pieces, 65 percent of which are provided by local suppliers. When start-ups begin product development, they are more concerned with speed and quality as opposed to cost. Being located near a strong supplier base that can turn around product very quickly is a priority.

Initial prototypes often come out of the university lab in rough form and need iteration, either within a lab setting or in partnership with suppliers. This process, although time-consuming and labor-intensive, must emphasize speed and quality. Thus, firms like to have their suppliers near at hand. In the case of one East Coast semiconductor firm, the loss of control and time that came with working with a third-party semiconductor fabricator in the United States pushed them to build their own fabrication plant. They did not consider going offshore because of the expense in time and money of transferring people and technology, as well as the fact that the novel work they were doing would have required eighteen months to transfer the process offshore. It took two years to get their prototype to be a fully functioning product. During this process, they benefited significantly from the proximity of talent and suppliers.

Another semiconductor equipment firm on the West Coast built a prototype in four months and continued to iterate it every six months for three years before they were ready to ship product to a potential customer. This is consistent with other semiconductor firms located in the Silicon Valley area. These firms could find a relatively strong local supply chain during the prototype stage. One firm described how it kept eight machine shops busy for two weeks at full capacity in order to ship a prototype system to a potential customer.

Financing and capabilities migration in an inflection band

The findings discussed previously paint a picture of a very robust regional innovation ecosystem for new firms that are in the exploration phase. For these firms, finding advanced skills across a wide range of disciplines, suppliers that can help them iterate prototypes, networks that can provide contacts with both funders and potential customers, and, most important, early stage capital to support the firm's growth are all readily available. This ecosystem helps incubate the early development of the technology and enables the firms to focus on quality and speed to market.

However, the local ecosystem falters as firms seek to scale production from the pilot stage to a commercial scale. To help explain this stage of growth, we have adopted a framework for the development of novel technologies from Lester and Hart (2012, see figure 4.1). As firms move from the exploration phase toward the exploitation phase, they are demonstrating the viability of their product and also building it at scale. The two activities are inseparable—as is often said in bioprocessing, "the process *is* the product." We call this space the *inflection*

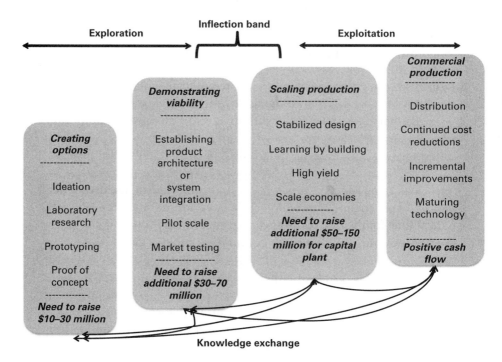

Figure 4.1
Inflection band during scale-up process. Adapted from Lester and Hart (2012). *Note:* The investment numbers relevant to our sample are orders of magnitude smaller than what Lester and Hart outline for energy technologies.

band to convey the critical nature of this stage for the firm and the fact that, rather than being a specific point in time, this stage can last for a relatively long period, up to several years.

Financing

During the early stages of development, the innovative companies we interviewed were able to raise significant amounts of risk capital over extended periods of time. However, as they moved into pilot and demonstration phases of their technology, they needed a new influx of significant capital to finish codifying their technology processes and bring it to commercial scale. Traditional venture capitalists, who invest in the earlier stages of the company, do not typically fund at this stage and at these levels (anywhere from $15 to $40 million), so these companies must look elsewhere for funding. We find that during this inflection band the money often comes from corporate investors or national investment funds of emerging economies. For example, an advanced materials firm that had withdrawn an earlier IPO received a $30 million investment from an Asian multinational firm twelve years after founding. At this stage, "venture investors [in the firm] look for certainty; they are willing to trade upside for certainty. The investors understood the possibility of acquisition by a foreign firm when they took the money [from the Asian multinational firm] in the last round."[14]

In another case, the CEO of an advanced materials company said, "The VC model does not work for manufacturing companies. VCs cannot make any money on something that costs $100 million and takes at least 10 years to build. The technological risk is high and there is a high burn rate. They are much more comfortable with a software deal that will cost them $20 million. They have to pull away at what is a critical time for the company—just as [the company] is trying to finalize the product and get it ready for commercial production . . . eventually people won't start companies like this because they can't get financing."[15] Ultimately, the company raised $40 million from an emerging economy government investment fund with a quid pro quo that some R&D and manufacturing would be set up in that country.

Those rare firms that went public offer a counterpoint to this pattern. A senior manager at one firm, an integrated surgical device manufacturer, stated that having the money from an IPO allowed them to get through an extended stretch to develop their technology for the market, after they had consumed most of the $125 million they had raised in venture funds. The tendency of the board was to sell the firm, "98

Box 4.1
Nanocompany*

Nanocompany is an advanced materials company working in nanotechnology. Put together by a "visionary" who sought out a network of researchers in this field and pooled their research through license agreements, the company was founded in 2000 in Boston and moved soon after to Silicon Valley. The company has one hundred patents. It currently has one hundred employees, a third of whom have graduate degrees.

Nanotechnology does not have a "big win." Markets are small and specific and there have not been any big "home runs." For many years, the company survived on funded research projects by the Department of Defense and other private companies as it searched for profitable applications of its technology. The company has developed multiple products and continues to develop new products in conjunction with one of their strategic partners. For their primary products, they have developed the prototype and done pilot production in rented space in a machine shop in the Midwest. Once they had the product to scale, they moved production to South Korea where there is established expertise in production at scale. All of their customers for their primary product are in Asia.

In terms of financing and future directions for the company, relatively early in its growth (within four years), the company attempted to go public, but the offering was withdrawn because of a lack of confidence in the application of the technology. The company went on to raise over $100 million in the past twelve years, approximately a third from strategic partners based in the United States and Asia. The company expects it will most likely be acquired by either its U.S. or Asian strategic partner, which they believe is the most appropriate strategy for the company. IPOs have not been particularly successful for tech companies (most of them trading down) and an acquisition provides certainty to investors. Scale issues would also disappear by being acquired by a large multinational. "There are very few benefits to staying independent," said one of the senior executives.

*Company name has been changed.

percent of the conversations in Silicon Valley are around an M&A [merger and acquisition] exit, not an IPO."[16] The firm remained independent, however, which may be the result of a product that fell in a crack between the diagnostics and interventional equipment industries as well as the willpower of management to resist the board of directors' desire to sell.

Life sciences firms seem more likely to follow this pathway. Eight out of the nine firms in the TLO sample that went public were in the life sciences sector. These companies benefited from an IPO, raising capital that has helped fund their long development cycles. For these firms, the complexity of the early stage scale-up of their products and the close interface with R&D teams leads them to develop capabilities in-house, even though they might work with a contract manufacturer on clinical production.

Capabilities migration

Although the firms we interviewed could find the skills and capabilities they needed during the initial phases of scale-up, they had greater difficulty finding the know-how and capabilities for production at scale. As described previously, the knowledge developed within the inflection band is not yet codified and becomes standardized only through iteration over months and years. To find the capabilities required at this stage to iterate the technology and develop it at scale, the TLO firms sought out partnerships to gather necessary complementary assets. Whether for reasons of a lack of skills ("in certain industries, a whole generation of engineers is missing," according to the CEO of a nanotechnology firm), pull from an industry where the center of gravity has moved abroad, and/or market demand that is growing faster outside the United States, more often than not, the TLO firms developed partnerships to scale production offshore. These factors, combined with financial resources, make the pull to scale abroad very compelling.

For example, in one biomedical device company we studied, we learned that it needed to design a product that could be manufactured at high volumes (involving precision injection-molded plastics and rubber components). First, the company tried to partner with small firms in the United States to develop this capability but ended up with a very low yield rate (less than 10 percent). Then it turned to large U.S. chemical and electronics companies. However, the product the start-up produced was so different from conventional technologies that the large companies had little interest. One large company executive called it "really stupid," another a "fool's errand," and a third company wanted $5 million for a feasibility study. After a global search for manufacturing capabilities at scale, the company settled on Singapore because it offered three things: capital ($30 million investment from the government), a willingness to draw on their semiconductor experience to build the right capabilities, and IP protection. The company was one of the first to move its production to Singapore and others have followed, creating a center of capabilities in biomedical manufacturing. The company has since gone public.

For several of the companies we interviewed, almost all of their future customers are in Asia. One company, a semiconductor equipment firm founded in 2007, has only ten potential customers in the world for its product, and the most important five of them are all in Asia. Volume is low for these high-margin systems and commercial production would represent approximately one hundred units a year. When looking for a partner for equipment testing they chose carefully, because some of these players are considered aggressive and would "eat you alive."[17] Their plan at this stage is to support their customer in the field while testing. The six months after completing the prototype are critical, so the CEO will be moving to Asia for a couple of months. They will have two to three people on site and set up an office next to the customer. Their partner has spent two years already evaluating the technology and paid $1 million up front for the demonstration phase. The pilot will cost $30 million and a full commercial production facility will cost $150 million. They expect to engage the customer for the investment going forward.

Suppliers as well as capital draw firms into overseas partnerships. In another case, a manufacturer of devices using specialized silicon inks was able to survive only by working with suppliers who had a long-term incentive to develop their technology together. The CEO says, "The only reason we are alive is because of several strategic partnerships."[18] They work with one Japanese company and one American company. The easiest way to ramp up the process is to find equipment that already fits with what they do, even if it is designed to work on a different process. The Japanese company they partner with has resources abroad for manufacturing, and it is cheaper for them to build a large-scale plant in Japan (although they have not done so yet). The CEO doesn't see a choice when it comes to building a fifty-billion-unit plant; it will have to be in Asia. The CEO further states that he believes this is common for many production-related companies because of the complexity of the technology coupled with the capital needs to develop it: "When they transition from the normal VC model, there is no other model to jump to, so they go abroad. They end up offshore 99 percent of the time. M&A deals happen at that point. The partner thinks 'we're going to manufacture this stuff, so why not acquire the company instead of being a partner?' Both manufacturing and technology companies go abroad looking for partnerships because it is easier for investors."[19]

Discussion and implications

The emergence of the high-tech entrepreneurial firm has created a new model for innovation in which these firms, trying to scale novel technologies and enter the global marketplace, must seek out complementary assets. The nature of the U.S. innovation ecosystem for these new technology firms, in terms of financing, demand from growing markets and customers overseas, and the lack of capabilities for scaling production in the United States, creates momentum for these companies to find these complementary assets offshore at a critical point in their scale-up process. The aggressive pull of emerging economies seeking to build capabilities in advanced technology reinforces this behavior. Of course, in a global marketplace, we would not expect all investment and all parts of a supply chain to be located within the United States Firms are acting rationally and taking advantage of a global economy that prizes innovation. But it is the crucial point in these firms' development at which they migrate offshore that raises concerns.

Although some might argue that the iterative process of innovation that we describe is not critical to the United States as long as the country continues to drive idea generation and early-stage research and development, we believe this is a mistaken view of the risks and stakes involved. The transfer or sharing across national borders of advanced knowledge, which often takes years to develop, risks the potential loss of the national competitive advantage early-stage capabilities have created in three ways. First, the loss of learning by building deprives the country's innovation ecosystem of new learning and thus reduces the accumulation of knowledge and capabilities, ultimately diminishing the potential for future and as-yet-unknown innovation. The "industrial commons" is made poorer for it. Second, as we have

Box 4.2
Semicompany*

Semicompany is a semiconductor equipment company founded in 2007. The company moved to Silicon Valley to be close to the large semiconductor cluster located there. The company has benefited from its proximity to strong universities as well as a good supplier network of machine shops that can quickly ramp up and turn around new prototypes.

The company has scaled quickly, raising over $75 million in five years. The company understood early on that the complexity of their product would require raising capital in this range and would take at least five to seven years to develop. As a result, they sought out investors who would understand this and stick with the company over time. For them, strategic partners have played a role on the technology development and evaluation side, providing knowledge and expertise in helping to scale the technology.

Because of the significant scale and cost of taking the product from prototype to pilot (approximately $30 million to build the pilot plant and $150 million to build a commercial production facility) and the benefits of iterating during scale-up in proximity to the customer, Semicompany is partnering with potential customers who are paying to be early adopters and help develop and evaluate the technology during a demonstration phase. Although the first machines will be made in California to perfect the process and keep some production close to R&D, they expect to build a pilot plant closer to the customer because of the lower costs. A commercial plant would also most likely be in Asia where there is expertise and where customers might insist they locate production. Subcomponents can be made anywhere and contract manufacturers are everywhere so the location of the commercial production is not dependent on proximity to any particular skill. They could potentially keep production in California and do the final assembly and testing closer to customers, but this seems unlikely.

Semicompany would like to stay independent and potentially go public, because they see a very large global market for their product.

*Company name has been changed.

seen in several industries, loss of learning by building increases the movement of the center of gravity for established and new industries away from the country, with implications for future industry growth. As underscored by others, where process innovation goes, product innovation follows (Pisano and Shih 2012). Finally, this loss limits the benefits the country could gain from economic growth generated by the downstream activities these firms will create with scaled production in terms of investments and jobs.

Independent of whether the company preferred to scale in the United States or not, many of the companies we saw have had little choice but to go overseas to continue the commercialization process. Although they are acting in the firms' best interest, as Teubal and Avnimelech (2003: 37) observe, "There is no *a priori* reason for the market solution to be optimal or adequate to the country." The loss of the capabilities generated by these leading-edge companies creates ripple effects for the country over time. Chesbrough et al. (2006: 1098), discussing a similar phenomenon, state, "It is open to debate whether local policymakers should have invested more in helping to create the complementary assets to allow *in situ* development." Given the outcomes we observe in our research, we would agree that there is a case to be made for private and public interventions to create complementary assets within the country that will enable more scaling locally.

We see four possible areas for exploration in terms of interventions: (1) increasing financing options for later stage development, (2) creating institutions and incentives that provide opportunities for firms to build capabilities through learning by building in advanced manufacturing in the country, (3) changing the contours of market demand through state procurement or standard setting, and (4) continuing efforts to encourage firms to raise capital through initial public offerings.

We believe initiatives in all four of these areas will extend the time and capital available for these firms to cross the inflection band and do so within their local economy. Given the country's focus on and investment in the early growth of innovative companies (university and company research grants, seed capital, tax incentives, etc.), we believe there should be an equal focus on the later-stage scaling of these companies and to encourage more of it to take place in the country. Likewise, many of these firms have benefited from U.S. R&D programs, whether in research grants, shared production facilities, or tax treatment. It is reasonable to ask whether the country should care how those investments pay off in the long run.

Appendix 4.1

Table A4.1
MIT TLO Companies Interviewed

Firm	Year Founded	Industry	Revenue	Public	SBIR
A	1997	Medical device	Yes	Yes	Yes
B	2001	Biomedical	Yes	Yes	Yes
C	2001	Semiconductor	Yes	No	No
D	2001	Semiconductor	No	No	No
E	2001	Biopharma	Yes	Yes	Yes
F	2001	Biopharma	Yes	No	No
G	2001	Medical device	Yes	No	Yes
H	2002	Battery manufacturing	Yes	Yes	Yes
I	2002	Biopharma	Yes	Yes	Yes
J	2003	Advanced materials	Yes	No	Yes
K	2004	Advanced materials	No	No	Yes
L	2004	Semiconductor	No	No	No
M	2006	Biotech	Yes	No	Yes
N	2006	Geothermal drilling	Yes	No	No
O	2007	Semiconductor	Yes	No	No
P	2007	Semiconductor	No	No	No
Q	2007	Advanced materials	No	No	No

Table A4.1
(continued)

Exploration	Exploitation	Foreign Corporate or (State) Investor	Amount Raised ($M)	Motivation for Offshore
CA	U.S./Mexico	No	56	Low-cost production of low-value parts
CA-R&D prototype	Singapore	Yes (Singapore)	216	Capital, Capabilities, Cost at scale
CA-R&D prototype	Japan	Yes	77	Capital, Supplier, Cost at scale
MA-prototype, pilot	MA, Asia, Europe	Yes (Russia)	108	Capital
MA-pilot	Multinational supply chain	Yes	120	Capital, Distribution Marketing
Germany	N/A	Yes	117	
MA	MA	No	74	N/A
MA	Asia/US	Yes	243	Capital, Capabilities, Cost at scale
MA-pilot, US-clinical	N/A	Yes	100	N/A
CA/OH	South Korea-production;?	Yes	95	Capital, Capabilities, Customers
MA-prototype	US-bulk, Taiwan-application	No	55	Capital, Customers
CA	Taiwan	Yes	153	Capital, Suppliers
CA	N/A	No	<10	N/A
CA	N/A	No	<10	N/A
MA	N/A	Yes	46	Capital
CA-prototype; S. Korea-pilot	Asia	Yes	75	Capital, Capabilities, Customers
CA-R&D prototype	US/Russia	Yes (Russia)	36	Capital, Natural Gas Supply

Appendix 4.2

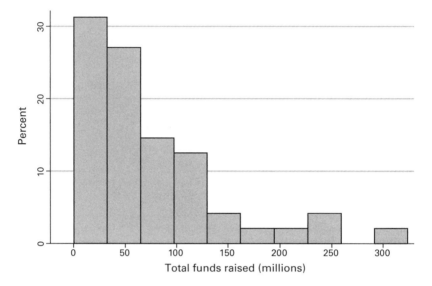

Figure A4.1
Distribution of funds raised by operating firms

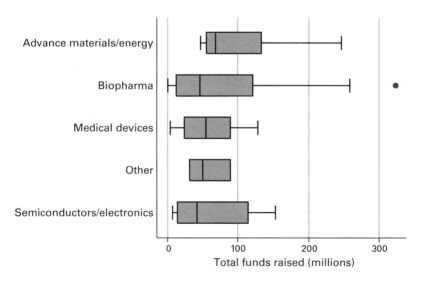

Figure A4.2
Total funds raised as of 2012 by industry for operating firms

Notes

1. The United States is second only to Israel in venture capital as a percentage of GDP (OECD 2011).

2. Chesbrough, Birkinshaw, and Teubal (2006) give an excellent review of this work on the occasion of the twentieth anniversary of Teece's seminal work on profiting from innovation.

3. See Delgado, Porter, and Stern (2012) for a substantive review of this literature.

4. See Grubb (2004) for a staged typology of technology development.

5. See March (1991) for a discussion of exploration and exploitation.

6. In all but a few cases, the firm was created based on technology developed at MIT. In a few cases, firms licensed MIT technology after a firm was formed.

7. See Information Technology and Innovation Foundation (2012) and see George and Bennett (2005) on critical case methodology.

8. We were careful to include those firms that integrated software into products with the proviso that the product was specifically engineered with this software in mind. We conducted extensive checks of archival records to determine the status of the unknown ten firms but were unsuccessful.

9. Of the eighty-two firms for which we have data, eleven closed and nineteen merged with or were sold to another firm by 2011, leaving fifty-two independent firms. Revenue for merged firms is not included, because unconsolidated sales figures for the acquired firms are not available. Appendix 4.2 contains figures of the distribution of funds raised by the fifty-two operating firms.

10. Venture funds are traditionally structured as partnerships, with the active fund manager serving as general partner and investors as limited partners. Most partnerships are structured with a seven-year investment cycle.

11. Revenue of $5 million exceeds the typical amount of research funds start-up companies report as revenue.

12. See appendix 4.1 for more detailed information on the companies interviewed. Interviews typically lasted between one and three hours with two or three PIE researchers present.

13. See Powell et al. (2005) for an excellent discussion of the role networks play in innovation ecosystems.

14. Interview with CEO, advanced materials firm, April 25, 2012.

15. Interview with CEO, advanced materials firm, December 13, 2012.

16. Interview with CEO, integrated surgical device manufacturer, April 25, 2012.

17. Interview with CEO, semiconductor equipment company, April 26, 2012.

18. Interview with CEO, silicon ink device company, June 14, 2012.

19. Ibid.

References

Chesbrough, Henry, Julian Birkinshaw, and Morris Teubal. 2006. Introduction to the Research Policy 20th Anniversary Special Issue of the Publication of "Profiting from Innovation" by David J. Teece. *Research Policy* 35 (8):1091–1099.

Delgado, Mercedes, Michael E. Porter, and Scott Stern. 2012. *Clusters, Convergence, and Economic Performance*. National Bureau of Economic Research. http://www.nber.org/papers/w18250.

Di Gregorio, Dante, and Scott Shane. 2003. Why Do Some Universities Generate More Start-Ups Than Others? *Research Policy* 32 (2):209–227.

Gans, Joshua S., and Scott Stern. 2003. The Product Market and the Market for Ideas. *Research Policy* 32 (2):333–350.

George, Alexander L., and Andrew Bennett. 2005. *Case Studies and Theory Development in the Social Sciences*. Cambridge, MA: MIT Press.

Gertler, Meric S. 2003. Tacit Knowledge and the Economic Geography of Context, or the Undefinable Tacitness of Being (There). *Journal of Economic Geography* 3 (1):75–99.

Grubb, Meric. 2004. Technology Innovation and Climate Change Policy: An Overview of Issues and Options. *Keio Economic Studies* 41 (2):103.

Hall, Robert E., and Susan E. Woodward. 2010. The Burden of the Nondiversifiable Risk of Entrepreneurship. *American Economic Review* 100 (3): 1163–1194.

Information Technology and Innovation Foundation. 2012. *The 2012 State New Economy Index*. Washington, DC: Author.

Lerner, Josh. 2012. *The Architecture of Innovation: The Economics of Creative Organizations*. Oxford: Oxford University Press.

Lester, Richard K., and David M. Hart. 2012. *Unlocking Energy Innovation Cambridge*. MA: MIT Press.

March, James G. 1991. Exploration and Exploitation in Organizational Learning. *Organization Science* 2 (1):71–87.

Moretti, Enrico. 2012. *The New Geography of Jobs*. New York: Houghton Mifflin Harcourt.

National Venture Capital Association. 2012. *NVCA Yearbook 2012*. Arlington, VA: Thomson Reuters and National Venture Capital Association.

OECD. 2011. "Entrepreneurship at a Glance." http://www.oecd-ilibrary.org/industry-and-services/entrepreneurship-at-a-glance-2010_9789264097711-en.

Pisano, Gary P., and Willy C. Shih. 2009. Restoring American Competitiveness. *Harvard Business Review* 87 (7–8): 114–125.

Pisano, Gary P., and Willy C. Shih. 2012. *Producing Prosperity: Why America Needs a Manufacturing Renaissance*. Cambridge, MA: Harvard Business School Press.

Powell, Walter W., et al. 2005. Network Dynamics and Field Evolution: The Growth of Interorganizational Collaboration in the Life Sciences. *American Journal of Sociology* 110: 1132–1205.

Teece, David J. 1986. Profiting from Technological Innovation: Implications for Integration, Collaboration, Licensing and Public Policy. *Research Policy* 15 (6): 285–305.

Teubal, Morris, and Gil Avnimelech. 2003. Foreign Acquisitions and R&D Leverage in High Tech Industries of Peripheral Economies. Lessons and Policy Issues from the Israeli Experiences. *International Journal of Technology Management* 26 (2): 362–385.

5   Energy Innovation

Richard K. Lester

The gap between how we imagine innovation occurs and what we expect from it may be widest in the case of energy. Innovators and their dilemmas are fodder for countless blogs, tweets, and media messages. Innovation, in the popular image, is driven by scientific breakthroughs in the lab, start-ups hatched in the garage, and audacious entrepreneurs disrupting old markets and creating new ones almost overnight. The archetypal innovator succeeds by meeting consumer needs today that no one could have imagined yesterday.

But in energy what we need from innovation has long been well understood, if not universally accepted. To forestall the worst effects of climate change, fossil energy systems will have to be replaced by low-carbon technologies that for the most part are not cost competitive today. Innovations are needed to make these low-carbon technologies competitive with the fossil fuel incumbents. Of course, bold ideas and audacious entrepreneurs are important here too. But for good new ideas to make an impact in energy they must be matched with the capital, skills, suppliers, and manufacturing facilities needed to bring them to market. This is true of other sectors, too, but in the case of energy the innovations must also be adopted on a very large scale. A huge infrastructure must be transformed in a process that will take decades. When it comes to climate change, unless energy innovations are adopted at scale, nothing of significance will have been accomplished.

A few randomly chosen facts begin to suggest the enormous scale of the energy innovation challenge:

• Today coal-fired power plants provide roughly 40 percent of America's electric power. Coal is delivered to these plants mainly by rail, and these shipments account for nearly half of the total freight tonnage moved by U.S. railroads. If all the coal delivered to U.S. power plants in one year were loaded onto a single train, it would be 95,000 miles long—nearly four times the circumference of the earth. To mitigate the effects of climate change, most of this coal will need to be replaced with lower-carbon energy sources.

• The need for major reductions in U.S. carbon emissions also implies significant cutbacks in petroleum use. One way to think about the magnitude of this task is to picture the physical scale of U.S. petroleum consumption—almost seven billion barrels a year, about half of it in the form of motor gasoline. This is the volumetric equivalent of the amount of water flowing over Niagara Falls at full-flow conditions continuously for seven days.

• One way of displacing petroleum is with agriculturally produced ethanol. U.S. output of ethanol from corn has increased sixfold since the early 2000s, but it is still only equivalent to about 4 percent of total U.S. petroleum consumption. Yet the U.S. bio-ethanol industry is already consuming more than 40 percent of the total U.S. corn crop.

• The International Energy Agency has estimated that preventing an increase in the global average surface temperature of more than 2°C by the end of this century would require a rate of investment in new energy infrastructure of about $1.5 trillion each year for the next twenty-five years (and probably for much longer). That $1.5 trillion is a difficult number to grasp. One way to think about it is that it is equal to the investment that would be required to stage one hundred versions of the 2012 London Olympic Games simultaneously. Two-thirds of this investment will be in emerging economies, and nearly half of it will be needed in the electric power sector for new generating capacity, better and smarter grid infrastructure, new transmission networks, and so on.

There is another sense in which scale matters in energy. Many new energy technologies are embedded in very large, complex, and capital-intensive systems. Even early-stage projects to explore technical feasibility may cost hundreds of millions or even billions of dollars and may also require large amounts of land as well as other resources. High financial risk complicates the process of bringing these technologies to market.

The contrast with the much faster-moving and lightly capitalized waves of innovation associated with, say, social networking or smartphone apps is obvious. In practice this line is blurred, because advances in information technology play a central role in energy innovation too. Still, for many energy technologies the journey from initial idea to impact in the marketplace is much longer and costlier. So in devising strategies for energy innovation it is important to consider not only what is needed for the early stages of the innovation process to flourish but also how to overcome the obstacles further down the road toward adoption at scale.

These problems of innovation scale-up are not unique to energy. Similar issues arise in other parts of the economy, notably the manufacturing sector, where concerns over the failure to capture the downstream economic benefits of American inventiveness stretch back decades (Dertouzos et al. 1989). In fact, even though the energy sector straddles the increasingly nugatory boundary between manufacturing and services, much of what is interesting and important about energy from an innovation perspective takes place in industries that seem to belong unambiguously in the manufacturing column. Wind turbines, solar panels, nuclear reactor pressure vessels, superconducting transmission lines, and coal-bearing railroad hopper cars are all manufactured products. And oil refineries and bioethanol plants, no less than semiconductor fabrication plants, are manufacturing.

So it is not surprising that many of the concerns about innovation scale-up in other manufacturing industries are echoed in the energy sector. The recent migration of solar and wind energy manufacturing from the United States to China to take advantage of the lower costs of labor and capital and more attractive market conditions there has prompted worries that the energy industry will join the long list of other domestic industries that have been unable to compete with China-based rivals, at the cost of American manufacturing jobs and profits and, potentially, the long-term sustainability of the United States' capacity to innovate in this field (Pisano and Shih 2009).[1]

But in other respects the innovation challenge in energy is atypical. Consider the anxiety over China "getting ahead" of the United States in innovation. Even as a general proposition, the idea that countries are engaged in a zero-sum innovation race is debatable. But in the particular case of low-carbon energy innovation the zero-sum description seems especially inapt. China's enormous and rapidly growing carbon emissions give the rest of the world—including the United States—a major stake in the success of its efforts to reduce these emissions. Even though Chinese innovation prowess in solar and wind may threaten some U.S. firms, United States interests will still be served if there are positive consequences for the global climate.

Moreover, rapid energy development and a more pliable regulatory environment mean that China is becoming an important source of new technology and market knowledge for American energy firms.[2] China is increasingly likely to host first-of-a-kind applications of some new low-carbon energy technologies. American energy firms can benefit from participating in these projects, or from conducting their own projects in China—projects which might take much longer or be more costly to carry out in the more complex U.S. regulatory environment and may not even be feasible at all. A current example is TerraPower, the advanced nuclear reactor development company cofounded by Bill Gates, which is reported to be negotiating with the Chinese to build its first full-scale demonstration project there. Similarly, GreatPoint Energy, an early-stage Massachusetts-based firm with an innovative process for coal gasification, will scale up its technology first in China. Indeed, it is not only American firms that stand to gain from China-based innovation. U.S. consumers, too, can benefit—in the form of lower energy bills—from China's willingness to deploy very large amounts of capital to drive down the costs of low-carbon energy technologies such as wind and solar.

There is another important difference between energy and many other technology-intensive industries from an innovation perspective. Whereas innovation in industries such as mobile computing and pharmaceuticals often involves the creation of fundamentally new products and services, energy is a commodity. Users care mainly about the cost and reliability of energy services. Innovators therefore face stringent, non-negotiable requirements on cost, quality, and reliability from the outset. Moreover, they must introduce their new products and services into mature markets, dominated by highly optimized energy systems honed over many decades and owned and operated by well-financed, politically influential incumbent firms with deep ties to Wall Street and Washington and, often, a strong commitment to the status quo. This is the toughest kind of innovation environment, and although it is not unique to energy, it is different from the conditions encountered in many other technology-intensive sectors.

A third important difference between energy and other sectors is that many of the major drivers of energy innovation are external to the energy marketplace. The actual and potential impacts of climate change are not now priced into the great majority of the millions of daily transactions between suppliers and consumers of energy. So, even though innovation can help to ameliorate those impacts, the economic incentives created by the play of market forces alone won't be enough to bring it about. The question is thus not whether to augment those forces, but how—and that makes the issue of innovation in the energy sector different from innovation in many other sectors of the economy.

For all these reasons, energy is a special case when it comes to innovation. The purpose of this chapter, therefore, is to augment the general discussion of innovation and manufacturing elsewhere in this book with some supplementary comments about the problem of energy innovation.

Energy and climate change

The threat of climate change and the need to transition to a low-carbon energy system is just one of several major challenges confronting the global energy industry. Underlying all else is the rapidly growing need for affordable, reliable energy supplies. The International Energy Agency recently projected that by the middle of the twenty-first century global energy use will have increased by at least 50 percent and that electricity use will have more than doubled, placing great pressure on energy supplies and prices.[3]

These projections might seem to imply profligate consumption, but that is hardly the case. The world is experiencing a period of extraordinarily rapid economic growth, unprecedented in human history, in which hundreds of millions of people in Africa, Asia, and South America are lifting themselves out of poverty and starting down the road to a middle-class standard of living, all within the span of a few decades. One of the consequences is sharply increased energy use. But the projected increase is scarcely extravagant. For example, if electricity use were indeed to double by the year 2050, this would mean, roughly speaking, that the richest billion of the world's population would be using electricity at that time at about the same rate as the average American uses it today, the middle seven billion would be using it at the rate of the average Chinese today (or about a quarter of the current U.S. usage rate), and the poorest billion would still have no electricity at all.

A second global challenge is the increasing worldwide dependence on imports of oil, natural gas, and other fuels, as well as energy technologies, in order to meet the rapidly growing demand for energy. This dependence is creating new economic vulnerabilities as well as the prospect of greater international tension and potential for conflict. As new sources of energy supply are discovered around the world, significant geopolitical shifts are likely. The possibility that increased production of unconventional domestic oil and gas resources will eventually lead to American energy self-sufficiency may have important implications for security arrangements in the Persian Gulf and elsewhere in the longer run. But the problem of global energy security will surely persist, and indeed seems likely to intensify.

A third global challenge is that of environmental pollution. Coal burning for electricity and industry and oil burning in vehicles, and the resulting emissions of sulfur dioxide, nitrogen oxides, hydrocarbons, and particulates, are the main causes of urban and regional pollution around the world. The impacts on public health and acid precipitation are often severe. According to one recent study of these health effects, outdoor air pollution, much of it associated with energy use, contributed to 3.2 million premature deaths worldwide in a single year (2010), including 1.2 million deaths in China alone.[4]

The fourth problem, as already noted, is that of climate change. How can the world meet the rapidly growing need for affordable, reliable, and secure energy supplies without wrecking the global climate?

That climate change is the most urgent, important, and difficult problem of all was the conventional wisdom among many American energy experts a few years ago. At the outset of his first administration, President Obama signaled his intention to make the issue a priority. He returned to it following his reelection in 2012, featuring it prominently in his inaugural address and in his 2013 State of the Union speech. But during much of the intervening four years the subject of climate change almost disappeared from energy policy debates.[5]

Part of the explanation is the series of shocks and surprises that marked President Obama's first term: the global financial collapse, the historic recession that followed, the worst offshore oil spill in U.S. history in the Gulf of Mexico, the nuclear disaster at Fukushima, and the political revolutions sweeping across the Arab world. Each of these developments focused attention on a different policy goal, at least for a while. At different times energy affordability, energy security, the trade deficit, local environmental impacts, and nuclear safety each became a principal topic in the energy policy debate. And throughout this period the job-creating potential of the energy industry was a primary focus for many politicians. In parallel, advocates for the fossil fuel industries actively tried—and to a significant degree succeeded—in changing the subject of the public debate away from the problem of climate change.

The last few years may turn out to have been an unusually volatile period for the energy sector. Nevertheless, more surprises can be anticipated over the next few decades, and for much of this period climate may well not be the most important issue on the energy agenda. Nature will send its own signals from time to time, and when those signals are strong enough there will likely be a policy response—possibly a very rapid and strong one. But at other times, just as in the recent past, more immediate issues will demand attention, and it does not seem likely that there will be an intense, uninterrupted energy policy focus on climate change for the next few decades—the key period for developing an effective response to the problem.

In fact, a number of energy analysts have recently been refocusing away from the problem of how to prevent climate change toward the problem of how best to adapt to its consequences.[6] If the expected social and economic costs of adapting to climate-related damage are lower than the expected costs of preventing it, that is a good reason to focus on the possibilities for adaptation and to examine which possibilities are likely to be most efficient.

In practice, the most effective strategy will involve mitigation and adaptation. As presidential science advisor John Holdren has aptly put it, "We need enough mitigation to avoid the unmanageable, and enough adaptation to manage the unavoidable."[7]

Designing and implementing such a strategy may well be the most challenging case of technological decision making under uncertainty that our society has ever had to face: the risk is of a high order and potentially irreversible; the underlying scientific issues are extraordinarily complex and imperfectly understood; the socioeconomic and ecological consequences are in many ways even more complex and uncertain; and preventive action, if it is to be effective, will require an unprecedented degree of international cooperation.

Decisions about what course of action to pursue must be informed by the best available scientific evidence concerning the following:

• The mechanisms—natural and anthropogenic—of greenhouse gas buildup in the atmosphere and, based on this understanding, predictions of how the atmospheric concentration of greenhouse gases will change over time;

• How different levels and rates of atmospheric greenhouse-gas buildup will affect the global climate;

• How climate change will affect physical, social, economic, and ecological systems at multiple spatial scales, from the global to the regional, with potential consequences including significant sea-level rise, increased frequency and severity of extreme weather events, alteration of disease vectors, disruption of water supplies, ecosystem transformation and its implications for habitat, population dislocations and migration, and economic risks to agriculture and coastal property.

Although difficult scientific questions must still be resolved and major areas of uncertainty remain, important advances in understanding have occurred since the 1990s. This progress has been tracked in the series of reports published at regular intervals by the Intergovernmental Panel on Climate Change (IPCC), which represents the closest approximation to a general consensus within the engaged scientific community. In its most recent synthesis report, published in 2007, the IPCC concluded that (1) the average global temperature has increased more rapidly over the past half-century (by roughly 0.6°C) than at any other time during the past two millennia; (2) this warming has coincided with a 35 percent increase in the atmospheric concentration of greenhouse gases (GHG) (mainly CO_2) over preindustrial levels; (3) this increase in GHG concentrations is mainly attributable to anthropogenic causes; (4) most of the warming is very likely due to the increase in anthropogenic GHG concentrations; and (5) the human influence has likely also extended to other aspects of climate, including observed sea-level increases, changes in wind patterns, and increases in temperature extremes. The IPCC further concluded that continued emissions of GHG at or above current rates would very likely induce warming and other climate changes considerably larger than those experienced during the past century.

In 2010 the U.S. National Academy of Sciences similarly concluded that the climate is changing and that the change is caused principally by human activities, particularly the combustion of fossil fuels. According to the academy's Panel on Advancing the Science of Climate Change, "[t]here are still some uncertainties, and there always will be in understanding a complex system like Earth's climate. Nevertheless, there is a strong, credible body of evidence, based on multiple lines of research, documenting that climate is changing and that these changes are in large part caused by human activities. While much remains to be learned, the core phenomenon, scientific questions, and hypotheses have been examined thoroughly and have stood firm in the face of serious scientific debate and careful evaluation of alternative explanations" (National Research Council 2010). The panel noted that the earth's average surface temperature in the first decade of the twenty-first century was 1.4°F (0.8°C) warmer than in the first decade of the twentieth century, with most of the warming occurring since the 1970s. It concluded that most of the warming since then has been caused by human activities resulting in the release of CO_2 and other GHGs into the atmosphere.

The atmospheric concentration of CO_2 currently stands at about 391 parts per million (ppm) and is increasing at a rate of about 2 ppm per year.[8] This rate of increase is accelerating, with the global expansion of fossil fuel use again the main culprit. In "business as usual" scenarios (i.e., with no additional efforts made to restrict CO_2 emissions), the concentration of carbon dioxide in the atmosphere by 2100 is projected to be roughly triple what it was before the Industrial Revolution began (i.e., about 270 ppm). How the earth's climate would respond to such an increase cannot be predicted with certainty, but recent estimates indicate that the global average surface temperature can be expected to rise by at least 4°C, and possibly by more than 6°C (Sokolov et al. 2009). The high end of that range is roughly ten times the amount of warming observed so far, and it is similar to the temperature difference between today's climate and the coldest part of the last Ice Age, when ice sheets covered much of North America.

The consequences of temperature changes of this magnitude are projected to be severe for natural ecosystems and human societies. The warming that has occurred in recent decades has already had observable effects, such as warming oceans, shrinking sea ice, more powerful storms, and the extinction of vulnerable species. Several more decades of business-as-usual will likely put large coastal populations at greater risk of inundation due to rising sea levels and storms. About 23 percent of the human population currently lives within 100 km of the coast and less than 100 meters above sea level. Changes to the climate will also likely make it more difficult for many people to grow their traditional crops. Public health will likely deteriorate because the range of pathogens will be extended. These burdens will generally fall most heavily on the poorest populations, who are least able to bear them.

The great complexity of the earth's climate system means that such projections are uncertain, and there is still a chance that the consequences of continuing down the business-as-usual path will turn out to be tolerable. But the weight of scientific evidence points in the other direction. Indeed, recent findings suggest that the most widely accepted projections underestimate the potential for damage.[9] In this context, a combination of mitigation to reduce greenhouse gas emissions as aggressively as possible and adaptation to protect the most vulnerable human and natural systems is the most sensible course.

Because of the many uncertainties involved, as well as the divergent interests of different stakeholders within and between nations, there can be no exact answer to the question of what would be an acceptable upper limit on the GHG concentration and the global average temperature. Many climate scientists have concluded that the worst risks of climate change might be avoided if the concentration of CO_2 and other GHGs could be stabilized between 450 and 550 ppm of carbon equivalent. At the lower end of this range, the IPCC has estimated that the average global temperature increase would be unlikely to exceed 3°C and would have a 50 percent probability of remaining below 2°C. At the upper end of the range (roughly twice the preindustrial GHG concentration of 270 ppm), the temperature increase would have a high likelihood of falling somewhere in the 1.5°C to 4.4°C range, a 50 percent probability of remaining below 3°C and a small but significant probability of exceeding 5°C. Some experts, weighing the risks involved, have concluded that this upper limit marks the outer bound of rational risk taking. Others advocate a more restrictive limit, arguing that to avoid unacceptably harmful consequences the average temperature increase should not exceed 2°C.

Stabilizing the GHG concentration in the 450 to 550 ppm range will be very difficult. The current atmospheric concentration of all GHGs is 430 ppm of carbon equivalent and is increasing at an accelerating rate. If no further preventive action is taken, the lower end of the range will be reached in about ten years and the upper limit within perhaps thirty to forty years. Deep cuts in GHG emissions will be necessary if we are to stay within these limits, and the longer we wait to take action, the deeper the required cuts will be. To avoid exceeding the lower bound, the global emission rate would have to peak within a very few years and then decline by several percentage points per year thereafter, and as a practical matter this goal has probably passed out of reach already. Even for the upper limit of 550 ppm, global emissions would have to peak in ten to twenty years and then decline at a significant rate. For example, stabilization at the 550 ppm level could be achieved if global emissions peaked in 2020 and then declined at an annual rate of 1 to 2.5 percent per year. If emissions continued to increase for another decade, however, the necessary postpeak reduction rate would almost double.[10]

In sum, the scientific evidence points to the need for a policy focus on stabilization scenarios in the 450 to 550 ppm range. Above 550 ppm, the chances of avoiding very serious economic, social, and ecological impacts appear slight, whereas scenarios below 450 ppm are probably no longer achievable. Remaining within this range would roughly correspond to an expected average global temperature increase of 2°C to 3°C by the end of the twenty-first century, and perhaps double that in northerly latitudes. If we fail to make the transition to a much lower GHG emission trajectory during the next twenty to thirty years, staying within this concentration range will be effectively impossible. Quantitatively, this will mean reducing the global emission rate by 25 to 50 percent by 2050.

Considerations of equity require that wealthy countries accept higher targets for emissions cuts than poor ones. The wealthy countries, with less than 20 percent of the world's population, have been responsible for 75 percent of the atmospheric GHG increment introduced since the preindustrial era, whereas poor countries will likely bear the brunt of the impact of global climate change and will certainly feel its effects earlier. Such considerations informed the negotiation of the Kyoto Protocol, under which most of the world's industrialized nations (though not the United States) agreed to limit their emissions, and the developing countries were exempt from emission restrictions. In the current round of global climate negotiations a different calculus is in effect. Even in the hypothetical case that the roughly one billion people who live in wealthy countries were to reduce their emissions to zero, the six billion people living in the rest of the world would still have much to do, because their emissions are growing much more rapidly and in any plausible scenario will account for the bulk of global emissions in the coming decades. (In a transition of more than symbolic significance, China in 2007 replaced the United States as the world's largest emitter of greenhouse gases.) Little has been accomplished in these negotiations so far, but it is clear that the advanced economies, including the United States, will need to commit to deep reductions in order to secure agreement on a global limit on carbon emissions. In 2009 President Obama joined with the leaders of the other G8 nations in pledging to cut emissions by at least 80 percent by 2050.

The only way for the United States to achieve such deep cuts in emissions is to engineer a transition away from its current heavy dependence on fossil energy resources. Today fossil fuels account for 85 percent of the nation's primary energy consumption, and the combustion of fossil fuels is responsible for almost 80 percent of total U.S. GHG emissions on a carbon-equivalent basis.[11] Because of the long lead time for turnover of the energy infrastructure, the United States will very soon need to begin the shift away from using petroleum for transportation and high-carbon fuels for electricity generation toward much greater energy end-use efficiency, much greater reliance on alternative fuels for transportation, and low- or zero-carbon power-generation systems.

Three waves of innovation

The United States' energy system will obviously not be transformed all at once, nor by a single "silver bullet" solution. It is helpful to think about this transition in terms of three separate waves of innovation, each breaking over the economy at a different time, each gathering momentum at a different rate, but all of which must be pursued in parallel.

The first wave is primarily composed of innovations designed to improve the efficiency of energy use. It is reasonable to expect that these innovations can begin to make a significant contribution within the next decade. Many can be implemented without major technological breakthroughs or even significant changes in consumer behavior, but rather by combining already available technologies with new business and financial models. Others, such as improvements to the fuel use efficiency of the automobile fleet, can be achieved through a series of incremental technical advances. These modest, relatively near-term innovations are crucial. The United States will need to accelerate, greatly, the pace at which it has been reducing its energy usage per unit of economic output if it is to have any chance of making the necessary deep cuts in carbon emissions.

The second wave will overlap with the first, but especially after 2020 we must begin to see adoption of the major low-carbon energy supply technologies—nuclear, wind, solar, geothermal, low-carbon biofuels, and carbon capture and storage—along with new electricity storage technologies, on a scale far exceeding anything previously achieved. But this will not occur in the absence of significant cost reductions in these technologies.

We might also hope to see a third wave of innovation, drawing on fundamental scientific discoveries in fields such as materials, catalysis, and energy transport, and in the best case overcoming longstanding physical limits on energy conversion and storage. This third wave might draw on ideas that seem impractical now or on developments in other fields that haven't previously been seen to be relevant in the energy sphere. Possible examples include advances in artificial photosynthesis, air capture of carbon dioxide, and nuclear fusion. But the long lead times required to translate foundational discoveries into commercially viable technologies, and then for these technologies to achieve significant penetration in the marketplace, mean that breakthrough technologies are unlikely to be making major contributions to the energy system before the mid-twenty-first century.

The problem of public action

Market forces alone will not push these waves of innovation forward fast enough. Public action of some kind will be required and will need to be sustained over several decades. What actions are likely to be most effective?

There are three broad possibilities. First, government can work to improve the environment for innovation of all kinds by reducing or eliminating obstacles to the flow of financial capital, knowledge, and people toward economically viable options. Policies affecting immigration, intellectual property protection, and capital market regulation belong in this category. Second, government can seek in a more targeted way to stimulate market demand for low-carbon technologies, thereby creating incentives for private sector investment in climate-friendly innovations. There is a wide range of possible mechanisms here, including (1) pricing carbon; (2) mandating the use of low-carbon technologies (for example by setting "portfolio standards" for those technologies); (3) implementing tax credits, subsidies, loan guarantees, or other incentives to encourage private investment in particular technologies; and (4) using the government's own procurement powers to create demand for low-carbon products and services. Third, government can intervene more directly in the innovation process by itself taking on some of the risks and costs of innovation—for example by funding or conducting research, development, and demonstration activities, or by entering into partnerships with private sector entities to advance particular technologies.

The rationale for a government role of the first kind—creating a generally conducive environment for innovation—is widely accepted in principle, even though some of the specific policies involved may be difficult to enact in practice. The second category is more controversial, especially to the degree that the policies involve targeting particular technologies or imposing additional costs on energy users or taxpayers. Even here, though, the idea that government has a legitimate role in stimulating demand for innovations whose value to society is underweighted in the marketplace enjoys fairly widespread support, at least in theory.[12] An important recent example is the Obama administration's rules, finalized in 2012, requiring the average fuel economy of new cars and trucks to increase to 54.5 miles per gallon by 2025.

The third category of government intervention—direct support of the innovation process—tends to generate the most skepticism, both in terms of the theoretical justification for government involvement in the first place and in terms of government's ability to be effective in practice. The traditional case for direct government support of commercially relevant innovation has chiefly focused on the "free rider" problem: private investment in innovation generally falls below the societally optimal level when businesses cannot prevent competitors from gaining access to the knowledge generated by their innovation activities and cannot force them to pay for it. Early-stage research and development is the canonical example, because it is particularly difficult for private firms to capture all the rewards of their investments in these activities. Firms therefore tend to underinvest in them and public investment is required to compensate. Energy is no different from other sectors in this regard, and the solution in most cases is the same: direct and indirect financial support from the government for fundamental research and early-stage applied R&D, along with incentives, such as tax credits, for private sector investment in R&D.

A second kind of market failure arises when energy prices don't reflect climate risks. In this case innovators will have few incentives to develop and deploy new technologies with a lower-carbon footprint. To remedy this problem, policies that attach a price to carbon—whether directly through a tax or via a cap-and-trade program—are essential. Pricing carbon creates immediate incentives for consumers to choose lower-carbon options, as well as longer-term incentives for private actors to invest in low-carbon innovation. Some economists have argued that once a carbon price is set at the correct level, there is no need for direct government support of innovation.[13] As a practical matter, however, pricing mechanisms are likely to fall short. Indeed, the conventional wisdom in Washington, D.C. today is that a carbon price cannot be implemented at all. Political wisdom is famously mutable, but even if a carbon price is eventually enacted, politicians will be reluctant to allow it to rise high enough to induce innovation at the necessary pace. Based on recent evidence, any future scheme adopted by Congress is likely to have escape ramps, price ceilings, exemptions, and other loopholes that will cause it to fall well short of establishing a universal, economy-wide price that ramps up at the societally optimal rate.[14]

Even with the "correct" carbon price in place, moreover, there is a case for direct government support of the innovation process. The MIT economist Daron Acemoglu and his colleagues recently showed that the optimal policy for economic growth subject to environmental constraints and limited resources involves carbon taxes *and* research subsidies (Acemoglu et al. 2009). They found that it would be excessively distortionary to rely solely on taxes to correct for the combined effects of (1) uninternalized climate risks from current carbon emissions, (2) the tendency of private actors to underinvest in R&D that could reduce future emissions, and (3) other market distortions that tend to favor more intensive use of existing technologies over the adoption of new technologies. Put differently, a strategy that uses government support to augment private R&D efforts will reduce the economic and political costs of achieving a low-carbon transition compared with a strategy that focuses solely on inducing faster take-up of low-carbon technologies through carbon taxes and leaving cost-reducing innovation entirely to the private sector.

But even with a sound theoretical rationale for direct government support of innovation, practical questions of effectiveness loom large— particularly when government involvement goes beyond support for early-stage R&D to include later-stage development and demonstration activities. It is at these stages when some of the most important barriers to innovation arise, when some of the most important cost-reducing advances are needed, and when government support may be especially crucial to success. The problem is that government is poorly suited to play a constructive role the closer technologies come to commercialization. Government decision makers are generally less informed than their private sector counterparts about the business and market considerations that come to the fore as technologies enter the marketplace, whereas their administrative procedures are often poorly adapted to market-based decision making. Compared with support for early-stage research, there is a greater risk that government intervention at this point will be inefficient and politicized and that it will crowd out private investment.

The mixed record of previous government programs to support energy technology in the later phases of the innovation process—including a number of high-profile failures at the U.S. Department of Energy (DOE)—provides ample basis for these concerns. Although there have been notable successes, there have also been prominent cases of failed or aborted commercial demonstration projects, of interest-group politics and interregional conflicts delaying and constraining Congressional action, of political accommodation to the loudest voices in the energy innovation debate, and of a sometimes-dysfunctional government bureaucracy pushing particular projects, technologies, and subsidies long after their unsuitability has become obvious. Troubled DOE projects have included the Clinch River Breeder Reactor Project, the synthetic fuels program of the late 1970s and early 1980s, and more recently the Yucca Mountain nuclear waste repository project and the still-unfolding FutureGen project. Numerous factors have contributed to these problems, from a systematic tendency on the part of government officials to underestimate project costs, to congressional interference, lack of consistency in policy direction and funding, inefficient business practices and restrictive bureaucracy, and the absence of a clear institutional mission at the DOE. One study of six large federal technology commercialization projects concluded, "The overriding lesson from the case studies is that the goal of economic efficiency—to cure market failures in privately sponsored commercial innovation—is so severely constrained by political forces that an effective, coherent national commercial R&D program has never been put in place" (Cohen and Noll 1991).

In other circumstances such critiques might be sufficiently serious to neutralize any argument for a direct government role in future energy innovation efforts, other than support for fundamental R&D. But the threat of climate change alters that calculus. Now the risk that government intervention will either fail outright or be costly and inefficient must be weighed against the possibility that success will substantially lower the cost—and increase the feasibility—of attempts to accelerate the energy transition. In this case, regrettably predictable attempts to exploit the risk of ecological catastrophe to promote ill-advised government interventions must be balanced against the uniquely large ecological and economic risks of *in*action given the nature of the climate threat.

A model of the energy innovation system

It is convenient to divide the problem of direct public support of energy innovation into its component parts. Although the process of innovation is complex and rarely unfolds in a linear fashion, it is nevertheless helpful to identify four distinct stages in the progression of an innovation from idea or concept to large-scale deployment, as shown in figure 5.1 (Lester and Hart 2012, 33).

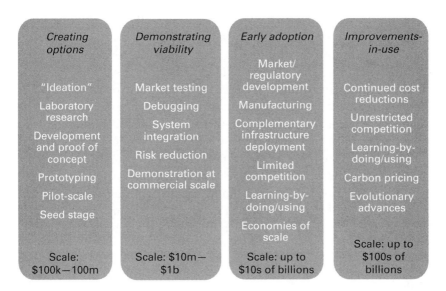

Figure 5.1
The four stages of energy innovation. *Source:* Richard K. Lester and David M. Hart, *Unlocking Energy Innovation* (Cambridge, MA: MIT Press, 2012).

Creating Options. System-level goals for this stage of the innovation process are to open up a broad range of innovation pathways by encouraging experimentation with new ideas and concepts, by attracting new entrants to participate in the process, by ensuring that knowledge about the options being explored is generated transparently, and by guaranteeing broad access to that knowledge. Creating options is closely associated with R&D, but the two are not synonymous. Although high-impact new technical developments frequently emerge from organized R&D programs, ideas for improved or entirely new products and services—including new business models—need not and often do not originate from formal R&D organizations, instead arising from encounters between developers and customers, in manufacturing facilities, or elsewhere in the supply chain. (Conversely, much R&D is not devoted to creating options but to supporting other stages of the innovation process.) An important objective at this stage is to create, maintain, and expand the technical communities and public spaces that facilitate new knowledge formation and concept development. Public funding for fundamental research and education is critical, as is venture investing to seed new ideas for products and services and businesses, although the enormous scale and long time horizon of many energy systems limits the role of venture capital in this case.

Demonstrating Viability. In the demonstrating viability stage the primary objectives are to enable technology providers, investors, and users to obtain credible information about cost, reliability, and safety under conditions that approximate actual conditions of use. This typically entails building, operating, and debugging full-scale prototypes. Other important tasks at this stage include settling on standards and infrastructure requirements for scaling the innovation and identifying key legal and regulatory barriers that will need to be overcome for widespread use. Private innovators and their investors assume an increasing share of costs and risks in the demonstrating viability stage, compared to the creating options stage. In some cases they may assume all the cost and risk. But the time horizon is often too long and the risk level too high for private investors to be willing to underwrite demonstrations for complex, large-scale technologies.

Early Adoption. Early adoption involves the most forward-looking users or perhaps those with the strongest need to use the innovation. The main goals at this stage are market development, accelerated learning, and early deployment of the infrastructures needed for scale-up. Innovators establish manufacturing and distribution capabilities and other key parts of the supply chain, and the early adopters (sometimes known as *lead users*) also play a key role, providing feedback that enables valuable features to be to enhanced and practical problems to be sorted out. Proprietary knowledge about processes builds up during early adoption and unit costs generally come down (although aggregate costs may mount rapidly as deployment of these early units proceeds).

Improvements in Use. The market and regulatory environments in this final stage settle into stable and predictable patterns. But designs continue to be refined, production systems and business models are improved, and the behavior of customers becomes better understood. Frequently the cumulative impact of evolutionary improvements to a technology during its life cycle in the marketplace greatly exceeds the performance gains achieved when the technology is first brought to market.

Again, it is important to stress that the innovation process is not linear, as might be suggested by the sequential presentation of these four stages. In fact, knowledge flows between the stages in both directions, and the boundaries separating them are in practice blurred. The central contention of this chapter, however, is that a strategy to accelerate energy innovation must address all four stages, and that it is not enough just to focus on one. For example, federal spending on energy research and development has frequently been criticized for being too low.[15] But much of the force that more R&D spending might exert at the front end of the innovation process will simply be dissipated unless effective measures are also in place to address the intermediate and downstream stages.

The remainder of this chapter explores the outlines of one such strategy. This strategy recognizes that energy innovation does not occur in a vacuum. There is a supporting system of institutions for research and education. There are well-developed markets for energy services, for labor, and for capital. There are codes and standards and rules for competition, for intellectual property, and for environmental protection. There are suppliers of equipment and of services. And there are mandates and subsidies for the development and adoption of specific technologies. In other words, the innovation process occurs within a dense network—or system—of institutions and incentives. The critical question is what kind of system will be capable of generating a sustained flow of innovations of many different kinds over a period of decades.

A practical energy innovation strategy must be cognizant of the institutional capabilities and constraints that exist today. But it is also useful to ask a different question. Suppose it were possible to begin with a clean slate and to build a system of institutions and incentives that would be capable of solving the energy innovation challenge. What might such a system look like?

Many of the basic attributes required for success are self-evident. The scale of such a system would need to match the true scale of the challenge. It should encourage competition and the entry of outsiders. As already noted, it should promote acceleration of all four stages of the innovation process. It should ensure timely and rigorous winnowing of options at each stage, so that noncompetitive technologies would not continue to receive support long after it was obvious that they could not compete. It should accommodate and exploit regional variations in innovation priorities—variations in natural resource endowments, economic conditions, institutional capabilities, and public attitudes toward different energy options. And it should not depend on crises to mobilize the necessary financial and other resources.

Building a new American energy innovation system

In a recent research project at the MIT Industrial Performance Center these attributes were used to sketch the outline of a far larger and much more dynamic energy innovation system than exists today (Lester and Hart 2012). The main elements of this system are summarized here.

New innovators

At the core of this new energy innovation system must be new market entrants: new firms and existing firms from other sectors. The U.S. energy industry today is dominated by large, risk-averse corporations with a history of underinvestment in innovation. The energy industry needs an infusion of new firms, new people, and new ways of doing things. Public policy can create space for new entrants and facilitate their access to resources. The most important and also most challenging arena is the electric power sector.

Expanded competition in electric power markets

The electric power industry is the central front in the low-carbon energy transition. This is because most low-carbon energy supply technologies are most usefully applied to the generation of electricity. So the transition to a low-carbon energy system will mean accelerating the historic shift toward electricity as the dominant energy carrier in the economy. Expanding the domain of market competition, promoting an open-industry architecture, and encouraging the entry of new competitors into newly opened segments of the electric power industry will all be powerful drivers of innovation. The most important spaces for competition and innovation lie at the edges of the power grid. Independent power producers will experiment with innovative generation technologies at one end of the grid. At the other end, specialist energy service companies, demand response providers, and distributed generators will explore new business models, new organizational configurations, and new kinds of services for end users. To promote competition, the process of vertical disintegration of the electric utilities that began in the1990s must be completed. The main objective at that time was lower electricity prices. Today accelerating innovation is the strongest argument for shrinking the footprint of the utilities. Expanded competition and new entrants to the power sector are the keys to all three waves of U.S. low-carbon energy transition.

Smart integrators

Smart integrator transmission and distribution utilities, working closely with a national network of regional transmission organizations and independent system operators (RTOs and ISOs) and with state and federal regulators, should manage the operations and development of the electric power system. Although no longer controlling the power system from end to end, the utilities that run the grid will remain the system's linchpins. They will manage the interaction of independent power producers, distributed generators, energy management service providers, customers, and many other players. Their responsibility will be to ensure that the diverse innovations arising at the edges of the grid work together to achieve the system's key objectives of lower carbon dioxide emissions, improved reliability, and greater affordability. Government regulation will still be necessary in order to prevent the grid's owners from exercising their monopoly power. But regulators, too, must become "smarter" in tandem with the firms they are regulating. The RTOs and ISOs are an essential part of this institutional complex.

They provide a transparent mechanism for operating wholesale power markets and for planning new and better transmission facilities. Congress should extend the system of RTOs to the entire country and should grant RTOs and ISOs greater authority to plan and site new transmission lines.

An invigorated energy efficiency marketplace
In the first, efficiency-driven wave of innovation, the largest target of opportunity is the building sector. In the near term, improving building energy efficiency is the most cost-effective greenhouse gas mitigation opportunity available to the United States. No technological break-throughs are necessary. The products and services already exist. But they are currently confined to relatively small customer segments. Until about the mid-2020s, the most important innovations will be institutional and organizational reforms that expand the marketplace for efficiency products and services. By 2020, it is reasonable to expect that a thriving marketplace will speed the widespread adoption of building energy efficiency products and services.

For new buildings and for new appliances, regulations that ratchet up energy efficiency in a predictable fashion will be the key to making these markets work better. The federal government must play a key role, defining baseline standards and ensuring national compliance with them in collaboration with state and local governments (in the case of new buildings) and manufacturers (in the case of appliances). Federal test beds (such as the DOE's building energy efficiency innovation hub), along with innovative private buildings, such as those certified to a high level by the U.S. Green Building Council, can serve as the proving grounds for each ensuing iteration of these standards. These buildings will be the leading symbols of the first wave of innovation.

For retrofits of existing buildings, regulatory mandates are impractical, and a combination of financial incentives, new financing institutions, new administrative structures, and new business models will be necessary. As utilities increasingly focus on the grid integration task, new opportunities to administer building retrofit programs may appear in many states. The administrators of these programs will encourage vigorous competition in the provision of products and services, facilitate the availability of energy consumption data to third-party service providers, and sustain public information and education efforts that aim at shaping behavior. Better and more accessible information, such as the equivalent of a miles-per-gallon-type label for all buildings, will support the deepening of efficiency products and service markets. The business model innovations of energy efficiency service providers, supported by public R&D and information provision programs, will enable the United States to begin to close the energy efficiency gap with Europe and Japan.

Regional innovation investment banks

A new group of institutions, centered on regional innovation investment banks (RIIBs), should be established to unlock the second wave of innovations that will enable low-carbon electricity to supplant other energy sources. The success of the second wave will depend on scaling up and cutting the unit costs of electricity-related services provided by low-carbon central station power plants, distributed generation technologies, and smart grid innovations. Financing for demonstration and early deployment of these innovations will be mobilized and allocated in new ways. The RIIBs, membership organizations composed of firms drawn from all segments of the electric power sector, will allocate funding to first-of-a-kind large-scale demonstration projects, "next few" postdemonstration projects, and early deployment programs. Teams proposing projects and programs will seek RIIB funding not as their sole source of finance but rather to augment their own investments and to lower their risks. In this way, RIIB investments will leverage larger amounts of private sector funding. The RIIBs will choose among competing projects based on the strength of the proposing team, the quality of its management, and the potential of the proposal to achieve energy innovation goals, as well as the extent of self-funding. The RIIBs will themselves compete with one another to build strong project portfolios in order to attract financial support from state-level trustee organizations. Over time each RIIB may specialize in areas of innovation of particular interest to its region.

State energy innovation trustees

Trustee organizations set up by each state should allocate funds to the RIIBs using the proceeds of an innovation surcharge on all retail sales of electricity within the state. The trustees will be free to allocate their funds to RIIBs in any region. The allocation will be based on the trustee's assessment of which RIIB portfolio of demonstration and postdemonstration projects and early adoption programs most closely matches its needs. The trustee organizations will be more broadly representative of stakeholders in the electricity system than the RIIBs themselves. Their members might include a variety of business sectors, government organizations and officials, environmental and labor groups, and technical experts. All proceeds from the surcharge will have to be allocated by the trustees to the RIIBs within a year of receipt.

A federal gatekeeper

A federal gatekeeper organization will certify that projects and programs presented to the RIIBs for funding have the potential to lead to significant reductions in carbon emissions at a declining unit cost over time. To receive certification, proposals will be required to create pressure on innovators to exploit learning to reduce costs. Public subsidies for projects and programs will decline steadily on a unit basis as experience with the innovation is gained. Certification will be granted for a limited period only, and may be withdrawn if progress proves too slow. The gatekeeper will be responsible for monitoring progress. The gatekeeper will also track projects and programs targeting the same innovations to guard against duplication and overlap. However, it will take into consideration the value of pursuing several different approaches in parallel as circumstances warrant.

Dynamic pricing

Some form of dynamic pricing (in which electricity prices change during the course of the day) will make it possible for customers to make choices that stimulate innovation. Dynamic pricing will reduce peak loads, and it will also incentivize central station and small-scale generators as well as providers of storage and other grid services to respond to supply-and-demand conditions on the grid in the most effective way. Customer decision making will also be informed by more extensive information about historical benchmarks, on bill comparisons with neighbors, and conservation tips. A federally sanctioned labeling program will validate the quality of meters and other equipment and help customers gain confidence that offers made by smart grid service providers are trustworthy.

Open grid architecture and customer control

An open architecture for distributed generation and smart grid technologies, supported by dynamic pricing, will promote innovation "behind the meter" and in the rest of the power system. Investments in distributed generation, grid-scale storage, and smart grid technologies will help to make the power system more reliable, less wasteful, and more responsive to customer choice. In the power grid of the future, many entities will compete to provide many different kinds of services to the smart integrator and to customers. They will be able to plug into the grid and play their roles with minimal difficulty. Regulators and standard-setting bodies will ensure that the interfaces among service providers, users, and the grid remain open and that pricing is fully transparent. On the customer side of the meter, the architecture of the smart grid will be customer controlled rather than utility controlled. Customer-controlled architecture will give customers and third-party service providers greater freedom to experiment with devices and behaviors and provide motivation to develop innovative business models.

Breakthrough innovations

A federal energy research structure, pluralistic in its styles, informed by user input, and larger and more diverse than today's system, will focus on the creation of new options for energy supply, delivery, and use with the potential to contribute on a large scale in the second half of the twenty-first century. The Department of Energy and its large laboratories will be an important part of the system, but other government agencies, including the Department of Defense, will play a larger role than today. Coordination of the federal research effort will be led by the Executive Office of the President. The federal long-term energy research structure will foster the open exchange of ideas, domestically and internationally, and will be linked to the downstream stages of the innovation system.

An energy innovation system with these characteristics would have many of the attributes described previously. It would be larger in scale than the current system, it would address each of the four stages of the innovation process—including, critically, the two intermediate stages—and it would be more open to new entrants. Also, it would rely more heavily on competitive processes to make resource allocation decisions, it would incorporate a "sunset" mechanism designed to ensure that innovations that were not progressing down the learning curve would not be eligible for continued RIIB funding, and by establishing a network of regional financial institutions it would create space for the exercise of competing regional interests and preferences regarding energy innovation. Indeed, over time the different RIIBs might come to specialize in technologies of particular interest to their regions—offshore wind in the Northeast, solar photovoltaic in the Southwest, carbon capture and sequestration in the Midwest, nuclear in the Southeast, and so on.

This is not the only scheme that would embody the basic attributes of a successful energy innovation system. There is plenty of room for other ideas. The key point is that in order to achieve the transition to a low-carbon energy economy, the need for creativity in developing, demonstrating, and improving specific innovations for energy supply and use, is matched by the need for creativity in the design of the innovation system itself.

Conclusion

America's innovation system is one of this country's great assets. That system must now be mobilized in support of a decades-long, global transition to a low-carbon energy economy. If the world is to have a chance of avoiding the worst consequences of climate change and still meet the need for abundant, reliable, and affordable energy, U.S. innovation leadership will be essential. Innovations in technology, business models, public policies, and regulatory institutions will all be required to bring about the fundamental transformation of current patterns of energy production, delivery and use that is needed. The United States is a long way from having an innovation system in place that is capable of meeting these challenges. In this chapter I have described some of the reforms that would help to create an environment within which entrepreneurs, investors, government leaders, and other participants in the innovation system could unlock the United States' enormous innovative capabilities in support of an accelerated energy transition.

Acknowledgments

This chapter draws extensively on several of the author's previous publications, including Richard K. Lester and David M. Hart, *Unlocking Energy Innovation* (Cambridge, MA: MIT Press, 2012); Richard K. Lester, "America's Energy Innovation Problem (and How to Fix It)," *MIT Industrial Performance Center Working Paper* MIT-IPC-09–007 (November 2009), available at http://web.mit.edu/ipc/research/energy/pdf/ EIP_10_003.pdf; as well as several recent public lectures. Sections of the chapter incorporate lightly edited passages from those earlier works. I am grateful to my colleague and coauthor David Hart for his many valuable insights and to the Doris Duke Charitable Foundation for its support of the Energy Innovation Project at the MIT Industrial Performance Center.

Notes

1. As Jonas Nahm has noted, by the year 2010, less than a decade after the first Chinese firms entered the wind and solar sectors, more than 50 percent of the world's wind turbines and 60 percent of the world's solar panels were manufactured in China. During that same period, America's share of solar panel production dropped from 40 percent to 7 percent, and by 2010 the United States was importing 54 percent of its solar panels from China (Jonas Nahm, PhD dissertation, Department of Political Science, MIT [in preparation]).

2. Jonas Nahm and Edward S. Steinfeld, in chapter 6 in this book, have pointed out the complementarities between U.S. and Chinese innovation capabilities in the energy sector.

3. International Energy Agency, *Energy Technology Perspectives—2012*, http://www.iea.org/etp.

4. "Global Burden of Disease Study 2010," *The Lancet* (December 13, 2012), http://www.thelancet.com/themed/global-burden-of-disease.

5. As just one example, in an article published in the *New York Times* in June 2012, one of America's leading energy analysts called for a new political discourse on energy in response to what the article characterized as "America's new energy reality"—largely brought about by the rebound in domestic oil and gas production. It is notable that the description of this new reality did not include a single mention of climate change (Daniel Yergin, "America's New Energy Reality," *New York Times* [June 9, 2012]).

6. See, for example, Alan Barreca, Karen Clay, Olivier Deschenes, Michael Greenstone, and Joseph S. Shapiro, "Adapting to Climate Change: The Remarkable Decline in the U.S. Temperature-Mortality Relationship over the 20th Century," *NBER Working Paper* no. 18692 (January 2013), http://www.nber.org/papers/w18692.

7. John P. Holdren, "The Energy/Climate-Change Challenge and the Role of Nuclear Energy in Meeting It," David J. Rose Lecture, Massachusetts Institute of Technology (October 25, 2010). Video recording at http://web.mit.edu/nse/events/rose-lecture.html.

8. In addition to CO_2, several other gases released into the atmosphere as a result of human activity are capable of absorbing re-radiated solar radiation in the critical wavelength window of eight to twelve microns—in other words, of behaving as greenhouse gases (GHGs). These include methane, nitrous oxide, and the chlorofluorocarbons. These gas molecules differ in their ability to absorb long wavelength radiation. Nitrous oxide, for example, absorbs 270 times more heat per molecule than CO_2. It is conventional to convert the atmospheric concentrations of each of these other GHGs to the equivalent concentration of carbon dioxide. The combined concentration of GHGs is then expressed in terms of ppm of "carbon equivalent." The current atmospheric concentration of GHGs is about 430 ppm of carbon equivalent.

9. A. P. Sokolov et al., op. cit. The MIT researchers estimated that the end-of-century temperature increase relative to 1990 for the business-as-usual scenario will lie in the range from 3.81°C to 6.98°C with 90 percent confidence. Though not strictly comparable,

the Intergovernmental Panel on Climate Change, in its 2007 assessment, estimated an increase in the range from 2.4°C to 6.4°C (Intergovernmental Panel on Climate Change, *Fourth Assessment Report*).

10. HM Treasury, *Stern Review on the Economics of Climate Change*, a report to the Prime Minister and the Chancellor of the Exchequer presented by Sir Nicholas Stern (October 30, 2006).

11. According to the federal government's latest inventory of GHG emissions, in 2010 the combustion of fossil fuels accounted for 94.4 percent of the CO_2 and 79 percent of total GHGs emitted on a carbon-equivalent basis. CO_2 from all sources accounted for 83.6 percent of total U.S. GHG emissions on a carbon-equivalent basis. The other main contributors were methane (9.8 percent) and nitrous oxide (4.5 percent) (see U.S. Environmental Protection Agency, "Inventory of U.S. Greenhouse Gas Emissions and Sinks: 1990–2010" [April 2012]).

12. Deployment mandates and subsidies are generally less efficient than pricing mechanisms. But politicians have tended to favor them, because their direct economic impacts may be smaller, at least initially, and because the costs are more likely to be hidden from those who are bearing them.

13. According to Professor William Nordhaus of Yale University, "[T]o a first approximation, raising the price of carbon is a necessary and sufficient step for tackling global warming. The rest is largely fluff."

14. The best recent example is the Waxman-Markey Bill, which sought to commit the United States to deep reductions in carbon emissions by introducing a cap-and-trade scheme. The legislation died in the Senate in 2010, after a bitter passage through the House.

15. See, for example, the recent report of the American Energy Innovation Council, a group of eight U.S. business leaders, which called for roughly a tripling of total federal energy R&D spending (American Energy Innovation Council, *A Business Plan for America's Energy Future* [June 2010]; available at http://americanenergyinnovation.org/wp-content/uploads/2012/04/AEIC_The_Business_Plan_2010.pdf). In a public letter to the president, a group of thirty-four U.S. Nobel laureates called for a similar increase (Paul Berg and others, "Letter to President Obama" [July 16, 2009]; available at http://www.fas.org/press/news/2009/july_nobelist_letter_to_obama.html).

References

Acemoglu, Daron, Philippe Aghion, Leonardo Bursztyn, and David Hemous. 2009. "The Environment and Directed Technical Change." Unpublished paper provided by the authors. http://economics.mit.edu/files/8076.

Cohen, Linda, and Roger Noll. 1991. *The Technology Pork Barrel*. Washington, DC: Brookings Institution Press.

Dertouzos, Michael L., Robert M. Solow, and Richard K. Lester. 1989. *Made in America: Regaining the Productive Edge*. Cambridge, MA: MIT Press.

Lester, Richard K., and David M. Hart. 2012. *Unlocking Energy Innovation*. Cambridge, MA: MIT Press.

National Research Council. 2010. *Advancing the Science of Climate Change*. Washington, DC: National Academies Press.

Pisano, Gary P., and Willy C. Shih. 2009. "Restoring American Competitiveness." *Harvard Business Review* 87 (7–8).

Sokolov, A. P. et al. 2009. "Probabilistic Forecast for Twenty-First-Century Climate Based on Uncertainties in Emissions (without Policy) and Climate Parameters." *Journal of Climate* 22:5175–5204.

6 The Role of Innovative Manufacturing in High-Tech Product Development: Evidence from China's Renewable Energy Sector

Jonas Nahm and Edward S. Steinfeld

China has been growing steadily since the late 1970s, but it is only since the new millennium that the country has surged forth as a global center for high-tech manufacturing. In the year 2000, China still accounted for only 5.7 percent of global manufacturing output (by value), about a quarter of the share held by the United States or Japan at the time. By 2011, China had vaulted to the top position, achieving an unparalleled 19.8 percent share, just ahead of the United States' previously world-leading 19.4 percent (Marsh 2011; UNIDO 2011). Gains for China have certainly come in mature industries such as textiles, steel, and consumer electronics. But in recent years, it is in emerging technology areas such as wind and solar power generation—the focus of this chapter—that the advance of Chinese manufacturers has been equally or even more astounding.

In 2005, wind turbine manufacturing in China was negligible. Just six years later, Chinese-made turbines accounted for 50 percent of the global total (Bradsher 2010). The ramp-up in solar panel manufacturing has been even more dramatic. Again, as late as 2005, China was only a marginal player in the industry. By 2010, the nation had emerged as the single largest producer and exporter of solar photovoltaic (PV) panels globally, a rise so striking that it has become a major source of contention between China and its trading partners in North America and Europe (Bullis 2012). Both the United States and the European Union have accused Chinese PV producers of engaging in product dumping, ostensibly enabled by excessive subsidization from the Chinese government. By late 2012, the United States had leveled punitive sanctions, and similar measures were pending in the European Union (U.S. International Trade Commission 2012).

But what does leading the world in manufacturing output, whether in solar PV or any other industry, really mean? Is such leadership primarily a reflection of favorable factor price conditions (i.e., low wages, subsidized capital, free land, etc.) or does it reflect the accumulation of real skills and expertise? What sorts of knowledge and capabilities, if any, does substantial national presence in manufacturing signify? And what sort of advantages, commercial or otherwise, does such status confer? To whom?

This chapter argues that China's centrality in new energy technology production has come about only because of extremely tight linkages between upstream innovation and downstream manufacturing. For many of these emerging technologies, a major obstacle to commercial viability involves the translation of an innovative, often new-to-the-world design into a reliable, reasonably priced manufactured product. As we demonstrate, that translation involves intensive communication and learning between upstream and downstream players. Particularly in these emerging technology industries, designs cannot simply be "thrown over the wall" to awaiting contract manufacturers.

At the same time, as the Chinese experience shows, intense interaction between upstream R&D and downstream manufacturing does not require geographic proximity. For many renewable energy technologies today—particularly in wind and solar—upstream innovation is still performed primarily by European and North American firms in their home environments. The manufacturing, however, takes place in China.

It takes place in China precisely because firms in that national business ecosystem have developed capabilities for a particular form of innovative manufacturing. That type of manufacturing is not primarily related to low factor costs or government subsidies. Rather, it stems from particular types of engineering skills that reside at the intersection of upstream design and downstream manufacturing. Those skills— unique in many respects to the Chinese production environment—are employed to translate outsiders' complex designs into easily manufactured and easily scaled final products. As we demonstrate, Chinese manufacturers and their in-house product developers are especially skilled in simultaneously managing tempo, scale, and cost. That is, they can with great rapidity translate an outsider's advanced design into a product that can be manufactured at scale, and all the while achieving cost savings as production volumes increase. The innovative mid-stream and downstream capabilities available now in China provide a critical bridge to commercialization for upstream innovators abroad. Thus, China in a national sense is playing a highly specialized and absolutely vital role in what amounts today to a global innovation ecosystem for new energy technologies.

Although we argue that upstream innovation and downstream innovation are tightly linked—an effective translation has to take place from one to the other for a product to achieve commercial success—our evidence does not suggest that upstream innovative capabilities grow out of downstream product development or manufacturing skills. Nor do we argue that the migration of manufacturing functions to new geographies necessarily pulls along with it upstream innovative capabilities. In fact, our evidence from the renewable energy technology sector suggests the opposite. Manufacturing in China today is highly innovative—it involves high levels of knowledge-intensive, proprietary skills—but it is distinct from the capabilities involved in upstream invention and innovation. At least in the renewable energy sector, we have uncovered little evidence to support the idea that Chinese innovative manufacturers are naturally developing upstream capabilities. Nor have we uncovered evidence that the ability of overseas firms to innovate upstream is somehow eroding because those firms are either doing less in-house manufacturing than in the past or no in-house manufacturing at all. It short, the world's entire energy technology production business is not somehow sliding over to China. But, because of its capabilities for innovative manufacturing, the Chinese ecosystem is playing a vital role in the broader global ecosystem for innovation.

China and broader assumptions about innovation, manufacturing, and competitiveness

In attempting to explain China's emergence in global manufacturing, a number of scholars have pointed to the country's low factor costs (Bergsten 2010; Krugman 1991). Regardless of whether those observers feel the cost structure reflects natural market forces or aggressive governmental subsidies, their argument has two underlying premises: first, that manufacturing simply migrates to the lowest cost environment, and second, that the know-how required to actually do manufacturing is either trivial or easily acquired.

Nonetheless, some observers then go on to assert that precisely because of China's position within manufacturing, the nation is developing proprietary know-how extending beyond manufacturing—ostensibly into everything from the design capabilities and innovative capacity needed to develop and commercialize entirely new products, processes, and services (U.S.-China Economic and Security Review Commission 2011). Knowledge, to the extent it is considered at all in this account, flows unidirectionally into China, and then somehow transforms from the trivial—physical assembly—into the truly sublime—innovation.

Proponents of this perspective have warned of the long-term consequences of China's rise in manufacturing for United States competitiveness in innovation. As manufacturing facilities relocate from the United States to China, they assert, the United States is not just losing jobs but also an essential ingredient for successful innovation. At the core of such arguments is not only the assumption that manufacturing and innovation are linked but also more specifically that it is their physical colocation that is so essential for the generation and commercialization of new ideas.

The importance of colocation has been elaborated on by a substantial and growing literature. Some recent studies argue that exposure to the actual process of making things provides R&D engineers with a better understanding of the limits and capabilities of existing technologies. And as a result, these engineers are better positioned to develop ideas for improved processes, new applications, and new technologies altogether (Ezell and Atkinson 2011; Helper et al. 2012). Other scholars claim that translating innovation into production relies on the exchange of tacit knowledge that cannot easily be transmitted over vast geographical distances, the type of knowledge that thrives in day-to-day interaction between research and production engineers (Tassey 2010). Still others find that innovation and the commercialization of new ideas rely on a dense network of suppliers with highly specialized capabilities, a so-called local industrial commons that supports and sustains innovative activities by supplying materials, production equipment, components, and the accompanying knowledge that helps turn an idea into a product (Pisano and Shih 2009; 2012). From this perspective, even if just factor cost advantages were behind China's initial successes in manufacturing, the country's vast manufacturing base now gives it a competitive advantage in innovation, one that the United States should respond to by "bringing manufacturing back" (President's Council of Advisors on Science and Technology 2012; Sperling 2012).

A decidedly different school of thought, though, draws the opposite conclusion. Scholars writing from this perspective agree that manufacturing has moved to China and other developing countries because of cost advantages, but they argue it could do so only because of an information technology revolution that has permitted physical fabrication and assembly to be separated from much higher value R&D, product definition, design, branding, and marketing (Baldwin and Clark 2000; Ernst and Naughton 2008; Sturgeon 2002). In today's world of globalized, highly deverticalized supply chains, China-based firms may be bending the metal and bolting together the parts, but those are no longer the production activities associated with true value creation, profitability, and proprietary know-how.

Proponents of this view argue that fabrication and assembly have never been as far removed from innovation as they are now, because digital technologies have largely erased the need for the type of tacit knowledge that could thrive only in close proximity to manufacturing and R&D. For Chinese firms, this means that manufacturing no longer offers an automatic path to innovative capabilities. Digital technologies have severed the links that once connected R&D and production, and in so doing have undercut many of the learning opportunities that once existed for manufacturing firms (Steinfeld 2004). For U.S. firms, such arguments imply that outsourcing and offshoring are sustainable—if not preferable—business models, because the majority of value continues to derive from innovation, regardless of where assembly and fabrication occur (Kraemer et al. 2011; Mankiw and Swagel 2006). Taking advantage of low-cost production environments in China, therefore, should not affect the long-term viability of innovative capabilities in the United States and Europe.

An alternative approach: Innovative manufacturing

On the basis of our findings from more than one hundred firm-level interviews conducted in China, Germany, and the United States between 2010 and 2012, we argue that the deverticalization of production in global supply chains has by no means severed the connection between upstream innovation and manufacturing, at least not in emerging technology sectors. As indicated previously, for many advanced energy technologies, a tight linkage between upstream innovation and downstream manufacturing is critical to the commercialization process. At the same time, as demonstrated by numerous cases presented in this chapter, innovation and production capabilities are inextricably linked in the product development process, but such links are often built and maintained across vast geographical distances. For foreign firms—whether they have in-house manufacturing capabilities or not—China's manufacturing infrastructure can be a platform for the commercialization of their ideas. Just as multinational firms have long operated R&D centers in foreign countries to take advantage of local research infrastructure and innovative specializations (Kitschelt 1986; Kogut and Chang 1991; Perrino and Tipping 1991; Porter 1990), foreign energy technology firms in their new product development and commercialization efforts now routinely rely on Chinese manufacturing capabilities.

We argue that what Chinese firms have achieved in high-tech manufacturing, particularly in emerging energy technology areas such as wind and solar power generation, stems from something more profound than just basic factor cost advantages and, particularly, subsidies. As is the case in many nations, including the United States, subsidies exist in China for manufacturers of renewable energy technology. A full discussion of this issue is beyond the scope of this chapter, but a brief examination of relative subsidization in the solar PV industry suggests at the very least that high levels of subsidies do not fully explain China's production footprint. As a recent report by the Congressional Research Service shows, the U.S. federal government for decades has supported both R&D and manufacturing in PV (Platzer 2012). Policies have included multibillion dollar advanced energy manufacturing tax credits, a $13 billion loan guarantee program for solar PV manufacturing firms, and the US Department of Energy's Sunshot Initiative to promote the domestic PV industry overall. Federal subsidies have then been complemented by additional state- and municipal-level subsidies—including land grants, tax credits, and loan guarantees—that are generally extended to manufacturing industries as a whole. The *New York Times* in 2012 estimated that these subsidies amount to $25.5 billion annually, though those are extended across all manufacturing sectors (Story 2012). Clearly, a number of U.S. PV firms have received such subsidies, but equally clearly, such subsidies have not guaranteed commercial success (Wallack 2011). The reality is that among federal, state, and local policies, the total amount of subsidization directed toward US renewable energy firms has yet to be calculated.

A similar situation is found on the Chinese side, though the levels of subsidization are arguably more modest—and the mechanisms for directing funds decidedly different from the United States case. A recent study by the Climate Policy Initiative calculates that Chinese central government support for the PV industry amounted to only 25 million euro from 2006 to 2010 (Grau et al. 2011). However, in China, extensive support has come through loans from state-owned banks and other local government financing vehicles. Recent journalistic reports have suggested that the state-owned China Development Bank extended $29 billion in credit to fifteen solar and wind companies, and $1 billion alone for the firm Jinko Solar (Bakewell 2011; Sustainable Business News 2012). There is no clear sense of what the actual interest rates charged are, though it is safe to assume that at least some of the credits are provided at below-market rates (Deutch and Steinfeld 2013).

The broader point is that in these industries, subsidization is rampant across a number of production environments, including China and the United States. However, in China, to a degree greater than in any other nation, production has not just grown but has substantially deepened its level of technological sophistication, now amounting to global "best in class" in several domains.

We argue that China's particular form of innovative manufacturing involves the simultaneous management of three production-related challenges: scale, tempo, and cost. China-based producers have demonstrated an unparalleled ability not just to scale up production, but to do so with extraordinary rapidity, and with steady unit cost reductions over time. From a manufacturing perspective, any one of these challenges could be considered formidable. Overcoming all three simultaneously represents a substantial achievement, one that involves firm-specific know-how and innovative capacity across a variety of production-related domains. Moreover, this know-how—although perhaps not directly associated with science-based upstream R&D or revolutionary, breakthrough innovations—is in fact proving to be a crucial enabler of the commercialization of a wide variety of high-technology goods, some of which are indeed new to the world, and some of which could be considered breakthrough products. It is in China's specialization in innovative manufacturing—the ability of Chinese firms to rapidly translate complex product ideas into mass-manufacturable products—that we see a continuation of close links between production and upstream R&D, even if such links now occur across continents.

The main attributes of Chinese innovative manufacturing

China's particular brand of innovative manufacturing, as evinced by the wind and solar industries, has four main attributes that link manufacturing tightly to upstream innovation: (1) it is based on engineering capabilities at the intersection of R&D and production, (2) it entails learning at the technological frontier, (3) it contributes to multidirectional exchange of knowledge between manufacturers and firms specializing in upstream R&D, and (4) it is deeply embedded in global production networks.

First, the know-how involved at the firm level is concentrated primarily in engineering design teams operating at the intersection between upstream R&D and actual physical fabrication. These engineering teams have unique capabilities to translate upstream designs, most of which come from beyond the firm, into commercially viable products that can be produced at scale. Because many of the designs initially lack essential information for commercializing the product—information, for example, regarding materials specification or subcomponent design for ease of manufacturability—the translation of these designs into viable products often requires China-based engineering teams to engage in combinations of process innovation, architectural innovation, and product innovation. The teams develop new approaches in areas as diverse as the fine-tuning of production equipment, the incorporation of new forms of automation, the redrafting of original product designs so as to allow greater modularity between components, and even the redefinition of the overall product and its functionality so as to permit new commercial applications. What links all of these efforts, though, is the consistent focus on ease of production scalability and reduction of unit cost.

Second, as indicated previously, this form of manufacturing specialization—and the learning surrounding it—is happening not just in mature industries, but in emerging technology sectors as well. This underscores the fact that the learning involved in innovative manufacturing entails more than just emulation of what outsiders are already doing (though emulation is certainly part of the picture). A number of Chinese manufacturers are learning at the frontiers of global technological development. Hence, in addition to their efforts at reverse engineering and imitative design, these firms pioneer creative reengineering, innovative changes to product architecture, creative modification of traditional production processes, and innovative applications of new materials and technologies.

Third, because the learning at the core of innovative manufacturing is happening at the technological frontier, a great deal of it is multidirectional. Chinese firms, of course, absorb know-how from partners, many of whom are overseas, and combine that know-how with their own firm-specific knowledge. But, interestingly, the solutions Chinese firms provide now frequently become important sources of learning for their overseas partners as well. This is different from unidirectional technology transfers from the advanced incumbents to latecomer aspirants so frequently described in the literature (Amsden 1989; Kim 1997; Kim and Nelson 2000). It is equally different from the tenor of the public debate in the United States, which has often pitted China's rise in manufacturing as a zero-sum game, one in which the development of any knowledge-based capabilities in China is seen as a direct threat to American innovation. What we witness instead is a process of multidirectional, simultaneous learning—a variant of what Gary Herrigel (2010) has described as industrial "co-development" —as overseas and Chinese firms cooperate to overcome challenges associated with the commercialization of emergent technologies.

Fourth, China's capabilities in innovative manufacturing are deeply embedded in multifirm, cross-border production networks. In such networks, upstream product designs and even key production technologies in many cases come from firms outside China.[1] Chinese producers, then, figure out how to take those designs and use that production equipment to mass-produce a product at a commercially viable price and within a market-determined time window. But the phenomenon is distinct from what has been described in long-established electronics and apparel industries, where the hand-off between upstream design and downstream fabrication is relatively straightforward and seamless. In other sectors, particularly the emerging industries at the core of this research, both the products and production processes are new. Rather than dealing with mature products, these industries are still wrestling with the initial commercialization of their technologies. Relationships among upstream design, manufacturability, scalability, cost, and ultimate product functionality are still highly uncertain. Therefore, the network of firms involved in product development and commercialization must involve more than just highly specialized firms focusing internally on their own assigned tasks and then handing off the results to the next partner in line. Instead, there has to be the capacity for multidirectional interfirm communication, learning, and collaborative problem solving. We argue that this capacity is central to Chinese innovative manufacturing.

Revisiting the literature on late development and innovation

Conceptually, our research builds on previous scholarship on innovation in Chinese industry (Ernst and Naughton 2012; Ernst and Naughton 2008; Ge and Fujimoto 2004; Thun and Brandt 2010). In many respects, we all bear the influence of the seminal theoretical work of Henderson and Clark (1990) and Baldwin and Clark (2000). Those scholars, in their efforts to conceptualize the (often unexpected) ways in which firms create value in advanced industrial economies, moved the discussion of innovation beyond the traditional focus on product innovation, and beyond the traditional distinction between radical and incremental innovation. Instead, they focused on "product architecture," the design information that determines how a product's subcomponents connect and interact to determine the product's ultimate functionality. Firm-induced shifts in this design information—essentially, "architectural innovation"—may not change the product's physical appearance or even functionality (at least in the near term), but may radically affect other aspects of the product, including its cost, its interoperability with other products, and in some cases its functionality over the longer run.

A number of scholars in recent years have identified important instances of architectural innovation in the Chinese business ecosystem. Ge and Fujimoto (2004) describe how Chinese motorcycle assemblers, through reverse engineering, effectively modularized the firm-specific, integral designs of Japanese lead firms. What the Chinese were doing was more than mere copying, because the newly engineered designs, though perhaps sacrificing some product functionality and quality, substantially lowered production costs and created new options for interoperability with after-market parts. Ernst and Naughton (2008, 2012) identify a similar pattern in their discussion of the information technology (IT) equipment industry and the rise of Chinese newcomers such as Huawei. Once again, it is not so much that wholly new products are developed, but rather that existing global products, through important changes in their underlying architecture, are now made available at significantly lower cost. That then permits the creation and exploitation of new markets, whether among more cost-conscious customers in advanced industrial countries, or across the developing world more generally.

Recent scholarship has also identified cases in which Chinese firms, even if they do not themselves initiate changes in product architecture, move quickly to exploit modularization pioneered by others. Hence, as Ernst and Naughton (2008, 2012) point out in the case of semiconductor design, Chinese fabless design houses such as Spreadtrum—by purchasing key integrated circuit design tools and intellectual property from abroad and also partnering with industry-leading foundry operators such as Taiwan Semiconductor—have become key suppliers to China's booming "Shanzhai" ("no brand") smartphone market.

As some scholars have reasonably argued, these instances of architectural innovation at least in some cases lead to actual product innovation. In their study of the Chinese automobile, construction equipment, and machine tool sectors, Thun and Brandt (2010) suggest that Chinese indigenous firms, by reengineering the focal models of global incumbents, have essentially created new "middle market" products, ones whose functionality and cost are particularly suited to what in many countries, including China, is the fastest-growing market segment. That Thun and Brandt's (2010) "new product innovation" may be indistinguishable from the architectural innovation, reverse engineering, and creative mimicry observed by Ge and Fujimoto (2004) or Ernst and Naughton (2008, 2012) hardly undercuts the point. After all, as Henderson and Clark (1990) emphasized in their original article, architectural innovation and product innovation frequently go hand in hand.

However, there are important differences between what we observe and what has previously been discussed in the literature, in part because much previous work focused on well-established industries. Such industries even today for the most part still follow the traditional product cycle. The newest, most sophisticated products get developed by global incumbents from advanced industrial economies, and it is in the home markets of those global incumbents that the products first get rolled out. Over time, once the wealthiest markets become saturated and production is standardized, the products—and the technologies necessary for producing them—migrate to developing locales, including China. As underscored by the existing literature, at that point additional forms of innovation take place, including modularization, cost reduction, and even incremental modifications to the products themselves. Thus, in the works of Ge and Fujimoto (2004), Thun and Brandt (2010), and Ernst and Naughton (2008, 2012), newcomer Chinese firms are accurately portrayed as innovative, but the kind of things they produce—whether we term them copies, knock-offs, or simply lower-cost variants—inevitably, and perhaps appropriately, come to be seen as derivative in nature. Even when new product innovation is said to take place in China, the illustrative examples pertain to the local adaptation and "down marketing" of existing global products, ones that are essentially simplified and made less expensive to meet the needs of a poorer, less sophisticated customer.

The scholars observing these phenomena rightly emphasize the significant challenges involved in mastering such forms of innovation. But given that the examples, drawn from mature industries, all take place within the traditional product cycle, the work can be interpreted in such a way as to reinforce a kind of conventional wisdom surrounding innovation that we believe is misleading. That is, though we do not believe this is the thrust of the authors' intended argument, the work implicitly supports the idea that "real" innovation—the creation of truly new products and truly new technologies—still takes place in advanced industrial economies (or at least is undertaken by advanced industrial firms), and it is only the follow-on duplications, simplifications, and modifications that take place in developing locales like China under the aegis of indigenous latecomer entrants.

Because our concept of Chinese innovative manufacturing pertains to emerging industries, ones for which the technologies globally are still rapidly evolving and the markets have yet to be defined, we are in a position to take issue with two latent assumptions in much of the existing literature. First, we challenge the idea that different forms of innovation should be judged hierarchically in either commercial or normative terms. That is, we disagree with the notion that new product innovation should be deemed superior, whether commercially or otherwise, to other forms of innovation, including the kind of reverse or reengineering associated with architectural innovation. In that regard, our approach bears similarity to the work by Breznitz and Murphee (2011) who, in a study of China's electronics industry, describe the ways in which Chinese firms have developed strong capabilities to enable and deliver products based on the latest technological innovation without themselves participating in new-to-the-world innovation. Yet, although Breznitz and Murphee argue that a focus on "real" innovation undercuts the significance of China's capabilities in the types of manufacturing innovation required to commercialize product ideas, they still see Chinese firms racing to keep up with technological developments in the West, rather than contributing to such innovation in their own ways. From their perspective, Chinese-style manufacturing innovation is an important enabler of product innovation, but still plays second fiddle to the upstream R&D capabilities in the United States and elsewhere (Breznitz and Murphee 2011).

And second, we challenge the assumption that different forms of innovation can be neatly disaggregated and understood to unfold in sequential fashion over time. These assumptions, it must be said, are powerfully embedded in the popular discourse on innovation. They are as ubiquitous in places like MIT, which regularly equate "innovation" with the generation of nascent technologies in university labs, as they are in China, where the government, ruing the absence of such nascent technology generation in its own country, has initiated a massive "indigenous innovation" drive in response (OECD 2008).

Our findings push in a very different direction. At the most fundamental level, they force us to return to a more basic understanding of what innovation, at least in a commercial sense, is all about. Innovation does not simply imply newness, whether that newness involves products, processes, or design architecture. Newness is "invention." Innovation, however, is the combination of invention and commercialization. In other words, for the new product idea, production process, or design architecture to qualify as innovation, it has to be able to command value in a commercial context. What often becomes apparent with new technologies—or even more established ones such as silicon solar cell (c-Si PV) fabrication that suddenly need to be scaled up to meet new, globally sized markets—is that the biggest challenges lie not in dreaming up the new product idea, but rather in translating the idea into a commercially viable product (Lester and Hart 2011). The engineering-related hurdles are often monumental. How can a new product idea be translated into something that can actually be manufactured? What combination of materials should be used? How should designs balance between maximizing product attributes (i.e., quality, reliability, performance, etc.) and maximizing ease of scalability on a manufacturing basis? And how can all of this be done quickly enough to accommodate markets that may be massive, but that open and close in narrow time windows, a condition quite common in the energy technology domain? Answers to those questions reside at the intersection between upstream R&D and production, the critical juncture that we identify as the core of contemporary Chinese innovative manufacturing.

Innovative manufacturing cannot be seen as a derivative of—or an afterthought to—product development. Rather, it is the critical, engineering-intensive enabler of such development. As such, it frequently involves the simultaneous management of architectural innovation, process innovation, and basic product definition itself.

This phenomenon differs in three key ways from how previous literature has described innovation in China. First, we observe not just the mimicry of overseas designs, but close interfirm—and generally cross-border—collaboration on the development of new knowledge and new designs. Second, we observe not just one-way learning (from advanced industrial incumbents to Chinese latecomers), but multidirectional learning, particularly as outsiders with upstream design knowledge learn to adjust in the face of the manufacturing and scaling knowledge they encounter in China (and vice versa). Third, we observe the continual emphasis on tempo. Particularly for the energy technology products we focus on in this chapter, cost in a static sense is not the issue. Rather, it is cost achievable in the narrow time frame within which the market is likely to be open. As the upstream originators know, new products in this area have to be developed rapidly. Speed for many of them is everything. Chinese innovative manufacturing often provides the answer, because what the Chinese partner brings to bear is the ability to translate upstream designs into manufacturable products extremely quickly, and without having to endure the repeated cycles of composition and decomposition that traditionally plague complex technological systems when first introduced.

The nature of Chinese industrial competiveness has unquestionably evolved since the 1980s. What began as comparative advantage based on low factor costs—namely low wages—had by the end of the twentieth century evolved into more knowledge-intensive forms of competitiveness. Those generally pertained to the types of follow-on reverse engineering, product repurposing, and local adaptation accurately described by the existing literature. Our notion of innovative manufacturing, however, suggests that at least parts of Chinese industry have reached a new stage of competitiveness, one situated at the frontier of global technology development, and deep within global innovation networks. Chinese innovators are no longer just finding ways to squeeze value from existing products. Instead, they have become critical players in a global, cross-border quest to commercialize new-to-the-world technologies, precisely the kinds of technologies that will be at least part of the solution to pressing global concerns surrounding climate change, resource scarcity, and urbanization.

Wind versus solar: Innovative manufacturing across diverse industrial and regulatory contexts

In this section, we provide a sense of the contours of Chinese innovative manufacturing across two different industries within renewable energy: wind turbines and solar PV. As noted previously, Chinese firms have established large-scale manufacturing capacity in both wind and solar industries with remarkable rapidity. China has been able to use its position as a manufacturing hub to build strengths in the development and commercialization of new-to-the-world innovation in both industries. To date, some of the most efficient solar PV technologies were first brought to market by Chinese solar firms, and many cutting-edge designs for wind turbines have been commercialized in cooperation with China's wind turbine manufacturers.

A number of Western politicians and journalists have reacted to China's rise in these sectors with concern, arguing that government subsidies have at once bolstered indigenous Chinese firms and imperiled competitors in the rest of the world (Bradsher 2011; Gold 2011). Although we do not deny that Chinese firms—much like renewable energy firms in the United States and Europe—have benefitted from favorable government treatment, we feel that four important distinctions between the wind and solar sectors cast doubt on the claim that factor prices or subsidies are the sole drivers of China's growth in these industries.

First, observers have pointed to China's low-cost labor supply as an explanation for China's rapid expansion of manufacturing capacity. Indeed, labor costs in China are a fraction of those in the United States or Europe. The (Bureau of Labor Statistics 2011, 2010) estimates that in 2008, hourly manufacturing wages averaged $1.36 in China, compared to $32.26 in the United States. Yet labor intensity differs across wind and solar industries, because the production of solar wafers, cells, and modules is increasingly automated, even in low-wage economies such as China. In a survey of studies on employment in renewable energy industries, Wei et al. (2010, 922) find an average of twenty-four manufacturing jobs per megawatt of wind turbines produced, compared to seven manufacturing jobs per megawatt of solar panels. Moreover, despite large and growing wage differentials within China, wind and solar firms have not chased labor costs to interior provinces, even as wages have risen rapidly in the coastal centers of industrialization, where most renewable energy manufacturing is located today (Li et al. 2012).

Second, observers have suggested that China's enormous domestic market has benefited Chinese firms in their developmental ambitions. Here, too, we observe large differences between wind and solar sectors. Because the Chinese central government only in 2011 established modest demand-side subsidies to encourage a solar market, China-based solar PV producers have expanded without the help of domestic markets. Instead, Chinese solar firms have exported virtually their entire production to locations such as Germany, which have employed demand-inducing regulatory interventions to create local markets. In the wind sector, the opposite occurred. In the mid-2000s, Beijing started enacting a series of demand-side regulations, including technology portfolio standards and a feed-in-tariff as part of the 2007 Renewable Energy Law, which turned China into the world's largest market for wind turbines (Schuman and Lin 2012). A large domestic market certainly benefitted local wind turbine manufacturers, not least by attracting international wind turbine manufacturers to China, which subsequently transferred technology and trained local suppliers. However, the success of solar firms in the absence of local demand suggests that domestic market demand cannot be the sole explanation for China's renewable energy success.

Third, proponents of antidumping tariffs to protect domestic renewable energy firms from Chinese competition have frequently argued that government support allows Chinese wind and solar firms to sell their products abroad below cost. Indeed, rapid scale-up of Chinese wind and solar manufacturing has been accompanied by unprecedented reductions in solar module and turbine prices. As indicated by figures 6.1 and 6.2, prices for wind turbines plummeted with increased localization of production in China. Price reductions in the solar sector were even more extreme. Solar module prices were approximately $2.75 per watt in early 2008. By early 2012, with China-based producers having multiplied production capacity to accommodate rapidly growing markets (figure 6.3), prices had fallen to roughly $1.10 per watt (IMS Research 2012).

However, price reductions and industry development in wind and solar sectors do not neatly correlate with government support. Since 2003, the Chinese wind sector has benefited from extensive central government support—for example, in the form of tech-transfer and localization requirements for foreign firms—whereas the solar sector

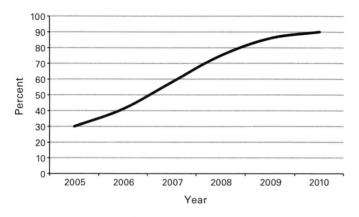

Figure 6.1
Domestic content in Chinese wind turbines (in percent)
Source: Chinese Wind Energy Association (CWEA). *Statistics of China's Wind Power Installed Capacity* (Beijing: CWEA, 2005–2010).

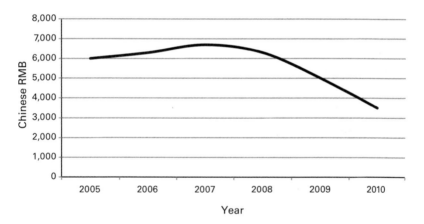

Figure 6.2
Wind turbine prices per KW (in RMB)
Source: Chinese Wind Energy Association (CWEA). *Statistics of China's Wind Power Installed Capacity* (Beijing: CWEA, 2005–2010).

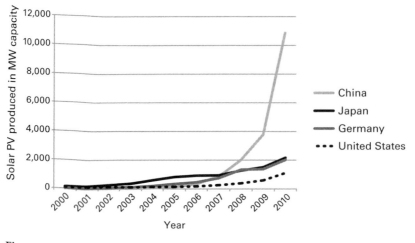

Figure 6.3
Annual solar PV production by country, 2000–2012
Source: Data compiled by Earth Policy Institute (2011).

has developed largely without targeted help from the central government. China's solar firms have instead relied on non-sector-specific
support offered to all manufacturing firms (including wind turbine
manufacturers) at the subnational level, for instance, in the form of
tax breaks, discounted land rates, and low-interest bank loans. Only
recently have Chinese solar firms enjoyed modest demand-side subsidies from the central level. Yet if firms in wind and solar sectors have
been able to rapidly reduce costs despite enjoying different levels and
types of policy support, government subsidies alone are insufficient to
explain their success.

Fourth, observers have argued that ownership structures in Chinese
firms—modern variants, basically, of traditional state ownership—
have provided incentives for governments at various levels to shield
firms from market forces. Supported by and integrated into the government bureaucracy, firms in many pillar industries have been protected
from bankruptcy, a situation that has allowed them to take investment
risks, access credit, and pursue aggressive pricing strategies.

However, we observe large variation in ownership patterns across
the wind and solar sectors, and these patterns by no means fall neatly
under the label *state owned*. Although many Chinese wind turbine
manufacturers have indeed maintained close ties to government—
either being state owned or spun off from a state-owned firm or power

company—virtually all of China's solar firms are privately owned, and many are listed on American stock exchanges. A number of major firms were not only started by returnees from abroad but are also largely foreign owned.

In short, the wind and solar industries display remarkable differences across a number of characteristics commonly used to explain their rapid growth trajectories. We argue that what these trajectories have in common is the presence of knowledge-intensive capabilities in manufacturing.

A taxonomy of Chinese specialization in rapid scaling

Knowledge-intensive manufacturing, particularly surrounding production scale-up, comes in a variety of forms, each of which involves distinct types of capabilities and distinct patterns of interfirm learning. In our research, we have identified four such patterns, each of which is described in the following section with firm-level examples. These patterns have in common a set of skills at the intersection of manufacturing and upstream R&D. All of the patterns we identify use these skills to improve tempo, volume, and cost. Three of them involve cross-border links between upstream innovators in a foreign country and innovative manufacturers in China. Although we present these four patterns as distinct elements of a typology, the patterns are not mutually exclusive. Many of the firms we interviewed were simultaneously engaging in several forms of knowledge-intensive scale-up, mastering different relationships between manufacturing and upstream R&D capabilities in order to achieve tempo, volume, and cost. This is frequently what it takes to survive in the highly competitive and volatile producer markets so characteristic of contemporary China.

Backward design and the reengineering of somebody else's existing product

In this first pattern of knowledge-intensive scale, capabilities at the intersection of manufacturing and upstream R&D are deployed to redesign an existing product in order to reduce manufacturing cost. This pattern, to a greater degree than any other we discuss, resembles traditional processes of reverse engineering. By creating versions of existing products that are simpler to manufacture at scale, new Chinese entrants have been able to outcompete established incumbents by undercutting them on the basis of price, and as a result, gaining domestic or global market share at their expense.

However, among Chinese firms, this cost advantage, rather than resulting from cheaper inputs and larger scale production as held by conventional views about reverse engineering, often stems from a distinct process of backward design that subjects product attributes to the demands of a particular cost curve. Product alternatives are weighed, but cost curves ultimately drive product selection even if this necessitates sacrifices in quality and performance. What results from this process is a product that resembles the original archetype, but, by way of simplified componentry, cheaper materials, and better manufacturability, can be scaled at low cost and incredible speed. Rather than imitation and emulation, backward design is a process in which a new product with distinct characteristics is created. Cost advantages do not stem primarily from advantages in factor costs, but instead from deliberate changes in product design. The relationships and interactions within which such processes of backward design occur are varied, in some cases permitting Chinese firms to command significant value and in other cases creating highly competitive environments that allow for only the thinnest of margins, particularly when other firms in the local ecosystem can quickly duplicate these new designs.

The wind turbine sector illustrates the range of backward design processes well. In one instance, a Chinese firm was granted a license by a German firm to produce a key wind turbine subsystem, the generator. Due to engineering constraints, the German firm had previously been unable to incorporate the most cost-effective fan model in the generator design. In this case, it was the Chinese licensee that, in the process of scaling production of the licensed generator, was able to redesign the original model to accommodate the cheaper fan, eventually relicensing this innovation back to the German firm.[2] The backward design capabilities of the Chinese firm permitted it to realize a product alternative that the German firm had considered, but had dismissed as unworkable. Once the alternative was demonstrated to be feasible, the German firm was willing to pay for this proprietary information through reverse licensing.[3]

Although in this example the Chinese firm was able to contribute production knowledge within a formal contractual relationship, in many other cases Chinese firms have used backward design skills to develop cheaper, mid-level products that compete directly with the product archetypes and their originator firms (Ge and Fujimoto 2004;

Thun and Brandt 2010). Particularly in the Chinese domestic market, many established multinationals have been unable—and to some extent unwilling—to engage in processes of cost-driven design, and have lost market share to cheaper alternatives as a result.

In the wind energy sector, where expanding domestic markets for turbines have attracted established foreign manufacturers and their key suppliers to China, domestic firms have employed backward design strategies to rapidly develop competing products at much lower cost. By sourcing important components from foreign suppliers, by licensing technology, and, in some cases, by buying smaller foreign competitors, Chinese wind turbine suppliers have been able to access technology relatively easily (Lewis 2012). Yet instead of producing these designs as they are, Chinese firms have subsequently employed backward design strategies to exploit cheaper materials, ensure easier manufacturability, and, where possible, use simpler components from domestic suppliers. As a result, market prices for turbines have dropped from 7,500 RMB per watt to 3,500 RMB per watt in just three years (Chinese Wind Energy Association 2011), leaving many foreign players unable to compete despite fully localized production.[4]

The speed at which they have been able to engage in backward design has provided Chinese turbine manufacturers with a competitive advantage even in instances when foreign firms have attempted to replicate this strategy. For example, a European turbine manufacturer followed the Chinese example and developed a cheaper, mid-level product for the Chinese market, using materials, components, and suppliers equivalent to those used by the Chinese competition. Although the firm was able to develop a product for a similar price, by the time it had completed the backward design process and established a local supply chain, the product was obsolete. By that point, the Chinese market had already moved on to larger turbine sizes.[5] In part, the European firm was slowed in its product development by lengthy negotiation and approval processes involving its European headquarters. Yet the speed advantage of its Chinese competitors also emanates from a more general willingness on the part of the Chinese firms to set a target price (one that often seems unrealistically low to outsiders), and then scramble improvisationally to figure out the feasibility and design details. Frequently, Chinese firms emphasize speed and cost at the expense of process and procedure.

Whether the ability to sell turbines at competitive prices in the Chinese market requires quality shortcuts that will affect their long-term reliability and whether Chinese wind turbine manufacturers are able to earn margins that make this industry desirable for themselves and their foreign counterparts remain questions open to debate. What seems clear is that on the relatively level playing field of fully localized production and domestic demand, Chinese firms have in rapid succession been able to engineer wind turbines that cost as little as 75 percent of the least expensive 4,500 RMB per watt models offered by their foreign competitors.[6]

Making somebody else's (new-to-the-world) product design come true

The ability of Chinese firms to move complicated products down the learning curve is also manifested in a different type of interaction with foreign firms, one characterized by mutual gains and multidirectional learning. In this second variant, the Chinese firm's knowledge about production, scaling, and reengineering is marshaled to make a foreign partner's product design commercially viable through large-scale manufacturing. The foreign firm provides the original design, and the Chinese firm figures out how to adjust the design and scale it to mass production. Again, capabilities at the intersection of manufacturing and upscale R&D are marshaled in support of tempo, volume, and cost, but these objectives are achieved primarily through preparing products for mass manufacturing.

The reasons foreign firms rely on Chinese innovative manufacturing capabilities are varied. The foreign firm may have no manufacturing capabilities at all, it may be unable to manufacture the product at a commercially viable price, or it may be deterred by the capital and tooling costs of commercializing a new technology. What these cases have in common, however, is their reliance on the production know-how of Chinese firms to replace, redesign, and substitute parts until the product can be manufactured at a commercially viable price. Rather than licensing or selling outdated technologies to Chinese firms for local manufacturing, as has been common in many developing economies including China (Vernon 1966), these instances of foreign-Chinese cooperation bring new-to-the-world innovation to China because of Chinese firms' expertise in completing the commercialization process for higher volume products.

In 2009, for example, a Chinese wind turbine producer acquired a ten-year exclusive license for the manufacturing of a groundbreaking, new-to-the-world wind turbine from a European engineering firm. The turbine employs a fundamentally different design concept offering greater reliability and versatility in offshore and onshore applications. What on the surface resembles a standard licensing transaction—the kind that has occurred countless times in the course of China's economic development—on closer examination reveals a much more complicated, multidirectional pattern of learning. Although the European firm developed the turbine design concept, the redesign for manufacturability and cost reduction occurred during small-batch production on the site of the Chinese manufacturer roughly two years after the initial contract was signed. The European design house specifically selected the Chinese partner among multiple potential licensees for the technology, choosing largely on the basis of manufacturing capabilities that would ensure reliability for the product and commercial viability for the project as a whole. Engineers employed by the Chinese firm made design changes to simplify tooling and assembly processes, and, in cooperation with other local firms, reduced costs by localizing sourcing and by introducing substitute materials. Additional design adjustments were then made during the process of scale-up to accommodate requirements for mass manufacturing.[7]

The Chinese engineering team acknowledged the learning benefits from this cooperation, and so too did the European partner. The European firm, without any manufacturing capacity of its own, placed great emphasis on being part of small-batch production and subsequent scale-up in order to maintain and improve its own design capabilities. This was especially important in the case of this particular turbine concept, because its novel componentry required all the components to be produced in-house. The engineers of the European firm came to understand that learning from Chinese partners to improve design-for-manufacturing is imperative for maintaining competitiveness and innovative capacity.[8]

Hence, the licensing agreement between the two firms is the legal manifestation of a much more deep-seated process of cooperation, in which both sides chose each other for particular capabilities and the potential for knowledge transfer. To the Chinese firm, the new design offered a commercial advantage in a highly competitive market environment, and the opportunity to learn to master a novel wind turbine technology. To the European firm, the Chinese licensee provided rich production experience and extensive capabilities for translating complex designs into cost-competitive products. The ability of Chinese firms to contribute critical knowledge to the commercialization of new-to-the-world innovation suggests a more pivotal role for China in the global division of labor than simply being the world's preferred manufacturing location due to the availability of cheap inputs. It also challenges, however, ideas about the feasibility of separating advanced innovation and production, showing how closely linked seemingly disconnected activities can be.

Rapidly scaled new-to-the-world product innovation

The ability of Chinese firms to move products rapidly down the learning curve is not applied exclusively to designs originally developed by foreigners, as was the case in the previous two examples. In some instances, Chinese firms use these capabilities to commercialize their own in-house, new-to-the-world product innovation. Because these firms have particular knowledge surrounding scaled-up manufacturing, they are able to see commercial potential in nascent technologies that may be available in the public domain, but have lain dormant because others deemed them too costly or risky to develop. In general, production knowledge and manufacturing capabilities play a particularly critical role when (1) manufacturability is a key constraint in bringing an idea or concept to market and (2) when scaling has to take place in a short time frame in order to take advantage of opportunities in fast-moving markets. This is particularly the case in emerging industries such as wind and solar, in which government policy and demand-side regulation strongly affect market demand, leading to volatility and short-lived commercial opportunities in global markets. Thus, although the new-to-the-world product in these cases is not the result of process innovation, manufacturing capabilities focused on tempo and speed are important to make the product commercially viable.

A case involving a Chinese solar PV manufacturer exemplifies this situation.[9] Similar to many innovations in the solar industry, where the conversion efficiencies of light to electricity for different processes are easily calculated but hard to achieve in practice, this particular innovation developed by the Chinese solar manufacturer was based on a commonly known theoretical principle that had not yet been made to work in a commercial solar application. The Chinese firm, similar to many of its competitors in China and abroad, was researching ways to commercialize this principle, which at least in theory promised higher efficiency solar panels. The firm's R&D center dis-covered a material produced by a third-party vendor that allowed the firm to run the process in the laboratory. The desired efficiency level was achieved after several months of trials. A key challenge, however, was to use existing production equipment to manufacture cells based on this new principle, and to do so very rapidly. Due to different material requirements, the new product was more expensive than tra-ditional solar cells. At the time, the extremely high price of silicon—the main raw material for solar cells—justified the additional expense to produce a higher efficiency cell. Speed was of the essence, however, because the innovation had to take advantage of a potentially narrow time window during which silicon prices would likely remain high and competitors researching the same technology would likely not realize breakthroughs of their own (the Chinese patent office had denied patent protection because the technology is based on a com-monly known principle).[10]

Through collaboration between the R&D team and production engi-neers, the firm was able to use existing production equipment to manu-facture the new product, and within months four production lines were churning out new, higher efficiency cells. Precisely because the firm found ways to use existing production lines to rapidly scale a new product, the initial invention became commercially viable in a very short period of time. Speed permitted the firm to capture the value of its innovative know-how. By the time many competitors developed a similar product, silicon prices had already dropped so far that the original firm decided to reconvert its production to a traditional product because the cost increase to achieve higher efficiency was no longer justifiable.[11]

Product platform for technology co-development and absorption

The presence of production scale and considerable know-how in vast Chinese manufacturing operations has provided a platform for a variety of international innovators to rapidly integrate their technology into an existing product. In many cases, the Chinese manufacturer produces a product at high volume that then incorporates an outside innovator's technology as a component. The external innovator, however, is more than just a high-end component vendor who sells a product at arm's length to the Chinese customer. In many cases the vendor actually commercializes the technology in cooperation with the Chinese customer. The vendor brings to the table knowledge about a particular technology that may have applications to a product the Chinese manufacturer has already scaled up. The Chinese manufacturer brings to the table knowledge about production, knowledge about how the component technology might be applied at scale while using existing production technology, and knowledge about how the original product will be improved as a result. Between the two parties involved, a component technology can be simultaneously commercialized and applied to an existing product at high production volumes.

In such cases, the interaction between global innovators and Chinese firms is not a simple commercial transaction, but instead a process of co-development that defines the very application of the technology itself (Herrigel 2010). Particularly for technologies with multiple applications—such as a liquid nanomaterial that may have potential uses in flat panel displays, solar panels, or LED lighting—integration into an extant, mass-manufactured product transforms the technology into a component with commercial value.[12] The new technology, therefore, has an instant market, because the Chinese co-developer becomes a high-volume customer. This type of technology absorption entails contributions of knowledge from the original innovator and the Chinese manufacturing firm, again resulting in a process of multidirectional learning. Yet in contrast to instances in which Chinese manufacturing capabilities make possible the commercialization of complex designs, in the cases of technology absorption described here, the Chinese product platform often determines the fundamental features—and markets—of the new technologies being fed in by outsiders.

The cooperation of U.S.-based Innovalight with the Chinese solar cell manufacturer JA Solar illustrates an interaction in which a foreign firm relies on China's manufacturing infrastructure as a platform for product development. A Silicon Valley start-up founded in 2002, Innovalight developed a nanomaterial with a number of potential applications in products ranging from integrated circuits and displays to solar PV. With Department of Energy funding and support from the National Renewable Energy Laboratory (NREL), the firm developed an understanding of how the nanomaterial, a silicon ink, might be applied in the solar PV industry. NREL research suggested that the ink could potentially increase the efficiency of solar cells by 7 percent. Yet, although Innovalight and NREL could together determine how the material might improve a single solar cell, neither had experience in large-scale manufacturing. Presumably, neither had the know-how required for applying the material in a cost-effective manner in high-volume solar PV production. Outside investors certainly seemed to doubt Innovalight's know-how in this area, because the firm was unable to raise the capital needed to build a solar PV production facility (Wang 2011).

In 2009, short of funds and nearly out of business, the company changed strategy, focusing on licensing its technology to solar manufacturers rather than building a production business itself. The same year, Innovalight found a partner in the Chinese cell manufacturer JA Solar. Looking for a way to gain an edge over its competitors, JA Solar was willing to invest in the collaborative development of a technology that could substantially improve the efficiency—and, thus, market appeal—of its main product. The idea would be to use the nanomaterial as a component, essentially applying it to a cell in order to improve the cell's efficiency. After a year of joint R&D, the two firms announced the successful production of high-efficiency solar cells using Innovalight's silicon ink technology. As a result, the two firms in 2010 signed a three-year agreement for the supply of silicon ink, as well as a strategic agreement for the joint development of high-efficiency cells (JA Solar 2010).

For JA Solar, the collaboration with Innovalight resulted in the ability to use foreign technologies for the production of a new line of high-efficiency solar cells. For Innovalight, JA Solar's manufacturing capabilities offered a type of expertise it could not gain from the collaboration with NREL. The process of joint development with JA Solar for the first time verified Innovalight's silicon ink technology as a product that can contribute value to solar PV. Established as a legitimate player in the solar industry, Innovalight subsequently began licensing its technology to other solar manufacturers.

With its record of successes, Innovalight in 2011 was acquired by DuPont and integrated into the global conglomerate's solar division. Innovalight's silicon ink will be coupled with other DuPont innovations in metal pastes and solar cell backing films. In January 2012, DuPont signed a $100 million supply deal with Chinese solar PV manufacturer Yingli (Stuart 2012). Although it is unclear whether JA Solar will be able to translate its cooperation with Innovalight into a long-term competitive advantage—particularly in view of the fact that Innovalight began licensing the product to JA's competitors as well—it is evident that JA's manufacturing capabilities played a critical role in developing silicon ink technology as a viable product in the solar industry. Through a global process of multidirectional learning and mutual risk taking, Chinese production knowledge provided a platform for the commercialization of American innovation.

From capabilities to institutions: The broader ecosystem for innovation

In this chapter we have sought to illustrate that the links between manufacturing capabilities and upstream R&D can in many cases be absolutely critical for innovation. The decline in U.S. manufacturing activity in many respects makes it more difficult for American firms to establish such links domestically. However, as we have demonstrated, American and European firms have succeeded in establishing such links with partners in China, taking advantage of China's distinct brand of innovative manufacturing without colocating upstream R&D capabilities. In the cases we have discussed in this chapter, upstream R&D and manufacturing, though geographically separated, remain tightly linked organizationally. This particular form of linkage has had a number of positive ramifications. For the firms involved, the possibility of creating links between R&D and manufacturing over vast geographical distances opens opportunities to access distinct specializations that have evolved in different ecosystems over time. For ecosystems, the possibility of physically separating R&D and manufacturing means that distinct specializations can be retained and enhanced, as multidirectional learning enables firms to mutually upgrade their capabilities without replicating each other's strengths and specializations. And for products, the ability of specialized firms to cooperate across long distances on product development leads to faster product cycles, lower costs, and added functionality.

Our examples have demonstrated that China's specialization in innovative manufacturing did not develop in an environment populated exclusively by domestic firms. Chinese innovative manufacturing relies on the contributions of outsiders. Sometimes these outsiders are physically present in China and sometimes they interact with Chinese counterparts from afar. Regardless, overseas firms are critical sources of technology and knowledge. But this is not a case of one-sided "technology transfer" or unidirectional knowledge flow. It is also not a case of a traditional supply chain in which a lead firm commanding the bulk of the revenue drives the behavior of subordinate suppliers or subcontractors (Gereffi et al. 2005; Nolan 2012). Rather, it is a more complex phenomenon involving multidirectional learning, one in which Chinese firms contribute indispensable know-how and capabilities for product development and commercialization. In the emerging technology sectors we have studied, foreign firms specifically seek out Chinese partners to access these forms of unique know-how.

It is not always clear who captures the most value in such cross-border interactions. Risk and reward are frequently spread in complicated ways, particularly given that many of the relationships are not clearly hierarchical. For all the benefits from accessing China's capabilities in innovative manufacturing, foreign firms have certainly taken risks by cooperating with Chinese partners. The process of mutual learning inevitably involves knowledge transfer, and for all the potential benefits, firms have reasonably worried about enabling new Chinese competitors. By sharing ideas and product designs, foreign wind and solar firms have enabled products to be commercialized through Chinese skills in innovative manufacturing, but, inevitably, they have also made themselves vulnerable to the possibility that their Chinese partners may one day be able to manage without them. In more than one foreign firm we visited, design blueprints and product ideas were only brought to China as paper copies so as to avoid the possibility of digital files getting illegally copied and distributed. Links between Chinese firms and their foreign partners may be close and cooperative, but not in all cases especially trusting. But for the majority of non-Chinese firms we interviewed for this chapter, the benefits in their view still outweighed the costs, seeing that they all deeply relied on Chinese partners in product development and commercialization.

As an ecosystem, China has done well in many respects. It has achieved sustained growth despite haphazard policy approaches on the part of the state. It has avoided the main pitfall associated with participation in modular production, the possibility—as some observers warned earlier—of getting eternally stuck in the lowest skill, lowest value pieces of global supply chains (Steinfeld 2004). The contemporary Chinese ecosystem has become a locus for considerable innovation. As a result, it has steadily attracted higher value production activities and higher status overseas commercial partners. Some of those partners today clearly feel that in order to maintain their own competitiveness and knowledge-based assets, they have to be in China.

Yet, despite these favorable outcomes, the specialization in innovative manufacturing also bears considerable costs and risks for Chinese firms. China's contributions to global technology commercialization have entailed enormous investments in manufacturing capacity.

Particularly in cases when the returns from innovation do not as clearly accrue to the manufacturer—a condition that applies to crystalline silicon PV—China's ability to benefit from large-scale manufacturing hinges on its ability to pull related, higher-value-added activities into the ecosystem. Additionally, Chinese firms have placed large bets on sectors such as wind and solar in which demand, almost regardless of any cost savings achieved by producers, depends ultimately on market stimulation by regulatory actors. Whether those regulatory actors are overseas (solar) or in China (wind), they hold in their hands the fate of these industries. And, in numerous industrial sectors, the rapid expansion of manufacturing has created the risk of overcapacity, potentially imposing financial losses on investors (and government subsidizers) as industries go through painful processes of downsizing and consolidation.

Regardless of how the costs and benefits are distributed, the contemporary Chinese business ecosystem has unquestionably developed specialized expertise and distinct patterns of multidirectional learning in production scale-up. Although we do not argue that these capabilities are rigidly determined by China's existing political order, we do believe that at least in wind and solar production, Chinese manufacturers have innovated at least in part in response to their government's highly improvisational, mercurial style of economic policymaking.

In a broad sense, China's political leaders have consistently emphasized economic growth as a fundamental imperative. Inconsistent, however, has been the manner by which actual policies to achieve such growth have been carried out. The Chinese state, across its myriad agencies and hierarchies, has tended to roll out policies informally, often allowing them to evolve organically with shifts in producer practices on the ground. In many cases, policy interventions are undertaken by local-level officials without apparent coordination and communication with bureaucratic superiors. Only after such improvisational practices get disseminated and prove successful do they get formally announced and institutionalized by the central state. Hence, those making policy in the state and those being affected by policy within the firm become accustomed to highly flexible and improvisational operations. Improvisation has become the norm in contemporary China. So too has interaction within extensive networks of entrepreneurs, suppliers, and policymakers. Such interactions facilitate information flows under ambiguous conditions, and spread risk by creating options for alternative paths that can be pursued at a moment's notice.

At the firm level, the nature of the policy environment has at least two consequences. First, producers learn to behave in an extremely flexible, highly networked manner. Learning and operating through continually evolving networks becomes routine. Second, given the fluidity of the situation, the boundaries between competition and cooperation become extremely ambiguous. Ambiguity is taken as normality. The sectors discussed in this chapter are extremely competitive. Numerous entrants compete bitterly for business, and all recognize that any given type of specialization—although necessary to secure profit—should always be considered fleeting. Firms cooperate extensively in networks, but so too do they compete. Thus, they end up in a mode of almost continual improvisational specialization, all within the general category of innovative manufacturing.

The Chinese manufacturing story, though, is about far more than just a policy environment. China's focus on manufacturing, and particularly its fostering of innovative manufacturing, has been taking place in the context of a vast industrial revolution, one whose scale and speed are arguably unprecedented in human history. This revolution and the market transition accompanying it have induced intense competition and extraordinary industrial diversification across many different municipalities and regions, each the size of a European country. And although we argue that China's specialization in innovative manufacturing is not primarily a story about factor costs, it has unquestionably occurred in an environment in which mass manufacturing has been a key avenue for improved living standards for hundreds of millions of workers, all within a few decades. In China, to a degree greater than in virtually any other nation, and certainly any advanced industrial economy, manufacturing *is* development, and innovative manufacturing will be a key to continued development for years to come.

But manufacturing, innovative or otherwise, is by no means the exclusive domain of China alone. In all its varieties and forms, manufacturing continues to be an important source of value creation across economies large and small, developing and developed, industrializing and postindustrial. As time goes on, these economies are becoming intertwined through increasingly complex cross-border commercial interactions and an increasingly fine-grained international division of labor. The boundaries between who is making what, who is earning what, and who is trading with whom are becoming ever-more ambiguous. And that, of course, suggests that our discussion about the tight linkages between innovation and production—even in the context of vast geographic separation—pertains not just to China, but to all of us, wherever we happen to be manufacturing, and wherever we happen to be engaging in upstream R&D.

Notes

1. For example, the American firm Applied Materials, the world's leading producer of PV manufacturing equipment, is a supplier to virtually the entire Chinese PV manufacturing sector. Over 90 percent of Applied Material's global customers in the PV area are located in China, and Applied Materials has an exclusive position in the supply of screen printing equipment, critical technology for all manufacturers in the crystalline silicon PV sector.

2. Interview, executive at Chinese generator manufacturer, August 26, 2011.

3. Interview, plant manager at German generator manufacturer, May 17, 2011.

4. Interview, head of China operations at multinational wind turbine manufacturer, August 30, 2011.

5. Interviews, manager, multinational wind turbine manufacturer, November 11, 2011; head of China operations at multinational wind turbine manufacturer, August 30, 2011.

6. Interview, head of China operations at multinational wind turbine manufacturer, August 30, 2011.

7. Interviews, head of China operations at European engineering firm, January 13, 2011; CEO, European engineering firm, May 20, 2011; chief technology officer, Chinese wind turbine manufacturer, August 29, 2011.

8. Interviews, head of China operations at European engineering firm, January 13, 2011; CEO, European engineering firm, May 20, 2011; chief technology officer, Chinese wind turbine manufacturer, August 29, 2011.

9. Interviews, chief technology officer and director of research and development at Chinese solar cell manufacturer, August 26, 2011.

10. Interviews, chief technology officer and director of research and development at Chinese solar cell manufacturer, August 26, 2011.

11. Interviews, executive at global production equipment manufacturer, August 08, 2011; CEO of Chinese solar cell manufacturer, August 10, 2011.

12. Interview, CEO of American nanomaterial manufacturer, October 13, 2011.

References

Amsden, Alice H. 1989. *Asia's Next Giant: South Korea and Late Industrialization*. Oxford: Oxford University Press.

Bakewell, Sally. 2011. "Chinese Renewable Companies Slow to Tap $47 Billion Credit." Bloomberg (November 16). http://www.bloomberg.com/news/2011-11-16/chinese -renewable-companies-slow-to-tap-47-billion-credit-line.html.

Baldwin, Carliss, and Kim Clark. 2000. *Design Rules. The Power of Modularity*. Cambridge, MA: MIT Press.

Bergsten, C. Fred. 2010. "Correcting the Chinese Exchange Rate." Hearing on China's Exchange Rate Policy, Committee on Ways and Means. Washington DC, U.S. House of Representatives. http://www.iie.com/publications/testimony/bergsten20100915.pdf.

Bradsher, Keith. 2010. "China Leading Global Race to Make Clean Energy." *New York Times* (January 30).

Bradsher, Keith. 2011. "China Benefits as U.S. Solar Industry Withers." *New York Times* (September 1).

Breznitz, Dan, and Michael Murphee. 2011. *Run of the Red Queen: Government, Innovation, Globalization and Economic Growth in China*. New Haven, CT: Yale University Press.

Bullis, Kevin. 2012. *"The Chinese Solar Machine."* MIT *Technology Review*. January/ February.

Bureau of Labor Statistics. 2010. *International Comparisons of Hourly Compensation in Manufacturing, 2008*. Washington, DC: U.S. Department of Labor.

Bureau of Labor Statistics. 2011. *International Comparisons of Hourly Compensation Costs in Manufacturing, 2010*. Washington, DC: U.S. Department of Labor.

Chinese Wind Energy Association. 2011. *Statistics of China's Wind Power Installed Capacity, 2005–2010*. Beijing: CWEA.

Deutch, John, and Edward S. Steinfeld. 2013. "A Duel in the Sun: The Solar Photovoltaic Technology Conflict between China and the United States." Report for the MIT Future of Solar Energy Study. Cambridge MA: MIT. http://mitei.mit.edu/publications/reports -studies/duel-sun.

Ernst, Dieter, and Barry Naughton. 2008."China's Emerging Industrial Economy: Insights from the IT Industry." In *China's Emergent Political Economy*, ed. Christopher A. McNally. New York: Routledge.

Ernst, Dieter, and Barry Naughton. 2012. "Global Technology Sourcing and China's Integrated Circuit Design Industry: A Conceptual Framework and Preliminary Research Findings." East-West Center Working Papers, Economics Series. Honolulu, HI: East-West Center.

Ezell, Stephen J., and Robert D. Atkinson. 2011. "The Case for a National Manufacturing Strategy." Washington, DC, The Information Technology & Innovation Foundation (ITIF). http://www.itif.org/publications/case-national-manufacturing-strategy.

Ge, Dongsheng, and Takahiro Fujimoto. 2004." Quasi-open Product Architecture and Technological Lock-in: An Exploratory Study on the Chinese Motorcycle Industry." *Annals of Business Administrative Science* 3 (2): 15–24.

Gereffi, Gary, et al. 2005. "The Governance of Global Value Chains." *Review of International Political Economy* 12 (1): 78–104.

Gold, Russell. 2011. "Overrun by Chinese Rivals, U.S. Solar Company Falters." *Washington Post* (August 17).

Grau, Thilo, et al. 2011. *Survey of Photovoltaic Industry and Policy in Germany and China*. Berlin: Climate Policy Initiative.

Helper, Susan, Timothy Krueger, and Howard Wial. 2012. "Why Does Manufacturing Matter? Which Manufacturing Matters? A Policy Framework." Metropolitan Policy Program. Brookings Institution. http://www.brookings.edu/~/media/research/files/papers/2012/2/22%20manufacturing%20helper%20krueger%20wial/0222_manufacturing_helper_krueger_wial.pdf.

Henderson, Rebecca M., and Kim B. Clark. 1990. "Architectural Innovation: The Reconfiguration of Existing Product Technologies and the Failure of Established Firms." *Administrative Science Quarterly* 35 (1): 9–30.

Herrigel, Gary. 2010. *Manufacturing Possibilities: Creative Action and Industrial Recomposition in the United States, Germany, and Japan.* Oxford: Oxford University Press.

Kim, Linsu. 1997. *Imitation to Innovation: The Dynamics of Korea's Technological Learning.* Boston: Harvard Business School Press.

Kim, Linsu, and Richard Nelson. 2000. *Technology, Learning & Innovation.* Cambridge: Cambridge University Press.

Kitschelt, Herbert P. 1986. "Political Opportunity Structures and Political Protest: Anti-Nuclear Movements in Four Democracies." *British Journal of Political Science* 16:57–85.

Kogut, Bruce, and Sea Jin Chang. 1991. "Technological Capabilities and Japanese Foreign Direct Investment in the United States." *Review of Economics and Statistics* 73 (3): 401–413.

Kraemer, Kenneth L., Greg Linden, and Jason Dedrick. 2011. *Capturing Value in Global Networks: Apple's iPad and iPhone.* Irvine, CA: Personal Computing Industry Center, UC Irvine.

Krugman, Paul R. 1991. *Geography and trade.* Cambridge, MA: MIT Press.

Lester, Richard K., and David M. Hart. 2011. *Unlocking Energy Innovation: How America Can Build a Low-Cost, Low-Carbon Energy System.* Cambridge, MA: MIT Press.

Lewis, Johanna I. 2012. *Green Innovation in China: China's Wind Power Industry and the Global Transition to a Low Carbon Economy.* New York: Columbia University Press.

Li, Hongbin, et al. 2012." The End of Cheap Chinese Labor." *Journal of Economic Perspectives* 26 (4): 57–74.

Mankiw, N. Gregory, and Phillip Swagel. 2006. "The Politics and Economics of Offshore Outsourcing." *National Bureau of Economic Research Working Paper Series* No. 12398.

Marsh, Peter. 2011. "China Noses Ahead as Top Goods Producer." *Financial Times* (March 13).

Nolan, Peter. 2012. *Is China Buying the World?* Cambridge: Polity Press.

OECD. 2008. *OECD Reviews of Innovation Policy: China.* Paris: OECD Publications.

Perrino, Albert C., and James W. Tipping. 1991. "Global Management of Technology: A Study Of 16 Multinationals in the USA, Europe and Japan." *Technology Analysis and Strategic Management* 3 (1): 87–98.

Pisano, Gary P., and Willy C. Shih. 2009. "Restoring American Competitiveness." *Harvard Business Review* (July).

Pisano, Gary P., and Willy C. Shih. 2012. *Producing Prosperity: Why America Needs A Manufacturing Renaissance.* Boston, MA: Harvard Business Review Press.

Platzer, Michaela D. 2012. *U.S. Solar Photovoltaic Manufacturing: Industry Trends, Global Competition, Federal Support.* Washington, DC: Congressional Research Service.

Porter, Michael E. 1990. *The Competitive Advantage of Nations.* New York: Free Press.

President's Council of Advisors on Science and Technology. 2012. "Report to the President on Capturing Domestic Competitive Advantage in Advanced Manufacturing. Executive Office of the President." http://www.whitehouse.gov/sites/default/files/ microsites/ostp/pcast_amp_steering_committee_report_final_july_17_2012.pdf.

Research, I. M. S. 2012. "Crystalline PV Modules Fall to Single Digits." http:// imsresearch.com/press-release/Crystalline_PV_Module_Profits_Fall_to_Single_Digits.

Schuman, Sara, and Alvin Lin. 2012. "China's Renewable Energy Law and its Impact on Renewable Power in China: Progress, Challenges and Recommendations for Improving Implementation." *Energy Policy* 51 (December): 89–109.

Solar, J. A. 2010. "JA Solar Signs Strategic Agreements with Innovalight for Joint Development of High Efficiency Solar Cells."http://investors.jasolar.com/phoenix .zhtml?c=208005&p=irol-newsArticle&ID=1446259&highlight=.

Sperling, Gene. 2012. "Remarks by Gene Sperling Before the Conference on the Renaissance of American Manufacturing." http://www.whitehouse.gov/sites/default/files/ administration-official/sperling_-_renaissance_of_american_manufacturing_-_03_27_12 .pdf.

Steinfeld, Edward S. 2004. "China's Shallow Integration: Networked Production and the New Challenges for Late Industrialization." *World Development* 32 (11): 1971–1987.

Story, Louise. 2012. "As Companies Seek Tax Deals, Government Pay High Price." *New York Times* (December 1).

Stuart, Becky. 2012. "DuPont and Yingli sign $100 million PV materials agreement." *PV Magazine.* http://www.pv-magazine.com/news/details/beitrag/dupont-and-yingli -sign-100-million-pv-materials-agreement_100005757/#axzz2bt0XRPsh.

Sturgeon, Timothy. 2002. Modular Production Networks: A New American Model of Industrial Organization. *Industrial and Corporate Change* 11 (3): 451–496.

Sustainable Business News. (2012). "JinkoSolar Gets $1 Billion Infusion from Chinese Development Bank." http://www.sustainablebusiness.com/index.cfm/go/news. display/id/24358.

Tassey, Gregory. 2010. "Rationales and Mechanisms For Revitalizing U.S. Manufacturing R&D Strategies." *Journal of Technology Transfer* 35 (3): 283–333.

Thun, Eric, and Loren Brandt. 2010. "The Fight for the Middle: Upgrading, Competition, and Industrial Development in China." *World Development* 38 (11): 1555–1574.

UNIDO. 2011. *World Manufacturing Production: Statistics for Quarter IV.* Vienna: Author.

U.S.-China Economic and Security Review Commission. 2011. "2011 Report to Congress of the U.S.-China Economic and Security Review Commission." http://www.uscc.gov/ content/2011-annual-report-congress.

U.S. International Trade Commission. 2012. "Crystalline Silicon Photovoltaic Cells and Modules from China." http://www.usitc.gov/publications/701_731/pub4360.pdf.

Vernon, Raymond. 1966. "International Investment and International Trade in the Product Cycle." *Quarterly Journal of Economics* 80 (2): 190–207.

Wallack, Todd. 2011. "Evergreen Solar Loses Tax Breaks Worth Millions." *Boston Globe* (May 20).

Wang, Ucilia. 2011. "DuPont Buys Solar Ink Maker Innovalight." http://www.reuters .com/article/2011/07/25/idUS165538390720110725.

Wei, Max, et al. 2010. "Putting Renewables and Energy Efficiency to Work: How Many Jobs Can the Clean Energy Industry Generate in the US?" *Energy Policy* 38 (2): 919–931.

7 Sustaining Global Competitiveness in the Provision of Complex Product Systems: The Case of Civilian Nuclear Power Technology

Florian Metzler and Edward S. Steinfeld

Much of the concern about America's decline in manufacturing focuses on mass-produced goods. This is understandable given that in the high-tech domain, such products cover everything from laptop computers and automobiles, to semiconductors and smartphones. But for all their diversity, these products share a common characteristic—they are produced in standardized fashion in high volumes. This chapter focuses on a very different type of good, one that a number of scholars have termed *complex product systems* (CoPS) (Hobday 1998; Davies 2003; Prencipe 2003). Examples include large-scale thermal or nuclear power plants, high-speed railway rolling stock, offshore oil and gas drilling platforms, and urban subway systems. These are all product systems that involve multiple technologies, multiple subsystems, and a wide range of componentry, all of which must operate in synchrony if the system is to be successful. Rather than being mass-produced, CoPS are developed and deployed on a one-off basis, or occasionally in small, tailored batches, usually for a specific governmental, institutional, or large industrial customer. These systems are all extremely capital, design, and engineering intensive, often requiring billions of dollars, multiple years of development and construction, and tremendous crossdisciplinary expertise to put into operation. For most of these systems, the product life cycle is measured not in months or even years, but in decades. The expectation is that once built, these products will remain in operation for a very long time. Given the mission-critical nature of many of them, perfect or near perfect reliability, safety, and timely delivery become as fundamental to their success as cost.

This chapter seeks to identify the range of commercial capabilities that are needed to design and deploy these societally critical product systems. What kinds of firms are involved? Where do these firms come from? What kinds of special skills or innovative capabilities do these firms bring to bear? How is the proprietary know-how that lies behind the successful design and deployment of complex product systems obtained, and how does it migrate across borders? Which forms of know-how are more likely to migrate than others? And how might these various forms of commercial knowledge be linked to geography, whether that of the country of origin of the lead commercial players or the country in which the system is actually being deployed?

Because CoPS tend to involve cutting-edge technologies, and because they are often purchased by public agencies, they frequently become instruments of governmental industrial policy. Countries that want to catch up technologically, and particularly those that seek to become global players in technology provision, use the purchase of CoPS to force technology transfer and production-related knowledge from the most advanced commercial vendors. In many cases, purchases are conditioned on localization of production in the buyer nation. Thus, not surprisingly, when rising powers purchase CoPS in great numbers, advanced industrial incumbents inevitably start to fear that their own days of leadership are numbered, that critical knowledge is flowing out the door, and that innovative capacity will surely migrate to where the systems are being manufactured and deployed.

This chapter makes a different argument. It acknowledges that, historically, determined nations have been able to pull in certain capabilities—particularly in manufacturing—by purchasing CoPS from overseas vendors. However, by carefully describing and differentiating the full range of capabilities that are actually required to produce and deploy CoPS, this chapter shows that many of the most critical capabilities actually do not move to the place of purchase or deployment. As we illustrate, procuring nations, through technology transfer agreements, can with relative ease push commercial vendors to transfer knowledge for the manufacture of heavy components. And simply by deploying a large number of systems locally, procuring nations can, mostly by learning through doing, enhance local skills in basic construction.

However, what procuring nations are much less able to do is force the transfer of system design and system integration capabilities. As we show, these knowledge-intensive skills are often at the heart of innovation in CoPS. Such skills do not naturally grow out of manufacturing or are necessarily located in close proximity to the place of production or deployment. Indeed, as we show, the design and system integration capabilities possessed by a handful of global technology leaders are often enhanced rather than undermined by the outsourcing of lower-level design work and component production to technology purchasers. For advanced industrial incumbents in the world of CoPS provision, technology transfer to ambitious, rising new powers is an inevitable price of doing business. But as we show, so too is it a way for incumbents to enhance their own innovative capacity and industrial leadership.

Complex technologies and systems integration capabilities

To a far greater degree than mass manufactured goods, CoPS depend on systems integration expertise. Such expertise entails more than just translating an upstream innovation into a downstream product. Rather, it involves the ability to design conceptually across multiple subsystems, execute those designs by decomposing the entire system and delegating specific development and production tasks to subsystem specialists, recomposing the completed subsystems, and doing it all on time and on budget. Rather than taking place within a single firm, this invariably unfolds across a multilevel hierarchy of commercial actors, including designers, system integrators (for the system as a whole and for key subsystems), component suppliers, and myriad subcontractors. The commercial and operational success of these complex product systems hinges on the ability to avoid repeated cycles of design, decomposition, recomposition, system failure, and redesign (Dugan 2011). It is precisely those repeated cycles of redesign and decomposition that drive up costs and lead to doubts about the operational viability of the system in question, a problem not unfamiliar to contemporary defense contracting, particularly for the most sophisticated systems such as advanced strike aircraft or attack submarines.

Systems integration for CoPS encompasses a wide range of tasks. Broad knowledge at the conceptual level must be coupled with specific product designs for core, critical subsystems—ones that in many cases will involve frontier technologies. The designs for those core subsystems must then be reconciled with architectural designs for the system as a whole, a system that in all likelihood will combine frontier technologies with existing, proven technologies. For the actual fabrication of subsystems and key components, product design information must be matched with manufacturing expertise and supply chain management. Matching often occurs simultaneously along multiple paths because a diverse variety of technologies, industries, and supply chains are involved. This all has to be coordinated through effective project management, thus ensuring that the appropriate subsystems—some of which require multiyear lead times to produce—actually show up at the right time and in the right sequence. Alternatively, coordination must be such that the project can still proceed when individual subsystems or components face difficult-to-predict but inevitable delays. Even in cases in which all the technologies involved are well proven, the coordination tasks simply to get the project built on time and within budget are monumental. Tasks as ostensibly straightforward as basic civil construction are for many of these projects neither simple nor totally commodified. Given the scale of the project involved, construction in this context entails substantial knowledge and learning by doing.

Once the complex product system is built, additional types of system integration knowledge are required for the provision of support services and technology upgrades, which is a key source of value for many of the firms operating in this domain. In recent years, movement toward service provision has been a major trend for leading firms such as Alstom, Areva, Westinghouse, Siemens, and Ericsson (Davies 2003). Designers of railway rolling stock such as Alstom, for example, have moved into the provision of railway signaling systems. Designers of nuclear power plants such as Westinghouse have expanded activities in fuel cycle management. And designers of mobile phone networks and networking equipment such as Ericsson have moved into the provision of value-added services for network operators. All of these shifts require interdisciplinary and often cross-industry knowledge about how the overall system and its various component technologies interact.

CoPS and broader concerns about national competitiveness

Although mass-manufactured products may drive concerns about trade imbalances or declines in overall manufacturing employment, CoPS are worthy of attention for several reasons. First, the commercial markets for some of these complex systems are substantial. In China alone in 2013, twenty-eight nuclear power plants are under construction, or just under half of the total number of new builds worldwide. The current "overnight" cost of an average-sized, one thousand megawatt (MWe) nuclear power plant built in China—that is, the cost of the plant less the cost of capital over time—is roughly between $2 billion and $3 billion (WNA China 2012). In the United States, the

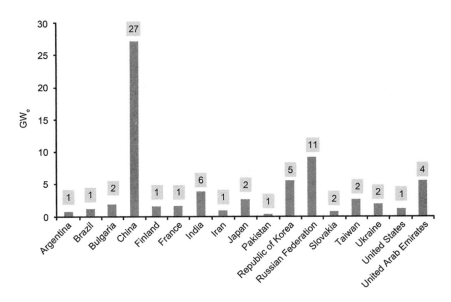

Figure 7.1
Number and Size of Nuclear Power Plant Builds Worldwide, 2011
Source: IAEA PRIS database (2011) and country submissions.

price—because of higher land costs, high capital costs, more lengthy construction time, and more extensive regulatory oversight—can be more than twice that figure. By 2030, the Chinese government aims to build two hundred such plants in China, whereas the Korean government intends to build eighty in Korea and abroad (WNA China 2012; WNA South Korea 2012). Given International Atomic Energy Agency (IAEA) estimates for the likely number of new builds globally by 2030, the worldwide market for civilian nuclear could be worth anywhere from $570 billion to $1.05 trillion until the early to mid-2020s. Figure 7.1 provides a sense of the geographic distribution of recent plant builds underway worldwide.

The commercial opportunities in other CoPS-related sectors have been significant as well. When China in the mid-2000s began rapid development of what would within a decade become the world's largest high-speed rail network, the Chinese Ministry of Railways signed deals with a variety of leading Japanese, European, and Canadian firms, including Kawasaki Heavy Industries, Siemens, Alstom, and Bombardier. The 2004 technology transfer deal with Kawasaki alone was worth $760 million (Shirouzu 2010). These are clearly substantial transactions for firms and national economies alike. For an advanced industrial nation such as the United States simply to take a pass on participating in these industries seems inconceivable.

Second, the capabilities involved in developing and delivering CoPS are strategic in nature. The systems themselves often involve strategic industries such as energy, aerospace, and transport. Furthermore, the systems integration capabilities involved in actually delivering these systems have obvious applications for the procurement of high-tech defense systems. There are clearly international security ramifications when nations either develop or lose the ability to produce CoPS.

Third, some of the world's largest buyers of CoPS today are emerging nations such as China, Brazil, and India, nations that at least some view as potential competitors with the United States in the future. Unwilling to be dependent over the long run on overseas suppliers, these nations all have ambitions to indigenize the technologies involved. Moreover, they have ambitions to become global suppliers themselves. Quite understandably, they are now leveraging the size of their domestic markets to push leading global firms to transfer critical technologies to indigenous firms. Indeed, for leading global firms involved in the sale of complex product systems, promises of technology transfer are a standard way to capture important deals in new markets. To see some of the world's most technologically advanced power generation systems, urban mass transit systems, or high speed rail networks today, one has to travel not to Western Europe, North America, or Japan, but to China. At least with respect to CoPS and China, the traditional product cycle (Vernon 1966) has largely been turned on its head. With China leading the way, several rapidly industrializing nations have become not just the largest markets for CoPS but also the most advanced markets technologically. And they have done so with an express ambition to develop national industrial capabilities.

The rise of indigenous providers in emerging economies has clearly raised concerns in advanced industrial countries that indigenous firms are undercutting long-term national interests by creating new competitors and by turning over strategically sensitive technical information. In 2010, the *Financial Times* reported somewhat ominously that in Westinghouse's successful bid to build four nuclear power plants in China, the U.S.-based (albeit Japanese-owned) firm turned over seventy-five thousand documents to China's State Nuclear Power Technology Corporation (Hook 2010). That figure of seventy-five thousand documents became somewhat of a trope, repeated frequently in media reports about China's rising technological capabilities and the West's decline.

In 2011, Senator James Webb sought to pass legislation to prevent U.S. nuclear firms from "giving away technologies to China" and placing "the competitive advantage of the American economy at risk" (Webb 2011).

This chapter will examine the validity of such concerns. What kinds of capabilities must firms have to be serious players in the CoPS domain, and in what ways are these capabilities linked to geography? To what extent does systems integration expertise migrate to those who procure complex technology systems? Can determined governments use the purchase of CoPS to force technology transfer and catalyze the development of innovative capacity in their own national business ecosystems? How, if at all, should advanced industrial nations respond? And last, concerns about technology transfer and the creation of new national competitors have long predated the era of globalization, particularly with respect to CoPS-related industries such as energy, transport, and aerospace. How, if at all, has globalization changed the nature of the game?

This chapter will explore these questions by delving deeply into one particular sector—civilian nuclear power—and one particular country, China. This focus is appropriate given that China today represents the largest single national market for civilian nuclear power technology worldwide, and China also happens to be a nation committed to developing its own indigenous capabilities in the sector. Nuclear power plants themselves share all the typical characteristics of CoPS: they tend to be purchased on a one-off or small-batch basis, they are extremely technology and capital intensive, they involve complex combinations of new and old technologies, and their product cycles tend to be very long. Further, the civilian nuclear industry, similar to many others in the high-technology domain, is experiencing considerable outsourcing and offshoring today.

At least in the case of the U.S. nuclear industry, the collapse of the home market after Three Mile Island; the growth of new markets in nations such as South Korea, China, and India; and the concomitant technology transfers demanded by those markets appear at least on the surface to be leading to the decline of a domestic civilian nuclear sector. In addition, the availability of inexpensive natural gas now in the U.S. market—essentially, the "shale gas revolution"—is undercutting demand for nuclear power in the United States. The number of U.S. firms technically accredited by the American Society of Mechanical Engineers to manufacture safety critical equipment for nuclear power plants dropped from about 440 in the 1980s to 255 in 2008 (WNA Heavy 2012). Our chapter will examine how declines like this should be understood in terms of the factors driving them and the implications of such declines for national innovative capacity in the United States.

The findings presented in the following sections have their origins in fieldwork we began conducting in 2006 and 2007 as part of the MIT Industrial Performance Center's project on global energy innovation. At that time, interviews were performed with a series of Chinese governmental regulators, engineering specialists, and academic researchers in the civilian nuclear sector. In 2010 and 2011, as part of MIT's Production in the Innovation Economy study, we focused our work directly on the firm level, conducting more than fifty in-depth interviews in forty commercial firms spread across the civilian nuclear supply chain in China. Included in the study were Chinese, American, German, Japanese, Austrian, and French firms, including some of the most prominent multinational incumbents in the industry. Respondent firms included reactor vendors, plant architects, EPC (engineering, procurement, and construction) service providers, project management specialists, nuclear construction firms, equipment manufacturers, fuel cycle managers, and inspection service providers. Our respondent firms effectively covered the full supply chain and the full range of commercial capabilities needed today to deliver a state-of-the-art civilian nuclear plant.

Technology transfer and localization in the nuclear industry

The U.S. government and a number of American firms have expressed increasing frustration with the Chinese government's industrial development efforts. Jeffrey Immelt, CEO of General Electric and an outspoken supporter of the US push to revive manufacturing, complained openly in 2010 of Chinese protectionism and technology theft from the West (Clark and Glader 2010). Similarly, in its *2011 White Paper on the State of American Business in China*, the American Chamber of Commerce in China (2011) openly protested Beijing's use of regulatory power to indigenize overseas technologies. In 2012, the U.S. Department of Commerce imposed anti-dumping sanctions on the Chinese solar photovoltaic industry after repeated complaints of inappropriate subsidization by Beijing (Bloomberg 2012).

A full evaluation of these complaints is beyond the scope of this chapter. However, what is important to recognize is that at least in the area of complex product systems, technology indigenization by purchaser governments has long been part of the game. Indeed, technology vendors have for decades made promises of technology transfer central in their marketing efforts to governmental customers.

Such commitments have unquestionably been prevalent in the nuclear power industry. Since the Eisenhower administration's 1953 Atoms for Peace Program, US firms such as Westinghouse, GE, and Combustion Engineering have built nuclear power plants and transferred nuclear power technologies to Belgium, France, Germany, India, Iran, Japan, Mexico, Pakistan, Slovenia, South Africa, South Korea, Spain, Sweden, Switzerland, and Taiwan. Among these customer nations, France, Germany, Japan, and South Korea later developed internationally competitive nuclear technology vendors of their own, firms that themselves today are involved in aggressive technology transfer efforts to follow-on nations and markets.

German reactor vendor Siemens/KWU in the mid-1980s was openly extolling its ability to offer "complete engineering technology transfer that could also be adapted to include complete manufacturing technology transfer to meet the demands and capabilities of the recipient country" (Hüttl 1985, 5). During that same period, GE celebrated its history dating back to the 1960s of establishing nuclear engineering capabilities worldwide, particularly through its cooperative arrangements with Japanese and German partners (Felmus 1985). Technical cooperation agreements in the 1970s led to Japanese-American joint development of the advanced boiling water reactor. And it is certainly not uncommon for former recipients of technology transfers to later become major global sellers and disseminators of technology themselves. The French nuclear firm Framatome, for instance, received extensive guidance on equipment manufacturing from Westinghouse in the 1970s. Several years later, Framatome would deliver reactor pressure vessels and manufacturing know-how to the United Kingdom as a partner of Westinghouse (George 1985).

One of the most interesting cases of technology transfer in recent times involves not China but South Korea. South Korea's first three nuclear reactors, all turnkey operations ordered from the United States and Canada, began operating between 1978 and 1983. Very few Korean firms were involved in these initial power plant projects, and the few that were involved focused on conventional tasks such as the construction of non-safety-related buildings. Between 1985 and 1989, six additional reactors were built in South Korea by U.S. and French firms, but this time with increasing participation by Korean industry partners and increasing amounts of training by Western vendors. Early in that period, the French firm Alstom alone transferred to Korean partners seventy-five thousand drawings and roughly one hundred thousand technical memos (Lemaire 1985), figures comparable to what Westinghouse some twenty years later would later be described as transferring to the Chinese. By the mid-1990s, Korean power plant deployment was being led by domestic firms that were then hiring U.S. firms as subcontractors (Berthélemy and Lévêque 2011).

Today, thirty-four years into its domestic nuclear power build-out, one that has involved the procurement of twenty-three plants at home and considerable governmental efforts to push technology transfer from abroad, Korea has developed important capabilities of its own. The country is well on its way to becoming the world's fourth largest vendor of nuclear reactors, behind the United States, France, and Russia (WNA South Korea 2012). In 2011, Korean utility KEPCO beat out French, Japanese, and American competitors to score its first international bidding success, a $20 billion contract to build four nuclear reactors in the United Arab Emirates. In the years preceding, Korean power equipment manufacturer Doosan had already developed a powerful international presence, receiving orders from Westinghouse to supply replacement steam generators in U.S. nuclear plants (Doosan 2008). And in 2007, Doosan became part of Westinghouse's bid to build four AP1000 reactors in China, with Doosan assuming responsibilities for transferring manufacturing technology to China First Heavy Industries (WNN 2011). The Korean newcomers, it seems, were already enabling the next generation of follow-on competitors.

Such is the nature of the international bidding process for CoPS projects. Just as in the past, today's nuclear reactor vendors offer comprehensive technology transfer packages when competing for new reactor projects, particularly in countries that aspire to build nuclear fleets or nuclear industries of their own. In their marketing efforts, reactor vendors do not tire of pointing out their track record for technology transfer and localization. In a 2012 brochure, French firm Areva claimed that it "embraced 'localization' long before the word became fashionable in business circles" (Areva 2009, 2). Similarly, Westinghouse vice president Tim Collier stated that "Westinghouse has a track record of technology transfers and localization that is unsurpassed around the world as evidenced by the long-term relationships we have built in places like France, Japan, Korea and other countries that have embraced nuclear energy" (Yuan 2012, 15).

As we argue in the next section, however, it is not simply the case that existing incumbents mortgage their future by enabling new global competitors. Nor is it the case that technology transfer is either unidimensional or unidirectional. The systems integration expertise required to develop and deploy nuclear power plants is complex and multifaceted, rarely residing within the hands of a single corporate entity. Indeed, for incumbents and newcomers alike, the capabilities frequently prove elusive, coming and going over time and from project to project. In a number of cases, technology transfer partnerships provide upgrading opportunities as much for technology originators as for those on the receiving end of transfer.

The multidimensional nature of value in the nuclear supply chain

By examining how the various costs of a nuclear power plant are distributed, one can get a sense of the range of firms, capabilities, and services that are involved in a typical plant build. Moreover, one can begin to get a sense of just how complicated—and, in some cases, tenuous—the relationships are at the firm level among innovative capabilities, systems integration capabilities, and manufacturing capabilities.

Approximately 25 percent of a nuclear power plant's total cost pertains to capitalized indirect services. These include engineering and design, project management, and construction and commissioning. Roughly 50 percent of total plant cost pertains to capitalized direct costs, which include reactor plant equipment, turbine generator plant equipment, and the balance of plant equipment (plumbing, non-safety-related pumps, etc.). Together, capitalized indirect services and capitalized direct costs account for the bulk of a power plant's "overnight" cost. An additional 25 percent of total plant cost pertains to financing. Figure 7.2 provides a sense of the types of corporate entities and tasks that are connected to these costs.

Design and related engineering services

In terms of the high-end design work that lies behind a nuclear power plant, an important distinction must be drawn between conceptual design and detailed design. Conceptual design determines the layout

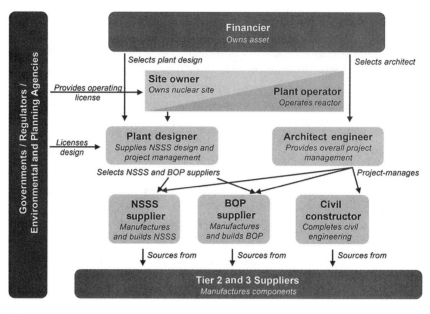

Figure 7.2
Organizational Chart for Nuclear Power Plant Projects (as Viewed by Rolls-Royce). *Note:*
NSSS = nuclear steam supply system; BOP = balance of plant.
Source: Molyneux (2008, p. 8).

of the reactor core based on physical principles, the choice of fuel type
and coolant materials, and related choices for building materials,
subsystems, and plant architecture. These conceptual designs—usually
including diagrams, drawings, and computer models, accompanied by
calculations and explanations—depend on extensive cross-disciplinary
knowledge, and tend to be heavily informed by academic research,
in-house R&D, and accumulated experience with previous designs.
Conceptual design and the innovative capacity surrounding it have
tended to be the domain of a handful of major multinationals generally
understood by the public to be leaders of the nuclear industry, firms
such as Westinghouse, Areva, and GE. Firms such as these correspond
to the designation *plant designer* in figure 7.2.

Conceptual designs, however, do not contain sufficient instructions
for engineers and workers to commence construction at the plant site.
The abstract concepts need to be broken down into work packages
that can be described in detail, procured, and scheduled. Required
equipment and inputs need to be identified and detailed drawings
must be created that can provide exact dimensions and locations for all

components. Such types of information generally fall under the category of detailed design. In Westinghouse's case, detailed designs for its China-based reactors have largely been the responsibility of the Shanghai Nuclear Engineering Research and Design Institute (SNERDI). In Areva's case, the Chinese partner for this task has been the China Nuclear Power Technology Research Institute (CNPRI). Though reactor vendors (the conceptual designers) tend to have in-house capabilities for doing detailed design work, these are the kind of tasks that are routinely outsourced as part of technology transfer commitments. It is by no means clear, however, that detailed design capabilities translate backward into conceptual design capabilities, a factor that drives the willingness of reactor vendors to hand over these tasks. Indeed, in the case of Korean firm KEPCO's successful bid to build four plants in the United Arab Emirates in 2009, KEPCO still relied on Westinghouse to provide intellectual property and engineering services related to the reactors' conceptual design (for which Westinghouse received up to $1.3 billion of the total $20 billion deal) (Berthélemy and Lévêque 2011).

Project management

Project management capabilities are required to convert conceptual and detailed designs into scheduled building sequences, to procure components, and to oversee the building process. Project management teams composed of experienced engineers determine the order in which various construction tasks need to be executed, taking into account the interdependence of different tasks and constraints such as space, labor, regulations, and the timing of major equipment deliveries. A central aspect of project management involves quality control monitoring over everything from the screening of suppliers, to the training of workers on site, to the inspection of completed construction stages. Given how important quality, reliability, and safety are in many CoPS— including, of course, nuclear power plants—purchaser governments, even when aggressively pushing technology transfer and localization, often prefer to have more experienced foreign firms handle overall project management.

As indicated by figure 7.2, project management functions are usually shared across several actors, often including the reactor designer and a specialized architect-engineering firm. It is indicative of the vast scope of activities involved in a nuclear power plant build that the reactor vendors—the ostensible leaders in the nuclear industry—have not proven able to maintain full project management capabilities in-house. Far from indicating failure on their part, this simply underscores the nonlinear fashion in which various critical capabilities in this industry evolve and interact. Just as detailed design expertise does not naturally lead to the development of conceptual design capabilities, project management skills do not naturally evolve from the ability to originate technology. These are all highly specialized capabilities commanding substantial value and involving considerable proprietary know-how. No single firm appears able to master them all, yet all are absolutely essential to the successful development and deployment of the technology system.

For example, for Areva's current reactor builds in China, the project management function is split between Areva itself (which manages the building of key equipment in the nuclear island), the French utility EDF, and the China Nuclear Power Engineering Company (CNPEC). Utilities such as France's EDF have long operated nuclear power plants in their home countries. In some cases, such as EDF's, this experience enables the utility to develop project management capabilities that can then be offered as a lucrative service in overseas projects. Korea's KEPCO is a similar example. For Westinghouse's builds in China, project management is being centered on Westinghouse, the global architecture-engineering firm Shaw, and China's State Nuclear Power Engineering Firm (SNPEC). In this case, the reactor vendor chose to work with a more generalized architecture-engineering firm such as Shaw or Bechtel.

It is reasonable to assume that the Chinese government, by pairing a state engineering firm with an overseas project manager for each of the Chinese nuclear power plant builds, is hoping that overall project management capabilities will be transferred. Historically, though, such skills have not always migrated easily or smoothly. The French and Koreans have been able to move into this area. However, in the French case, the most experienced firms have run into trouble with project management, particularly when they have attempted to improvise on established practices and partnerships. In both its domestic and overseas builds, reactor vendor Areva traditionally handled project management in close partnership with EDF. With its current reactor build in Olkiluoto, Finland, though, Areva has chosen to undertake project management largely on its own. The plant's construction, involving more than 1,900 subcontractors, is now considerably behind schedule and substantially over budget (Aalto University 2010). Initially intended to enter service in 2009, the plant as of early 2013 was still not completed. The plant's initial estimated cost of 3.7 billion euros (WNN 2012) had by 2010 already been exceeded by 2.7 billion euros (Brett 2010).

The reasons for the delays and cost overruns are manifold, but at least some analysts have traced them to the main contractor's inexperience in dealing with complex construction projects (Aalto University 2010). The point is not to point the finger at Areva per se, but rather to emphasize that project management challenges often elude even the most sophisticated global leaders in the nuclear power industry. At the very least, it is fair to say that the ability to design a complex system—whether within a national industrial ecosystem or in a single major multinational firm—by no means translates directly into the ability to manage the overall construction of that system.

Construction

Although global firms generally take the lead in overall project management, the actual construction itself—the pouring of the concrete, the welding of the metal, and the installation of equipment—is generally undertaken by local firms wherever the project is undertaken. In figure 7.2, those firms fall under the category of *civil constructor*. Most of these tasks in a nuclear power plant barely differ from those at any other large construction project. But all large, infrastructure-scale construction projects involve tremendous complexity and managerial challenges. Such challenges include knowledge of—and adaptation to—local environmental, seismic, and meteorological conditions. This kind of knowledge, then, affects everything from the kinds of construction materials that are used to the methods of construction that are employed. Through repetition and accumulated experience, construction firms can develop techniques for speeding the building process and reducing cost. Some of these techniques—including the subtle understanding of which practices must bow to local conditions and which can be standardized—translate into global competitiveness.

In recent years, Chinese construction firms have been involved in one of the largest national infrastructure build-outs in human history, including everything from a nationwide high-speed railway network, a national highway network, numerous municipal subway system projects, hundreds of large-scale power plants, and multiple large-scale airports. It is worth noting that several of these firms are now taking their skills abroad, undertaking construction projects not only in the developing world, but also in advanced industrial economies. Chinese state-owned construction firms have been notably involved in several recent bridge builds in California and New York (Semple 2011; Barboza 2011). Thus, it seems that although design and project management skills do not necessarily migrate to nations procuring complex systems such as power plants, construction skills often do. Concomitantly, those skills arguably erode in economies that cease to engage in major infrastructure expansion and renovation.

Equipment manufacturing and sourcing

Design, project management, and construction account for roughly a quarter of the cost of a nuclear power plant. Equipment, by contrast, accounts for about twice that share. Such equipment includes everything from small off-the-shelf valves to vast machined forgings, from conventional Portland cement to highly specialized alloys. Some of this equipment is particular to the nuclear industry and some is not. In figure 7.2, plant equipment suppliers are placed in two categories, those managed by the NSSS (nuclear steam supply system) supplier and those managed by the BOP (balance of plant) supplier. In order to get a better sense of the know-how that various suppliers possess, we will categorize equipment more precisely as commodity materials, key equipment, or nonkey equipment.

The most common commodity materials used in a nuclear power plant build are concrete and rebar. In most cases, there are no special requirements for these basic inputs, and they are provided by the same mills that provide such commodity materials to other sectors. The amounts of concrete and steel required in a typical one thousand MWe nuclear plant build are vast—about two hundred cubic meters of concrete and forty metric tons of steel per MWe (Peterson 2005). Together, however, these basic materials account for only about 4 percent of total equipment cost of the plant.

Key equipment is much more specific to the nuclear industry and much more expensive. This category pertains to discrete items that perform key functions in the operation of a nuclear plant. These items, or even just their main components, generally cost more than $10 million each. Examples include steam generators, reactor pressure and containment vessels, pressurizers, control rod drive mechanisms, reactor coolant pumps, turbines, and generators (Tong 2010). As

Table 7.1
Examples of Commercial Participants in Each Major Category of Nuclear Power Plant Deployment

	Examples of Companies Active in This Domain	
Category	International	Chinese
Design and related engineering services	Areva, Westinghouse	SNERDI/SNPTC, INET/ Tsinghua University
Project management	EDF, Westinghouse/Shaw	CNPEC/CGN, CNPE/CNNC
Construction	Bouygues	CNEC
Key equipment	Alstom, Curtiss Wright, Doosan, Rolls-Royce, Siemens	Dongfang, Harbin Electric, Shanghai Electric
Nonkey equipment	Emerson, Endress+Hauser, Flowserve, Garlock, Halfen, Nexans, Schott, Vanatome	Ansteel, Bohai Shipyard, China Valves Technology, IDT Sealing, Sichuan Star Cable

Note: This list is far from comprehensive. A typical nuclear power plant build can involve 1,500 to 2,000 suppliers and subcontractors.

indicated in table 7.1, a number of major multinational firms operate in this domain. And many of these firms play a central role in the technology localization programs that reactor vendors advertise to customers. In other words, for those governments that seek technology transfer when procuring a nuclear power plant, they generally seek know-how surrounding the design and manufacturing of key equipment. Such equipment accounts for roughly 20 percent of the total cost of a typical plant (Tong 2010).

Most suppliers to a nuclear power plant project, however, produce neither commodity materials nor key equipment. Rather, they produce all the additional equipment—the pipes, valves, pumps, seals, tanks, vessels, sensors, motors, and so on—required to keep a nuclear power plant functioning. Such nonkey equipment is extremely heterogeneous, often including products that are used in a variety of non-nuclear-related industries. Thus, many of the suppliers in this category are not purely nuclear industry firms. Nonetheless, the breadth of the category underscores the wide range of manufacturers that must be mobilized in order to get a plant built successfully.

As they organize supply chains across these various equipment categories, project managers must balance several considerations. First, they must take into account long-term partnerships that they have established with key equipment suppliers. For example, Westinghouse works closely with reactor coolant pump manufacturer Curtiss Wright (whose reactor coolant pump division Westinghouse previously owned). Westinghouse has no formal obligation to source reactor coolant pumps from Curtiss Wright, but the latter works closely enough with the reactor vendor to be involved in the reactor's actual design process.[1] In other cases, in return for contributing to new reactor designs through the provision of capital, human resources, or test facilities, key equipment manufacturers receive exclusive supply agreements or design interfaces that are specifically tailored for their components.[2] It is not uncommon that, when bidding for overseas projects, reactor vendors such as Westinghouse or Areva try to involve their key equipment suppliers directly in the deal.

Second, while performing their project management role, reactor vendors and architecture-engineering firms have to consider the technology transfer commitments they have made to the plant purchaser. Because many of these commitments involve the transfer of manufacturing know-how for key equipment, the relationship with long-term suppliers becomes critical. In other words, as part of the reactor vendor's overall bid, key equipment suppliers must be persuaded to transfer some of their technology to host country entrants. For Westinghouse's AP1000 builds in China, Doosan has been transferring know-how to China First Heavy Industries for the production of forgings for Doosan's reactor pressure vessels. Thus, China First Heavy has effectively been brought into Doosan's supply chain as part of Westinghouse's overall technology transfer agreement with the Chinese. The situation can become complicated for the reactor vendor because it has to balance purchasing commitments made to key suppliers against technology transfer commitments made to governments.

Third, project managers have to take into account the internationalization strategies that key and nonkey equipment suppliers undertake on their own. Larger, more complex pieces of equipment—some of which are key and some nonkey—have their own project management and sourcing issues, ones that are handled by the equipment supplier. Similar to many other manufacturers today, some nuclear equipment suppliers distribute their operations globally in order to take advantage of capabilities in particular locales. For example, a senior manager of a U.S.-headquartered power plant equipment supplier described what he termed his firm's "global division of labor."[3] The firm, he explained, has an "innovation center" in Europe staffed with the "lead technical guys, the grey-haired staff," as well as detailed engineering and design teams in Shanghai and actual manufacturing operations in Guang-dong. The detailed engineering and design facility in Shanghai employs two hundred Chinese staff, one hundred of whom are engineers. Today, even for this firm's projects in the United States, conceptual engineering takes place in Europe, detailed engineering in Shanghai, and equipment manufacturing in Guangdong. The former U.S. location for detailed engineering and design was "no longer needed."

For this particular firm, as in numerous others we interviewed, the attraction of China was not just the availability of low-cost labor. Rather, it was the availability in the same regional ecosystem of low-skill, low-cost labor and top-notch, high-end engineering talent. In this particular firm's Shanghai design office, all employees are university graduates, and most have a master's degree as well. Our interview respondent praised Chinese product development engineers for their high efficiency and young age, noting that they "have a very strong technology background and great design abilities." He also said that graduates from top Chinese universities such as Fudan and Tsinghua are better trained than many graduates from universities in the West.

Although outsourcing and offshoring may make sense as a matter of specialization, the manner in which suppliers undertake this is potentially of great concern to project managers of nuclear plant builds, especially when project managers are not dealing with trusted, long-term suppliers.[4] In the Chinese case, despite pressures from their home government to localize equipment sourcing, even China's state-owned nuclear firms are often reluctant to buy from domestic producers for fear that those producers will outsource indiscriminately to low-cost, low-quality secondary suppliers or overestimate their own manufacturing capabilities.[5] Chinese project managers worry that substandard materials and equipment will find their way into the plant. They also worry that supplied products will deviate from designer specifications or that late deliveries will lead to schedule holdups. Therefore, the desire often becomes to source from more transparent overseas-owned suppliers with proven track records. Some of these companies are in their home countries, but some are also in China trying to marry the best of both worlds and provide high quality at low prices. Some of these overseas suppliers are in China because of Chinese localization requirements, others to take advantage of certain design and manufacturing capabilities of the Chinese production ecosystem, and still others to be close to their customers. In all these cases, being an overseas firm with a proven track record in the nuclear industry accords them competitive advantage over local entrants.

As the preceding discussion suggests, quality assurance to a large extent drives equipment sourcing choices for complex product systems, whether in the nuclear industry or other safety-intensive sectors such as aerospace. But quality assurance especially in civilian nuclear power has several particular attributes that are worth considering.

Nuclear power plant equipment must comply with the national quality regulations of the country in which the plant is located. Historically, nuclear regulators and inspection organizations in different countries have emphasized different aspects of the manufacturing process. As a result, a variety of different national standards have evolved. In the United States, for instance, nuclear power plant equipment manufacturing has to comply with standards set by the American Society of Mechanical Engineers (ASME). In France, however, a different set of standards—the Règles de Conception et de Construction des Matériels Mécaniques des Ilots Nucléaires (RCC-M)—apply. The differences across national standards are more than just nominal. For example, the American standards focus more on monitoring the manufacturing process of the product, whereas German standards emphasize postproduction testing of the product.[6]

When nuclear power plants are built in third-party nations according to American or French designs, a common practice on the part of nuclear reactor vendors is to follow the national standards used in their home market. In countries such as China, this is required by law. Beijing essentially outsources its nuclear equipment quality standards to nations that have long-established histories in the industry. But this practice itself leads to complications because the Chinese are currently sourcing designs from three different overseas vendors. Thus, China's French-designed, Russian-designed, and U.S.-designed power plants are all built to different national standards (Xu 2010).

For equipment suppliers, this poses a problem. Many suppliers possess only one set of national compliance certificates, because the financial and time expenditures required to acquire and maintain such certificates are onerous[7] (Kwon 1985). Typically, therefore, a French valve producer with only RCC-M accreditation will not be able to sell valves to a U.S.-designed plant that requires ASME accreditation.

When combined with other commitments to honor long-term supplier relationships and technology transfer agreements, these regulatory compliance issues makes sourcing choices all the more difficult for project managers. The complexity of the decision-making process underscores why so few players prove globally capable of handling project management in the nuclear (and other comparable) sectors, and why established incumbents prove so difficult to displace.

Apart from regulatory compliance concerns, safety, reliability, and timely delivery are so important in the nuclear sector that they frequently trump cost as a driver of purchasing decisions. Modern nuclear power plants are generally designed for a lifetime of sixty years, with the integrity of key equipment guaranteed across that period.[8] A key equipment supplier's competitiveness, therefore, is often driven by the ability to demonstrate quality assurance through extensive and transparent testing.[9] Moreover, on-time delivery becomes as important as the initially agreed-on price. Delays in the delivery of plant equipment have far-reaching financial consequences due to the high up-front capital costs of nuclear power plant builds.[10] Such delays also undermine the intricate sequencing of the plant's construction process. Given the importance of quality and time criticality, therefore, procurement departments often hesitate to replace an established and trustworthy supplier with a cheaper, but relatively unknown alternative. Again, though, such hesitancy has to be balanced against commitments for technology transfer and, at the upper limits, cost considerations.

Although quality issues encourage the building of longer-term procurement relationships, the number of established suppliers has shrunk since the 1980s because of the small number of new builds that have taken place in the advanced industrial world. In the United States alone the number of firms with ASME N-stamp accreditation has dropped from about 440 in the 1980s to 255 in 2008 (WNA Heavy 2012). However, since the late 2000s, markets for nuclear technology have picked back up due to demand from newly industrializing nations such as China and India. In response, a number of firms from advanced economies are taking a fresh look at the industry, often entering or returning from other sectors. Completely new entrants from the countries purchasing nuclear technologies are also appearing on the scene. Equipment procurers must negotiate this new environment, opting in some cases to stick with the few traditional suppliers still in the market and in other cases to aid in the development of entirely new producers.

Many components required for the operation of nuclear power plants need to be regularly monitored and replaced at fixed intervals. These components tend to fall into the nonkey category, including items such as non-safety-related pumps and valves, stainless steel piping, and basic instrumentation. Nonkey components are relatively inexpensive, and they do not require as much regulatory documentation as key equipment related to the nuclear steam supply system. Nonetheless, many of them are important and demanded on a steady, ongoing basis. Thus, some players argue that physical proximity between component suppliers and the plant is desirable.[11] Colocation can lead to the development of nuclear technology industrial clusters, such as the Haiyan Nuclear Power Industrial Park and the Rongcheng Nuclear Power Industrial Park in China. As one nuclear expert described,

Haiyan is a supermarket. It's close to the Qinshan Nuclear Power Plant, and all the firms that come here are like a supermarket for CNNC [China National Nuclear Corporation]. You come here, and I buy from you. They all want to have local manufacturers, so they can get reliable supply.[12]

Both domestic and overseas-owned suppliers of nonkey components have sought to take advantage of the cluster effects now available in China.

Other firms cluster around suppliers rather than buyers. A fairly typical example is a European pump firm that produces metal machinery in Guangdong province. The firm's China division is a wholly foreign-owned entity with 1,300 employees as of 2011. The firm had added two hundred new employees in China every year.[13] Today, the firm produces pumps for a variety of sectors including the nuclear industry. In a fashion typical of such producers, the firm takes existing product designs from its various European branches and transfers them to China. In China, engineering teams redesign the products, adapting them to the local environment to speed production time and reduce cost. According to the president of the firm's China operation, location in Guangdong is a key source of competitiveness, but so too is tacit in-house knowledge involving make-or-buy decisions in the complex production environment. For this firm, about 70 percent of the parts for a typical product are sourced externally. In this respect, being situated in Guangdong is critical because the region hosts an incredibly dense array of potential suppliers. In this environment, a core capability for the pump firm involves optimizing make-or-buy decisions and organizing local supply chains in a manner that achieves large cost savings for some parts, and guaranteeing quality and reliability for other parts. A key aspect of the firm's China-based engineering and design capability involves understanding which parts from the original

European designs can be swapped out for lower cost alternatives and which cannot. For cases in which quality and timely delivery are crucial, the European firm has capabilities for internalizing production of previously outsourced components. For example, when the firm repeatedly encountered problems with externally sourced steel casings for pumps, it eventually decided to build its own foundry to forge the casings in-house. This foundry, built in cooperation with another European firm, is located next to the firm's Guangdong manufacturing facility.

Chinese domestic firms in the nonkey equipment category have also moved aggressively to exploit cluster effects in their home country. One example involves a privately owned pipe manufacturer located in coastal Jiangsu province.[14] A national leader in the production of a particular type of piping, the firm is the first Chinese private firm that has been able to manufacture respective piping that complies with United States and European regulatory standards for use in nuclear power plants. The firm entered U.S. and European markets in 2011 and now produces for the nuclear, chemical, oil and gas, shipbuilding, papermaking, medical, food processing, aerospace, and defense sectors, all industries that are growing rapidly in China as well. Starting in the late 2000s when the quality of domestically produced pipes of this type was low throughout China, the firm began its upgrading efforts by purchasing an Italian machinery firm and production lines from German machine tool firms. In its most recent development efforts the firm has focused on the nuclear industry, in part because of proximity to rapidly expanding demand and in part because of the Chinese government's willingness to support the growth of the nuclear supply chain. The firm was able to expand its factory floor threefold and introduce twenty new foreign-sourced production lines in part due to investment that came with the firm's being designated a key industry project of the 2011 central governmental investment plan. With the promise of sustained demand from the domestic nuclear sector, the firm has been able to invest with a long-term outlook, enjoy substantial governmental support, and recruit high-end design talent from a local metallurgical design institute. Moreover, the firm has been able to draw on previous experience it had garnered through participation in China's rapidly growing petrochemical and gas industries.

A similar example of a Chinese firm that has upgraded in response to a growing domestic market for nuclear-related technologies involves a graphite seal supplier.[15] Graphite seals are used in many areas of power plants to prevent leakage in pumps, valves, pressure vessels, and between pipes. Until roughly four years ago, the market for nuclear power plant seals in China had been dominated by French and American firms. Chinese firms produced seals only for conventional industries because the quality requirements were lower. According to our respondent, Chinese firms since 2008 have won virtually every tender for nuclear seals.[16] The domestic firm we interviewed in this sector produces seals that are one-third the price of foreign suppliers' seals. The bulk of the cost savings come from sourcing the graphite raw material from local as opposed to overseas suppliers. The actual manufacturing process, though, is essentially commodified, relying on extensive automation imported from abroad. According to the firm's engineers, very little tacit knowledge is required. In some respects, therefore, the firm's growth patterns resemble what has occurred in the solar photovoltaic industry (Nahm and Steinfeld, chap. 6, this volume). Firms enter the business by purchasing expensive, highly automated production lines from abroad. They then seek to compete by scaling up and trying to eke out cost savings in the supply chain, often by squeezing raw material suppliers. These are tough, narrow margin businesses, but the firms are willing to plunge in and enter the fray. Whether these firms will find long-term sources of competitive advantage remains to be seen, but at least in the near term, the reality of rapid demand growth from civilian nuclear power and other CoPS-related sectors makes their aggressive expansion efforts in China seem more reasonable.

As these examples indicate, numerous pathways exist by which firms can seek sustainable competitive advantage in the nuclear power business. As shown in table 7.2 and table 7.3, even if one considers only China's new plant builds, one can see the extraordinarily diverse array of domestic and overseas commercial actors that have been involved. Among the overseas players, some have operations in China, and others do not. And this figure provides only a small sampling of the firms involved. The actual numbers are much higher. In Areva's ongoing build in Finland, more than 1,900 suppliers and subcontractors are involved (Aalto University 2010).

In the civilian nuclear sector, as in many industries involving complex product systems, the pathways to commercial competitiveness are extremely diverse, spanning the spectrum from upstream design and project management to heavy equipment fabrication, commodity material production, and basic civil construction. Therefore, the

Table 7.2
Different Reactor Types under Construction in China and Related Chinese and International Actors

Reactor Type	CNP-600	CPR-1000 and EPR	AP1000	HTR-PM
Main contractor	CNNC	CGN	SNPTC	Chinergy
Design (Chinese actor)	BINE	CNPRI	SNERDI	INET
Design (foreign partner)		Areva	Westinghouse	
Project management (Chinese actor)	CNPE	CNPEC	SNPEC	CNPEC
Project management (foreign partner)		Areva/ EDF	Westinghouse/ Shaw	Sargent & Lundy

Table 7.3
Explanations of Acronyms

Acronym	Full Name
BINE	Beijing Institute of Nuclear Engineering
CGN	China Guangdong Nuclear Power Group
CNNC	China National Nuclear Corporation
CNPE	China Nuclear Power Engineering Corporation
CNPEC	China Nuclear Power Engineering Group Co.
CNPRI	China Nuclear Power Technology Research Institute
EDF	Électricité de France
INET	Institute of Nuclear and New Energy Technology
SNERDI	Shanghai Nuclear Engineering Research and Design Institute
SNPEC	State Nuclear Power Engineering Company
SNPTC	State Nuclear Power Technology Corporation

industry cannot be characterized by straightforward linkages among competitiveness, innovative capacity, participation in manufacturing, and proximity to demand markets. To base industrial promotion policy on a presumption of straightforward linkages, at least in these kinds of industries, would clearly be problematic.

Pathways toward competitiveness in the global nuclear industry

In this section we review the categories of nuclear industry players discussed previously and comment on their future trajectories given market conditions in the early 2010s.

The reality is that in the nuclear industry, as in a number of CoPS-related sectors, there has been a considerable amount of technology lock-in over the years. From the 1950s onward, light water reactor designs have thoroughly dominated the market, accounting for over 95 percent of the more than four hundred commercial power reactors operating worldwide today (IAEA 2012; Cowan 1990). For better or worse, the basic product architecture of these reactors—the arrangement and design of the steam generators, reactor pressure vessels, reactor coolant pumps, and turbine generators—has barely changed over the decades. As a matter of public relations and safety, nuclear reactor designers are not shy about emphasizing the proven nature of their designs and the continuity with a previous track record (Westinghouse 2003; Teller 2010). Westinghouse describes its "most advanced, yet proven" nuclear reactor, the AP1000, as being "based on standard Westinghouse Pressurized Water Reactor (PWR) technology that has achieved more than three thousand reactor years of highly successful operation" (Westinghouse 2009, 2). Thus, despite ongoing research into radically different designs (i.e., sodium-cooled fast reactors, high-temperature gas-cooled reactors, etc.), incremental product improvement rather than radical innovation overwhelmingly characterizes the nature of the business.

What this means for reactor vendors is that they are not competing primarily on the basis of new technology. They are really competing on the basis of a proven track record of safety and a proven record of delivering extraordinarily expensive product systems on time and on budget. Moreover, for the most lucrative customers—namely, governments planning on building a fleet of reactors and an indigenous nuclear industry—the vendors are competing on the very basis of their ability to transfer technology. In this sense, it is not quite so simple to suggest that incumbent vendors undercut themselves by transferring designs or particular technologies to newcomer nations and rising aspirants in the industry. The vendors often win deals precisely because they know how to transfer technology. As we have described, though, because the entry barriers to the conceptual design and project management functions of this industry are so high (and so dependent on proven track records of success), even despite extensive technology transfer since the mid-twentieth century, there still exist only a handful of established reactor vendors worldwide.

The additional reality is that the reactor vendors' real source of proprietary know-how lies not so much in the technology itself, but rather in their ability to manage the technology system's deployment through the organization of a wide array of commercial actors and tasks. That is, the incumbents compete to a large extent on the basis of proven records of systems integration capabilities.

Only a handful of global firms have developed these capabilities since the 1950s. Participation in a large number of plant builds in the firm's home market seems to be a necessary, but by no means sufficient, condition for the development of systems integration, supply chain organization, and technology transfer capabilities. It is neither inconceivable nor guaranteed that a Chinese firm may one day compete globally in nuclear plant design and overall project management. The Koreans (KEPCO) today do so only in partnership with the Americans (Westinghouse), and the Japanese, despite their substantial domestic program, have tended to lag internationally.

For firms such as Areva and Westinghouse, given that their home countries are no longer engaged in extensive new plant builds, winning international deals in major markets is critical. Such deals are often won on the basis of a proven track record of system reliability, successful technology transfer, on-time project delivery, and reasonable cost. This combination inevitably requires coordination between reactor vendors and their key equipment suppliers. In many cases, key suppliers have to be persuaded to manufacture in new locales and transfer technology to rising commercial aspirants. In still other cases, key suppliers—and even new entrants from rising nuclear markets—are brought in as co-investors in third-country overseas projects. For example, Westinghouse and Areva have teamed up with their Chinese partners (SNPTC and CGN, respectively) to bid for the six GWe Horizon project in the United Kingdom (Xu and Schaps 2012). For nuclear reactor vendors, going global and working with rising aspirants on new plant builds may have its risks, but so too is it critical for continued commercial viability.

At the same time, the reactor vendors have moved aggressively downstream into the provision of high-end services for existing nuclear plants. Westinghouse, for instance, although maintaining its engineering and design functions, has sought to expand its plant maintenance and fuel cycle management businesses. By moving into service provision, the reactor vendors are proceeding down a path pursued by a number of major multinationals involved in CoPS-related sectors. Of course, some firms prove more willing and adept than others in negotiating this evolution. In the case of China's high-speed railway build-out, for example, for every Kawasaki Heavy Industries that complains about technology theft, there are the Alstoms and IBMs of the world that are quietly and steadily selling signaling systems, maintenance programs, and tailored software. The basic point is that in many CoPS-related sectors, the path to future competitiveness for major incumbents lies not necessarily in manufacturing per se, but rather in the ability to deliver—and ultimately service, maintain, and upgrade—sophisticated technology systems. In the United States, for instance, more than six thousand MWe in nuclear power–generating capacity were added since the 1990s without any new reactors having been built. Power uprates through upgrading to advanced equipment or more efficient processes often prove more attractive than new plant builds. For key equipment suppliers, the path to the future is arguably more precarious. They are deeply reliant on extremely capital-intensive manufacturing processes, ones for which know-how is increasingly becoming codified and embedded in sophisticated production equipment. Industry leaders such as Korea's Doosan grew in part because they enjoyed substantial financial backing from the state, substantial support from the state in pushing technology transfer from overseas incumbents, and a rapidly growing domestic market for their products. These conditions, however, now can be obtained in China. It is not surprising, therefore, that we witness the rise of new entrants such as China First Heavy Industries. Doosan, Curtiss Wright, or numerous other major equipment suppliers appear to be holding on by more deeply partnering with reactor vendors on reactor design and overall project financing. By helping to design reactors or finance projects, some of the larger global equipment suppliers are binding themselves more tightly to the reactor vendors. In that kind of arrangement, the equipment supplier becomes more than just a vehicle for the reactor vendor's overseas technology transfer commitments, a vehicle that can be dispensed with once a new crop of equipment suppliers, the technology transfer recipients, arises.

For nonkey equipment producers, manufacturing is again the heart of their business, but prospects for the ongoing competitiveness of incumbents appear more varied. As a number of successful European machinery producers have discovered, proximity to major global manufacturing ecosystems—such as those represented by a number of regions in China—is essential. First, it provides immediate access to an extraordinarily diverse array of suppliers across multiple price points and quality levels. Second, it provides access to important engineering talent, particularly for product development and cost reduction. As we have repeatedly seen with the more successful European equipment suppliers, their overall product designs come from high-end markets at home, but then China-based design teams reengineer those products to reduce costs and ease manufacturability. This often involves localizing the supply chain to China. By adapting the original product design in this fashion, lower cost variants become attractive for emerging mid-tier markets, some of which are in China but many of which extend worldwide. Third, maintaining at least some production in China affords critical proximity to particular kinds of customers that require ongoing quality assurance, service provision, and delivery on demand. As discussed previously, such conditions apply in the nuclear sector. The overall point is that although Chinese domestic firms are clearly rising in these areas, overseas incumbents also can maintain competitiveness by developing a presence in China and by effectively marrying new capabilities and opportunities available in China with existing capabilities back in the home market.

In the area of construction, however, firm-level capability development does seem tied to where the complex system is built. To a greater degree than in any other value activity surrounding nuclear power plant deployment, construction depends on local knowledge. And, capabilities accumulate through repetition. "Learning by doing" is critical in construction. Although the basic principles may be straightforward, the actual techniques and choices of materials often are not, especially when large-scale projects are involved. Chinese firms in recent years have built tens of thousands of kilometers of railway and highway systems, and hundreds of power plants, dams, airports, and bridges (Vickridge and Lu 1999). Over time, these firms have adopted competitive bidding practices, advanced construction technologies, efficient management techniques, and advanced quality control. When combined with abundant skilled and semiskilled labor—and generous state funding—this accumulated experience has led to considerable learning and skill upgrading. In 2011, twenty-two Chinese firms featured in the *Engineering New-Record's* top-one-hundred list of global construction contractors (ENR 2011). It is not surprising that several of these firms are now expanding into international markets, including the most developed economies such as the United States. Local knowledge is important in construction, but some of the learning by doing clearly is transferrable across borders. Firms that get involved in a large number of infrastructure builds in their home country often prove capable of doing similar builds in other locales. In part, they develop tacit understanding of which techniques can be generalized, and which must be modified to meet local conditions. And, as they go abroad, they learn to manage local subcontractors. Previously, we have witnessed this with Korean construction firms. Now, we are seeing it with the Chinese. The basic point is that nations resisting large-scale investment in infrastructure expansion should not be surprised when they increasingly find themselves relying on the construction capabilities of those who do.

Conclusion

Governments can indeed force technology transfer through the procurement of complex products and technology systems. When countries have national fleet ambitions in the nuclear sector, they can build themselves into global technology suppliers. We have witnessed this first with France, Germany, and Japan; then with Korea; and now, perhaps, with China. In all likelihood, Chinese firms will become global suppliers of at least certain pieces of capital-intensive key plant equipment.

But the full range of capabilities needed to develop and deploy nuclear power plants is vast. No single firm today can do it all. Moreover, the most challenging, difficult-to-duplicate capabilities involve not the physical fabrication of technology subsystems, but rather the management and integration of the overall project. By focusing on particular aspects of the nuclear supply chain, firms today face many different avenues by which they can exert commercial leadership worldwide. It is by no means clear that competitiveness in one area—say, key equipment manufacturing—leads to competitiveness in another, such as conceptual design or project management. A major goal of this chapter has been to separate out these distinct capabilities and activities so as to avoid wrongheaded conclusions about the ostensible selling (out) of know-how through cross-border commercial interactions in this industry.

As this chapter has suggested, some capabilities, particularly in heavy manufacturing, clearly can and do get transferred through international procurement deals brokered with governments. Such is the nature of the industry—technology transfer is simply a basic cost of doing business. But other capabilities, such as detailed design work, reengineering for cost reduction, and supply chain optimization, are willingly transferred by lead firms not as a quid pro quo, but rather as an effort at overall skill enhancement and competitiveness building. That is, by establishing a presence in particular overseas markets—ones that involve proximity to key buyers, key sources of engineering talent, and dense supplier networks—the technology transferor aims not to sacrifice its capabilities, but instead to enhance them. It often accomplishes this by transferring technology to entities in which it has ownership, whether subsidiaries or joint ventures. As we have illustrated with the cases of European nonkey equipment suppliers, we believe that operations in China have enhanced rather than detracted from these suppliers' overall global capabilities and competitiveness. New Chinese competitors are undoubtedly arising, but for many European and North American suppliers, that's not necessarily the heart of the "China" problem. Rather, it's that their own home country competitors—whether from Europe or North America—are becoming better at what they do by selectively absorbing production and design capabilities from the Chinese system. In other words, Western producers are competing among themselves to make best use of capabilities that can be absorbed by maintaining a presence in China. Thus, effectively managing a China-based subsidiary or joint venture, and successfully integrating it into global operations, has itself become a key differentiator of overall competitiveness for certain advanced industrial firms.

We have seen how sticky systems integration capabilities are in the civilian nuclear power sector. Only a handful of firms worldwide have developed and maintained these capabilities over the long term. Though they may have had their origins in national fleet-building efforts, these capabilities today do not seem particularly tied to specific geographies, manufacturing activities, or national investment practices. Today, as a growing number of equipment suppliers emerge from industrializing countries, the options for various sourcing and partnering arrangements grow. This creates new opportunities for incumbent systems integrators to innovate, and in some ways raises barriers against aspiring competitors. For a given nuclear plant build now, whether in the UK, South Africa, or anywhere else, firms such as Areva or Westinghouse have the option of partnering globally with new equipment suppliers or detailed design firms, including ones hailing from new markets such as China. By partnering with these new suppliers and effectively sourcing globally, reactor vendors may be able to add lower cost to their existing source of competitiveness, namely proven track records. That is, some emerging global suppliers, including ones from China, can produce at lower cost (in large part because of the scale economies they are achieving in producing for their rapidly expanding home market). It is still a bit early to say whether this has become a factor in the nuclear sector, but it has clearly become a factor in the delivery of other complex product systems, including conventional thermal plants worldwide and large bridge constructions.

Finally, the reactor vendors, through their control over conceptual designs, can increase their degree of sourcing freedom by moving toward more modular product architectures, a trend currently pursued by Westinghouse. Advanced industrial incumbents today still enjoy many options. The point is that it is by no means clear that incumbent reactor vendors or other systems integrators in the nuclear sector (firms such as France's EDF or America's Shaw) are in retreat or about to be completely supplanted by new entrants. The incumbents may prove to be best positioned to exploit the new opportunities represented by an evolving production and sourcing environment.

What is already clear is that even as the industry continues to globalize and new competitors emerge, the incumbent systems integrators also face opportunities to upgrade and capture new revenue streams. Complex product systems, given their nature, create demand for value-added services, maintenance, and technology upgrades. These services in recent history have involved such things as the provision of railway signaling systems, subway fare collection systems, and nuclear fuel cycle management. In many cases, these are extremely high-value activities that depend on long-standing commercial partnerships, and that require extensive cross-disciplinary, systemwide knowledge. Moreover, these services are needed on an ongoing, iterated basis. By moving forward rapidly into service deployment, incumbents at once build competiveness in future growth areas and ensure themselves against the emergence of lower cost and often substantially state-supported entrants in their traditional areas of business.

What seems to be the case for virtually all firms involved in complex products and systems provision is that withdrawal from the outside world is simply not an option. In the nuclear technology industry, no national competitors—whether the Chinese, the Koreans, the French, the Americans, or any others—appear to be getting ahead by reining things in, refocusing their activities on home geographies, or retreating from cross-border partnerships. Particularly given where complex product systems are being built today (see figure 7.1), the question is not whether to retreat, but rather how to stay involved in enough worldwide project builds so that the most difficult-to-duplicate skills—namely those involving systems integration—remain fresh, up-to-date, and increasingly tied to the kinds of knowledge-intensive, follow-on services that will be demanded for decades to come.

Notes

1. Interviews, project manager at international consulting company, September 14, 2011; executive at international nuclear reactor vendor, October 14, 2011.

2. Interview, executive at international nuclear reactor vendor, October 14, 2011.

3. Interview, CEO of American engineering, procurement and construction company, September 7, 2011.

4. Interview, head of international strategy at medium sized American equipment manufacturer, October 22, 2011.

5. Interview, business development associate at international consulting firm, November 19, 2012.

6. Interview, international business development director at American materials supplier, October 20, 2011.

7. Interview, head of international strategy at medium sized American equipment manufacturer, October 22, 2011.

8. Interview, engineer at American engineering, procurement and construction company, September 18, 2011.

9. Interview, head of international strategy at medium sized American equipment manufacturer, October 22, 2011.

10. Interview, project manager at international consulting company, September 14, 2011.

11. Interview, executive at international consulting firm, October 18, 2011.

12. Interview, executive at international consulting firm, October 18, 2011.

13. Interview, head of China operations at European equipment manufacturer, September 5, 2011.

14. Interview, import and export department director at Chinese equipment manufacturer, September 20, 2011.

15. Interview, deputy general manager at Chinese equipment manufacturer, September 20, 2011.

16. Interview, deputy general manager at Chinese equipment manufacturer, September 20, 2011.

References

Aalto University. 2010. *Case Olkiluoto 3 Nuclear Power Plant Project in Finland*. Project Business Research Group, Aalto University, Helsinki, Finland.

American Chamber of Commerce in the People's Republic of China. 2011. "2011 White Paper on the State of American Business in China." http://www.amchamchina.org/article/7914.

Areva. 2009. "Did You Say 'Localization'?" *EnergyBusiness* (Quarter 1). http://www.areva.com.

Barboza, David. 2011. "Bridge Comes to San Francisco with a Made-in-China Label." *New York Times* (June 25).

Berthélemy, Michel, and François. Lévêque. 2011. "Korea Nuclear Exports: Why Did the Koreans Win the UAE Tender? Will Korea Achieve Its Goal of Exporting 80 Nuclear Reactors by 2030?" Cerna Working Paper.

Brett, Patricia. 2010. "Safety Fears Raised at French Reactor." *New York Times* (July 26).

Clark, Jennifer, and Paul Glader. 2010. "GE Chief's Remarks Show Growing Irritation with China." *Wall Street Journal* (July 2).

Cowan, Robin. 1990. "Nuclear Power Reactors: A Study in Technological Lock-in." *Journal of Economic History* 50 (03): 541–567.

Davies, Andrew. 2003. "Integrated Solutions: The Changing Business of Systems Integration." In *The Business of Systems Integration*, ed. Andrea Prencipe, Andrew Davies, and Mike Hobday. New York: Oxford University Press.

Doosan. 2008. "Doosan Wins a USD 288 Million Order for a New-Type of Nuclear Power Plant in the U.S." Doosan Heavy Industries and Construction Co. Seoul, South Korea.

Dugan, Regina E. 2011. "Just Make It." Talk presented at MIT (November 29).

ENR. 2011. The 2011 Top 400 Contractors. *Engineering News Record*. May 16. http://enr.construction.com.

Felmus, Neil L. 1985. "Transfer of Engineering Technology." In *Transactions of the Third International Conference on Nuclear Technology Transfer: ICONTT-III*. Madrid, Spain.

George, B. V. 1985. "The Establishment of PWR Technology in the United Kingdom in Support of the Sizewell B Project." In *Transactions of the Third International Conference on Nuclear Technology Transfer: ICONTT-III*. Madrid, Spain.

Hobday, Michael. 1998. "Product Complexity, Innovation, and Industrial Organisation." *Research Policy* 26 (6): 689–710.

Hobday, Michael, Andrew Davies, and Andrea Prencipe. 2005. "Systems Integration: A Core Capability of the Modern Corporation." *Industrial and Corporate Change* 14 (6): 1109–1143.

Hook, Leslie. 2010. "US Group Gives China Details of Nuclear Technology." *Financial Times* (November 23).

Hüttl, Adolf. 1985. "Ten Years of Experience in Technology Transfer for Turnkey Power Plants." In *Transactions of the Third International Conference on Nuclear Technology Transfer: ICONTT-III*. Madrid, Spain.

IAEA. 2011. "Power Reactor Information System." International Atomic Energy Agency. http://www.iaea.org/pris.

IAEA. 2012. "Nuclear Power Reactors in the World." International Atomic Energy Agency. http://www-pub.iaea.org.

Kwon, Joong-Kyou. 1985. "Transfer of Manufacturing Technology for Nuclear Power Plants. In *Transactions of the Third International Conference on Nuclear Technology Transfer: ICONTT-III*. Madrid, Spain.

Lemaire, Michael. 1985. "Alsthom's Experience with Technical Cooperation in Nuclear Power Plants." In *Transactions of the Third International Conference on Nuclear Technology Transfer: ICONTT-III*. Madrid, Spain.

Molyneux, John. 2008. "Presentation to Supplier Conference." Rolls-Royce. https://www.ukap1000application.com.

Peterson, Per F. 2005. "The Future of Nuclear Energy: A California Perspective." Berkeley: California Energy Commission 2005 Integrated Energy Policy Workshop.

Semple, Kirk. 2011. "Bridge Repairs by a Company Tied to Beijing." *New York Times* (August. 10).

Shirouzu, Norihiko. 2010. "Train Makers Rail against China's High Speed Designs." *Wall Street Journal* (December 2).

Teller, Andrew. 2010. *The EPR^{TM} Reactor: Evolution to Gen III+ Based on Proven Technology*. Areva.

Tong, Michael. 2010. "China Power Equipment, February 2010." Deutsche Bank Global Market Research.

Vernon, Raymond. 1966. "International Investment and International Trade in the Product Cycle." *Quarterly Journal of Economics* 80 (2):190–207.

Vickridge, Ian, and Youjie Lu. 1999. "Civil Engineering in China." *Civil Engineering* 132 (February): 14–23.

Webb, Jim. 2011. "Senator Webb Introduces Legislation to Stop "Giving Away" Taxpayer-funded Technologies to China." Office of Sen. Jim Webb, D-Va.

Westinghouse. 2003. "The Westinghouse AP1000 Advanced Nuclear Plant." Westinghouse Electric Co. Butler County, PA.

Westinghouse. 2009. "Westinghouse Teams with Shaw Group/Laing O'Rourke for UK Nuclear New Build Effort." Westinghouse Electric Co. Butler County, PA.

Wingfield, Brian, and William McQuillen. 2012. "U.S. Imposes Anti-Dumping Duties on Chinese Solar Imports." *Bloomberg* (May 18).

WNA China. 2012. "Nuclear Power in China." World Nuclear Association. http://world-nuclear.org.

WNA Heavy. 2012. "Heavy Manufacturing of Power Plants." World Nuclear Association. http://world-nuclear.org.

WNA South Korea 2012. "Nuclear Power in South Korea." World Nuclear Association. http://world-nuclear.org.

WNN. 2011. "Major AP1000 Component Arrives at Sanmen." *World Nuclear News* (July 27).

WNN. 2012. "Partial Ruling on Olkiluoto 3." *World Nuclear News* (July 6).

Xu, Wan, and Karolin Schaps. 2012. "China Nuclear Firms Team for UK Project Bid-Sources." Reuters (June 21).

Xu, Yi-chong. 2010. *The Politics of Nuclear Energy in China*. Basingstoke: Palgrave Macmillan.

Yuan, Xiao. 2012. "Company Special: Westinghouse Talks Benefits of Nuclear Energy." *China Daily* (February 15).

8 Innovation and Onshoring: The Case for Product Variety

Donald B. Rosenfield

Offshoring and onshoring are major strategic questions for firms as well as major public policy issues. The questions are critical ones for almost any firm. Offshoring often reduces some costs in the short term but might create some competitive challenges in the long term as overseas competitors gain market share. Offshoring part of a portfolio in the belief that the firm can then focus on higher-value items, or the more lucrative parts of the product and service value chain, can lead to erosion of market position in these other parts of the business. However, continuing to produce in a high-labor-cost environment such as the United States can lead to loss of market position for cost reasons, as many U.S. based firms can attest.

From a macroeconomic and public policy perspective, the offshoring question is also of great importance. The great debates we have been engaging in about U.S. competitiveness are focused on questions of offshoring. Increased manufacturing productivity and offshoring are cited as major reasons for the significant decline in manufacturing in high-cost countries such as the United States. In addition, there are calls for supporting domestic firms and for developing conditions that would permit domestic manufacturing to flourish. There are frequent suggestions that manufacturing is very important to U.S. competiveness and the standard of living (Pisano and Shih 2009; Helper, Krueger, and Wial 2012; Grove 2010).

Offshoring questions are often posed as outsourcing questions but the concepts are different. Offshoring simply means producing overseas for a firm's domestic markets, whereas outsourcing means having another independent firm produce specific products. Outsourcing can take place either in the United States or abroad, and it is possible to offshore using one's own facilities and assets. The two concepts are related but imply different strategic choices that can lead to different outcomes. From a macroeconomic and public policy point of view, offshoring is the predominant issue.

From the point of view of an individual firm the decision to offshore or onshore often becomes a question of cost. Firms may look at total product cost, particularly labor costs, and decide to offshore based on the cost differences in producing domestically or abroad. In industries with high labor content such as clothing, firms will frequently go offshore. If the extra transportation costs, duties, and other additional costs are sufficient to reduce the difference, firms will stay onshore.

Using this lens of onshoring versus offshoring, when can manufacturing jobs and productive capacity be developed in a place such as the United States? The approach of the PIE study is to explore the relationship of innovation with production. In the current debates on onshoring and offshoring, innovation and the linkage to manufacturing are frequently cited as the critical factor in the determination of where to locate manufacturing. Many suggest that the key to domestic competiveness is continued innovation (Hockfield and Liveris 2012; Pisano and Shih 2012; Tassey 2010). There is some evidence that offshoring results in a decrease in innovativeness (Fuchs and Kirchain 2010). Furthermore, there are claims that the United States is losing its advantage in innovation (Atkinson and Ezell 2012). The challenge for policymakers is to foster an environment of innovation, and a strategy for firms is to develop competitive advantages in manufacturing that are linked to innovation.

To explore the relationship between innovation and manufacturing, our research strategy is two-pronged. We first interviewed eight operations leaders at a set of seven large firms in the United States that have substantial manufacturing presence in the United States. Most (but not all) are headquartered in the United States and they encompass different industries. We explored how these firms make decisions about production location. Although the relationship between innovation and manufacturing is an important factor in production location decisions, our research uncovered other reasons as well. For example several of our interviewees cited the need to locate production close to customers, in some cases because of transportation cost, in other cases to provide product customization or service.

The companies were selected to encompass a wide range of industries (automotive, electronics, aerospace, consumer products, medical devices, construction, and biopharmaceutical). They are all relatively large companies and are also all successful companies by some measure. Furthermore they all have a major presence in the United States and abroad. We sought to determine how these companies make decisions at each stage of development and production, and what factors influence location decisions and when they might onshore.

In addition we built an analytic model of the total cost of a product and how various product characteristics might affect that cost. The standard approach to developing cost models is to look at the costs of direct product costs, duties, and transportation. But this simple trade-off of direct product cost with transportation and duties fails to take into account a variety of other costs that are often critical. These costs include inventory, handling, markdowns, the impacts of delays, and so forth.

The apparel industry provides an illustration of these issues. The industry sees large forward buys (advance purchases) for many items that are then dispensed to distribution centers and stores in large lots. This approach capitalizes on economies of scale in purchase and transportation. However, this model also entails high inventory costs, frequent markdowns, and even write-offs for products that do not sell. Some firms, such as the Spanish company Inditex (Zara), replenish some of their products on a more frequent basis and offset increased production costs by cost reductions in inventory costs and less frequent markdowns. The firm also does a much better job in fulfilling sales demand. The standard cost models ignore the kinds of strategies around which Zara has constructed its business model. The standard approach also ignores the enhanced service and significant product variety that Zara offers. By building a model of total product cost that depends on the set of key product characteristics, we can develop inferences about the types of conditions that support offshoring versus onshoring.

The next section discusses the linkage between innovation and manufacturing by summarizing the findings derived from the interviews in our sample of large, innovative firms with strong manufacturing presence in the United States. We then present an analytic model for total product cost that identifies innovativeness as a factor that supports onshoring but also identifies two other factors—the ratio of product value to weight and the degree of product variety—that support the decision to onshore. Although others have cited the ratio of value to weight, our analytic model explicitly quantifies this factor as a cost driver.

The second factor, product variety, is significant for two reasons. First, it is closely related to the costs of inventory and service for companies such as Zara. Second, product variety is a form of innovation. It requires flexible production processes, advanced supply chain management, and information technology capabilities. Companies that provide such variety must be innovative in all these ways. By linking high variety to innovation, this type of manufacturing strategy fosters onshoring. So innovation does not just mean product and process innovation, but also the development of a variety of products and processes.

In summary both the model and the interviews suggest that there are three factors that foster onshoring: (1) innovation in products in processes, (2) low ratio of value to weight, and (3) high variety of products. We address all three factors and provide additional focus on variety and its implications.

Onshoring to maximize innovation

Innovation can affect sourcing decisions in a number of ways. First, if the basis of competition is through innovative products and services, production costs might not be as significant a factor in sourcing as it is for other types of products. In this case, other factors such as collocating manufacturing with R&D to maximize innovation might affect profitability more than cost does. Pisano and Shih (2012) suggest that the key determinants of innovation are the degree of linkage between manufacturing and R&D (or alternatively how separable or modular they are) and the maturity of the manufacturing process. For example if manufacturing is closely linked to R&D and process innovations are evolving rapidly, then offshoring can be risky.

Second, there are strong linkages between product development and manufacturing. If design and development are taking place in high-cost locations such as the United States, there may be an incentive to locate manufacturing operations there as well. Manyika et al. (2012) suggest that the need for colocating R&D and manufacturing and the linkage between innovation and manufacturing depend on the particular industry as well as the phase of development. They also cite data to suggest that a high level of innovation (measured in R&D intensity) and a high level of production complexity (measured in the cost of capital relative to revenue) are often associated with the need for colocating R&D and manufacturing. Others have cited this linkage of R&D

and manufacturing in the debates about government policy. For example, Tassey (2010), in developing the case for government support of R&D, cites the importance of colocation of manufacturing and R&D in many industries and in particular emerging industries. As he notes, "because much of the knowledge is tacit in nature . . . co-location synergies are critical" (Tassey 2010, p. 289).

Third, highly innovative products will have significant product development costs and possibly significant capital costs for manufacturing operations, and thus labor costs as a percentage of total costs are not as significant. Helper, Krueger, and Wial (2012) suggest that industries in the United States that are most likely to retain or grow employment are those with high wages. But high-wage industries are also the most innovative. Four industries they study (computers and electronics, chemicals, transportation equipment, and machinery) pay high wages and rank highly on more than one measure of innovation.

Interview evidence: Onshoring for innovation

To explore the linkage between innovation and manufacturing further, we interviewed eight operations leaders at a set of seven large firms in the United States. All of these firms have a substantial presence in the United States and all but one are headquartered there. These firms— Amgen, Caterpillar, Honeywell, Intel, Johnson & Johnson (Medical Devices and Diagnostics), Toyota (Toyota Motor Engineering and Manufacturing North America, or TEMA), and United Technologies (UTC)—are all considered to be innovative. For example, Toyota and Intel were rated number five and number twelve among the world's most innovative firms in 2010 by *Business Week*.[1] United Technologies and Honeywell International were among the top one hundred innovators in the Thomson Reuters rankings.[2] Johnson & Johnson and Caterpillar were ranked number twelve and number nineteen respectively by *Fortune* magazine and Amgen was fifth among pharmaceutical companies in *Fortune*'s evaluation of most admired companies.[3]

The firms we studied covered a wide variety of industries, including automotive/vehicles (Toyota, Caterpillar), pharmaceutical (Amgen), medical devices (Johnson & Johnson), consumer (Johnson & Johnson, Honeywell), construction (Caterpillar, UTC), aerospace (UTC, Honeywell), materials (Honeywell), and electronics (Intel). At each of these companies we asked operations leaders to describe the process from concept through ramp-up for specific products. What drove location decisions to each stage of development? How did the availability of critical assets such as skills drive location decisions at each stage of development? We also asked about manufacturing location decisions—specifically how important colocation of R&D product development with manufacturing was for their firms. Finally, we asked what other factors drove location decisions at their companies.

What we uncovered in these interviews was that manufacturing matters for innovation and is a source and enabler of innovation. However, the linkage to innovation does not drive all manufacturing location decisions—there are other considerations, such as proximity to the customer for purposes of variety and customization and the impact of transportation costs, that also influence location decisions. In addressing these concerns, these companies not only think about process and product innovation but also about how product variety links to manufacturing capabilities.

Our interviewees at the seven different firms cited several aspects of innovation. First, there is often the need for the close relationship between product development and manufacturing, at least for parts of manufacturing. Second, manufacturing processes themselves can be the source of innovation, particularly when the product is complex. Finally, our interviewees often cited the need to locate close to the customer with variety and customization as a strategic goal, thus suggesting a third form of innovation. Locating close to customers enables firms to better understand market needs for their products and how well the products fit the market. It thus enables these firms to better develop the type of product variety that their markets will need.

In terms of specific location criteria, table 8.1 summarizes some of the specific numbers of responses that cite primary location criteria for at least some of their products.

Some of the details of these responses are worth discussing. Several firms cited the colocation of manufacturing, at least part of manufacturing, with development as important for their strategies. Because of this, locating manufacturing in the United States becomes an important strategic option. Our interviewee at the Toyota (TEMA) stated that colocating development and the lead factory is significant. Toyota's Venza, Tundra, and Sienna models for example, were developed for the U.S. market, were styled in California, were developed at the company's center in Ann Arbor, Michigan, had manufacturing engineering in Cincinnati, and were manufactured in the United States.

Table 8.1
Fraction of Companies Citing Specific Reasons as Being Important for Production Sourcing

Manufacturing Location Criterion	Fraction of Companies Citing Specific Reasons for Production Sourcing
Colocation of manufacturing and development	4/7
Process technology development capability	4/7
Being close to customer to know product, customize, or provide variety	3/7
Reduce transportation costs	2/7
Reduce production factor costs	2/7

Our interviewee at Johnson & Johnson (Medical Devices and Diagnostics) also described the importance of having manufacturing closely linked to development, which is largely located in the United States. For UTC, the linkage and the importance of colocation vary considerably by the business. The firm has several centers of excellence around the world. Many, such as Pratt & Whitney, are located in the United States, although that is changing. For Honeywell the importance of the development-manufacturing linkage varied by product and line of business. For aerospace assembly and chemical products, a tight linkage is critical. It is also important for complex products such as boilers and combustors. Within the performance materials and technologies business at Honeywell, development teams work closely with production. Although manufacturing being located next to development is not critical, locating the development teams within the same geographical region such as the United States can have advantages.

Several other firms noted that colocation is not as significant or that it might apply only to a limited extent. For example, at Intel, the development group for wafer fabrication works closely with the lead production fabrication plant, but our interviewee claimed that these two functions do not need to be colocated. At Johnson & Johnson, new contact lenses are developed and produced in Florida, but high-volume production is done mostly in Ireland. For many of these firms, components and standardized products, such as Honeywell thermostats, are typically produced in lower-cost locations.

The second area of innovation that might support manufacturing in the United States is process innovation. Although the design-manufacturing innovation is critical to innovation in products, the process itself can also be a source of innovation. Amgen, Intel, UTC, and Honeywell specifically cited this situation. The use of an advanced process technology often can be the reason for locating in the United States. As our Intel interviewee suggested, "When you have an innovative process technology, it is easier to be in the United States." In a capital-intensive industry in which labor cost is a small percentage of overall cost, the advantages in process improvements can offset any factor-cost disadvantage. However, in some cases, particularly for the pharmaceutical industry, tax considerations can drive locations outside the continental United States.

Although manufacturing matters for innovation, and manufacturing in the United States can enable innovation in the United States, the interviewees at these firms suggested other reasons for locating manufacturing in specific locations. Standard commodity products will generally be located in low-cost areas, but other reasons are important as well. Caterpillar, Honeywell (for some products), and Toyota stated that it is important that they produce where they sell or where products are consumed. There were a variety of reasons for this. First is the need to be close to the customer in order to understand the precise customer expectations and aspirations for the new product. A second reason, which Honeywell cited for complex products such as combustors and boilers, is that locating production closer to consumer markets might allow the firm to tailor the product to the market. Finally, locating close to customers reduces transportation costs from manufacturing sites to customers. These alternate rationales suggest additional reasons for sourcing in high-cost locations such as the United States, which we explore in the next section.

Additional location factors

Our interviews at these seven different companies, although emphasizing the importance of the linkage between innovation and manufacturing, also suggested three other factors: regulatory factors, transportation costs, and product variety.

Regulatory factors are often straightforward (e.g., certain defense-related products must be sourced in the United States), but they can also be subtler. For example, there might be some regulation on local content or product standard that affects location decisions. Although recognizing its importance, we will not explore that factor in detail.

Others (e.g., Manyika et al. 2012, pp. 53–54) discuss regulatory issues in more detail.

A second additional factor favoring onshoring is high transportation costs. The determining factor is the ratio of product value to product weight, which we refer to as the value density. The reason is that the product cost savings from offshoring are often closely related to the value of the item whereas transportation costs are generally proportional to the weight. When the weight is high for a given value (e.g., chemicals) the transportation premium is higher for a given level of savings for the direct production of the offshored product. For products with a high-value density such as electronics or biotech, there is little transportation penalty for offshoring. Helper, Krueger, and Wial (2012) identified this issue and compare value per unit weight (dollars per ton) with job losses during the period from 2001 through 2009. Their data for job losses correlated positively with value density with a coefficient of correlation of 19 percent.

The third additional factor favoring onshoring is when product or service variety is significant and important competitively. Some of the large firms we interviewed as part of this strategy emphasized the need to be close to customers to customize the product. But variety is not something that is easily implemented. Providing variety requires a firm to be innovative in a number of ways. First, it may need flexible production systems to allow frequent changeovers. Second, it needs flexible production scheduling to respond quickly to varying requests. That could involve a highly capable workforce that could manage a wide variety of equipment and varying volumes. Third, it might need highly capable information technologies and supply chain management systems to allow inventories to respond quickly to varying requests and to allow responses to a wide variety of items in stock.

A few examples illustrate these concepts. Consider the Spanish company Inditex and their Zara brand. Zara replenishes products much more frequently than other apparel companies, and the firm does this through a flexible and innovative production system that has significant capacity within reasonable proximity of their Spanish headquarters.

Yet this strategy is not limited to foreign firms. For example New Balance Athletic Shoe does final assembly of 25 percent of its running shoes in the United States (Bowen and Huckman 2008). There is very little production of shoes of any type in the United States, and the New

Balance example is a stunning one in this context. On what basis does New Balance produce in the United States? The answer is wide variety. New Balance provides a wide variety of its product at production sources relatively close to the customer, so it can replenish its product on a regular basis with a short lead time.

For any given item, product can be replenished a number of ways. If customized, then production must be close to the demand source. Otherwise expedited transportation such as airfreight must be used, or the lead time must be long. In the New Balance case, which represents build to stock, the firm must provide inventory support with a plant or warehouse relatively close to either customers or retail channels. This inventory support depends on the lead time from the production source to the inventory stocking point. The longer the lead time the more significant the inventory investment. For items with high variety and hence low demand per item, the required inventory support is higher (the actual mathematical relationship is discussed in the following section). Thus a long lead time would result in prohibitive costs. In other words, if New Balance were providing wide variety and were sourcing products in Asia, it would have very high costs to support its inventory because of the long lead time to Asia. Hence they set up some production in the United States.

However, as is the case for the other companies cited, providing high variety requires capabilities and innovation. The key requirements are a flexible process technology and close alignment of development and manufacturing to develop the wide variety of products and an advanced supply chain management system (as well as information technology system) to deliver the variety. For example one might have to provide the flexible processes to provide the variety or quick response such a strategy requires. Thus some might not view a variety strategy as any different from other types of innovation. The analytic model that follows shows how variety affects product cost.

An analytic model for total costs

To better understand the relationship between onshoring and innovation, we developed an analytic model of total product costs. We consider the following general relationship:

Product costs = manufacturing cost + transportation cost + inventory cost

Note that we are not separately including handling costs (these can be assumed to be the same functional form as transportation in that they will likely be proportional to product weight) and any duties (obviously, higher duties support onshoring).

The model's main contribution is in identifying and explaining the effects of product volume (or alternatively, product variety, which increases as volume decreases) on the onshoring decision. Two additional key variables in the onshoring decision are the identified labor dependence of the product (fraction of product costs that depend on labor) and the ratio of product value to product weight (the value density).

Based on the impact of each of these variables, onshoring becomes more desirable as labor dependence decreases, value density decreases, and variety increases (or alternatively volumes decrease).

The approach of looking at total product costs has some limitations. A product may have a moderate or small cost disadvantage if produced in the United States or similar high-cost location, but location in the United States might be better from the point of view of product development, colocation of product development and manufacturing, or innovation in general. Furthermore, the advanced technologies for the product or process might make offshoring to a low-cost location difficult. Finally, from a competitive point of view, the firm might be focusing on a strategy of innovative products or a strategy of fast service or delivery, so a modest disadvantage in cost may be acceptable if an advantage exists in one of these other areas. However, the approach to understanding the total costs is still important, because too high a cost disadvantage can negate any advantage in other areas.

Manufacturing costs

We first model manufacturing costs. What is the driver of manufacturing cost when innovation is the key to competitive advantage? When innovation is significant, the fraction of costs that are dependent on labor and other factor costs will be lower, which might mitigate the effects of higher wage rates that might exist. With frequent process innovations, for example, costs are usually changing rapidly, and the basis of competition is elsewhere, such as in the availability of the latest features or performance measures. It then follows that any cost advantages from offshoring might not be very large. In addition, when manufacturing is closely linked to R&D, this is an indication that changes in

design are critical to competitive advantage and costs are less significant. Finally, if development costs are high, the impacts of labor costs
are lower. Semiconductors and biotech products are good examples of
this type of phenomenon. For innovative products that may be early
in their life cycles, much of the cost is product and process development
rather than in repetitive production of mature products.

The approach we chose to use to model is to assign a certain fraction
of the manufacturing cost to be dependent on factor costs, and in particular labor. The fraction attributable to labor will be lower for more
innovative products.

To analyze the production cost compared with other costs we consider a unit of product sales or value (e.g., the costs of a dollar of sales).
So the production cost for a unit of sales is

$$C_p = r (1-f + fL) \tag{1}$$

where C_p = production cost per unit value
r = base production cost as a fraction of the sales value
f = labor dependence of product (what fraction of costs is proportional
to labor)
L = labor cost index with $L = 1$ representing a base location.

The assumption is that if innovation is high then the fraction of cost
attributable to labor content is low and the advantage, if any, from
offshoring is lower. When the dependent labor cost fraction is lower
due to the effect of innovation, the situation favors onshoring.

Transportation costs

We next model transportation costs. Recognizing that weight is the key
driver of transportation costs, we get a straightforward expression for
transportation costs. (In some cases product volume drives transportation costs, as exemplified by the situation in which a product might fill
a truck before it reaches maximal weight. In these cases cost is not a
linear function of weight. In most situations the driver is weight.) Then
transportation cost can be equated to

$$C_{tu} = BW$$

where C_{tu} = transportation cost per unit
W = weight per unit
B = unit transportation cost.

As a fraction of the value and hence cost-per-unit value, we can express transportation cost as

$$C_t = BW/V = B/V_D \qquad\qquad (2)$$

where C_t = transportation cost per unit value
V = value per unit
V_D = value density = V/W, value per unit weight.

Thus, if the value density is lower and the impact of transportation is higher, onshoring has an advantage. The relative value of V_D can thus offset higher values of f, the fraction attributable to labor.

Inventory cost

The final component of the cost model is inventory. The inventory model is the most complex part of the model and is also the part of the model that is affected by variety. Modeling inventory cost involves a specific assumption that product variety is provided by having finished goods inventory. An alternative model would be to assume variety is provided by customization. Both approaches will yield the result that high variety increases costs.

The basic concept of the model is straightforward. When product variety goes up (and individual volumes go down) the costs of inventory go up to maintain a given level of service. In a build-to-order system without inventory of finished goods, the effect is similar in that it is costly to provide customized products and this cost goes up as the options increase. One might use build-to-order if demand is hard to predict or forecast error is high. Although inventory costs may be low in this case, other costs, such as a flexible manufacturing system or expedited transportation, will significantly increase.

The purpose of this section is to model the cost of inventory as a function of the parameters that drive it. The driver of inventory is forecast error. If forecast error is high, then more inventory is required to address the uncertainties. To establish how inventory varies with variety we will explore the impact of variety on forecast error. Specifically we need three types of relationships:

• The relationship between inventory and forecast error

• The relationship between forecast error and the lead time over which it is calculated

• The relationship between forecast error and product volume

These three relationships together determine how inventory varies with lead time, which is very different for the onshoring and offshoring cases and high product variety. First, inventory increases as forecast error increases, because reserve stocks or safety stocks are generally proportional to the magnitude of forecast error. Because reserve stocks or safety stocks are typically the predominant part of inventory, we assume that inventories will behave as reserve stocks behave and thus be proportional to the magnitude of the forecast error. We can thus use standard inventory models for safety or reserve stocks. The constant of proportionality will depend on the level of service provided. This is sometimes referred to as the z-factor, which is drawn from the relationship between service and inventory using a normal or Gaussian distribution.

The relationships between forecast error versus lead time and product volume are more complex, but they can be considered from theoretical and empirical points of view. From a theoretical point of view, a probability model can describe how product demand is built up. For example, a demand model will equate demand over time as the sum of independent increments based on the individual time periods. This implies that the variance of demand over the lead time is proportional to the length of the lead time. Hence, the standard deviation of demand variation is proportional to the square root of the lead time.

Similarly one can build a model that represents demand as the sum of independent demands from individual sources or geographic areas. When the forecasting and demand process behave in certain ways[4] then the forecast error is the same as the standard deviation of demand, and we can determine the forecast error as it relates to lead time and product volume. This type of probability model will give guidance to measure the effect of variety when considering offshoring.

We thus model inventory and hence reserve stock as

$C_i = ze$

where C_i = inventory cost

e = forecast error
z = service level multiplier (for example $z = 2$ represents 97.7 percent for a normal distribution).

The expression represents a multiplier of the forecast error. The question is what drives the forecast error? In particular what is the specific effect of lead time and the average demand level? For time, if one models demand as a sum of independent demands from individual time periods, then

$$Y_t = x_1 + x_2 + x_3 + x_{4...} + x_t$$

where x_i = demand in period i
Y_t = demand in periods one through t
or var $Y_t = t$ var x_i

if the individual demand periods are independent and identically distributed.

So the standard deviation of demand is proportional to the square root of the length of the time period,

$$\sigma_t = \sqrt{\mathrm{var}Y_t} = \sqrt{t}\,\sigma_i \tag{3}$$

where σ_i is the standard deviation of demand in any period i and t is the length of the time period.

If forecasts are not biased and forecast error is not correlated over time, then forecast errors are also proportional to the square root of the length of the forecast horizon.

Similarly, if one considers the demand for an individual item that is composed of the sum of all demands from separate geographical areas, then the variance and hence the squared forecast error for that one item for all areas is proportional to the number of geographical periods that are being summed. Thus when one compares items for a single firm one might then expect that the variation or the standard deviation demand will be proportional to the demand.

Formally, suppose demand is the sum of geographically distinct but independent and identically distributed variables. So the total demand D_n is

$$D_n = d_1 + d_2 + d_3 + \ldots + d_n$$

where d_i = demand in geographical area i and the variance of D_n is equal to

var D_n = var d_1 + var d_2 + $\ldots$ + var d_n = n var d_i
if the d_i are independent and identically distributed,
where n is the number of terms in the sum and var d_i is the variance of any of these.

We can rephrase this as

$$\mathrm{var}\, D_n = n\bar{d}_i \left(\mathrm{var}\, d_i / \bar{d}_i \right) = \bar{D}_n \left(\mathrm{var}\, d_i / \bar{d}_i \right)$$

where $\bar{d}_i$ = average demand for each region

$n\,\bar{d}_i = \bar{D}_n$ = average demand for all regions

Because $\bar{D}_n$ is the average total demand, the variance of demand is proportional to the average total demand and the term $(\mathrm{var}\, d_i / \bar{d}_i)$, which is a constant independent of n.

Hence the square root of the variance, the standard deviation, is proportional to the square root of the average total demand:

$$\sigma_{D_n} = \sqrt{\bar{D}_n}\ \sqrt{\mathrm{var}\, d_i / \bar{d}_i} \tag{4}$$

If the forecast errors are unbiased and uncorrelated in time, then forecast error is proportional to square root of total demand.

Because variation is proportional to the square root of demand and is proportional to the square root of time from relations (3) and (4), then it must be that the functional form is the one in **equation (5)**. (One can also derive this relationship by considering the increments of demand over time and distinct areas, that is, demand is the double sum over time and area subdivisions.)

$$\sigma_{\bar{D},t} = K_1 \bar{D}^{.5} t^{.5} \tag{5}$$

where
$\sigma_{\bar{D},t}$ = standard deviation of demand over time t,
K_1 is a constant,
$\bar{D}$ is average demand, and
t is the time horizon.

In summary, theory suggests that for an individual firm, forecast error and hence inventory might be proportional to the square root of the lead time being considered and the average volume of any item.

Theory of course does not always match reality. These models may not be accurate for a number of reasons. First there may be a consistent bias in the forecast or the demand increments could be correlated in time or geography. That is, demand variation and forecast errors may not show these behaviors, so the effect of variety (specifically, the relationships among inventory and time and volume) can also be explored empirically. Specifically, the suggested relationship can be tested with the database of demands for an individual firm. The author and others have actually tested these models in a wide variety of corporate settings (see Rosenfield 1994; Lehman 2011; Amati 2004; and Vega Gonzalez 2009). Although the precise relationships between forecast error and demand variation with lead time and average demand might not show square root relationships, there is typically a strong and concave relationship between demand variation and these two variables. The relationships are between demand variation (either forecast error or the standard deviation of demand) and two independent variables: the time over which the variation is calculated and the average demand. The general form of the relationship is

$$\sigma_{\bar{D},t} = K_1 \bar{D}^\alpha t^\beta \tag{6}$$

where $\sigma_{\bar{D},t}$ = standard deviation of demand for average demand $\bar{D}$ and lead time t

$0.5 < \alpha < 1$

$0.5 \le \beta < 1$.

Rosenfield (1994) shows the relationship for a consumer products company for a wide range of items and shows an alpha value of around 0.7. Figure 8.1 presents the relationships between forecast error variation and demand for a set of items for a period of close to a year for a major biopharmaceutical company. Note that the alpha value is 0.80. Figures 8.2 and 8.3 show the sample relationships between variation and demand and time horizon respectively for a major apparel

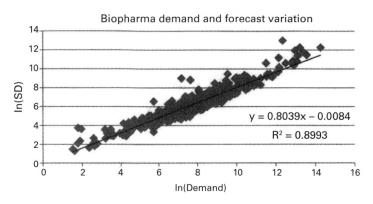

Figure 8.1
Biopharmaceutial firm, variation, and demand relationship
Source: Adapted from Lehman (2011).

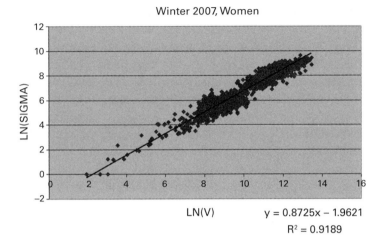

Figure 8.2
Apparel firm, variation, and demand relationship
Source: Vega Gonzalez (2009). © MIT. Reprinted by permission.

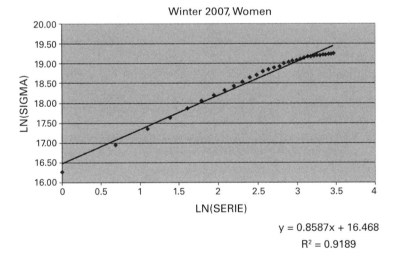

Figure 8.3
Apparel firm, variation, and time relationship
Source: Vega Gonzalez (2009). © MIT. Reprinted by permission.

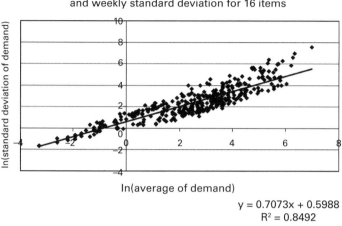

Figure 8.4
Relationship between standard deviation and average demand—food distribution
Source: Amati (2004). © MIT. Reprinted by permission.

company. The relationships are for the winter season for women and with an alpha value of 0.87 for the demand and a beta value of 0.86 for time. For the two seasons and three product categories explored, the alpha values ranged from 0.61 to 0.86 and the beta values ranged from 0.84 to 0.91. Finally, figure 8.4 (Amati 2004) shows the relationship between the demand standard deviation and demand for a major food distributor where the alpha value is 0.71.

Note that the square root relationships that derive from the theoretical model (5) fit within the empirical model (6) with α and β each equal to 0.5. As we see these values are higher and are typically 0.7 or 0.8. Although forecast errors, which actually drive inventory, may result in still higher values of α and β if there is a consistent forecast bias, the general empirical model will illustrate the impact of variety and lead time on inventory costs.

We modify relationship (6) to determine inventory units rather than demand variation (assuming proportionality) and to determine inventory level on a percentage basis by dividing by demand $\bar{D}$. We get the following relationship for percentage inventory as a function of lead time and demand:

$$\text{Inventory} = K_2 \bar{D}^{-(1-\alpha)} t^{\beta}$$

where K_2 is a constant of proportionality depending on the variability of the demand and the service level. Thus inventory costs go up as demand goes up, but in a concave relationship, not as fast as demand. Thus when we divide by demand, we see that per-unit inventory costs go down.

So if we multiply the left side by the annual inventory cost (e.g.,15 percent) and we divide each side by the unit value the left side becomes percentage inventory cost.

Thus,

$$C_i = K_3 \bar{D}^{-(1-\alpha)} t^\beta / V \qquad\qquad (7)$$

where
C_i = inventory cost per unit value
K_3 = constant that depends on service level demand variation and inventory
V = unit value.

Thus if demand decreases, inventory costs on a percentage basis go up.

So the significance of the expression is how variety relates to individual item demands. Assuming that total demand does not change, then as variety increases, individual item demands decrease and inventory costs go up. If these costs significantly increase, then onshoring might become somewhat more favorable.

This analysis is for build-to-stock items. What happens if the firm uses a build-to-order system? The actual effects are somewhat similar in that building to order nearly always represents high variety. In the high-variety build-to-order case, offshoring requires either a long lead time or expedited transportation. The former is unusual and undesired and the latter involves a large premium, which would favor onshoring. Thus, the ultimate high variety of customization would favor onshoring.

Full model

Adding the production, transportation, and inventory costs from **equations (1), (2) and (7)**, we get the following expression:

$C_S = C_p + C_t + C_i$
$C_S = r\,(1\text{-}f + fL)$
$+ B/V_D$
$+ K_3 \bar{D}^{-(1-\alpha)} t^\beta / V$

where

C_S = total or sum of production, transportation and inventory costs as a percentage of sales
C_p = production cost as a percent of sales
C_t = transportation and handling cost as a percent of sales
C_i = inventory cost as a percent of sales
r = base production cost as a percent of sales
f = labor dependence
L = labor cost index
B = unit transportation cost
V_D = value density
$\bar{D}$ = average demand
t = lead time
V = unit value
K_3 = constant that depends on service level demand variation, and inventory.

In summary the full cost of production and distribution includes direct production, transportation, and inventory. There are three major inputs that affect total cost:

• As labor content increases the cost of offshoring through production goes down.

• As the ratio of value to weight goes up, the cost of transportation goes down and the relative cost of offshoring goes up.

• As product variety goes up and individual product volumes go down, the cost of inventory and service goes up, and the relative cost of onshoring decreases.

Innovation is closely linked to onshoring in two ways. First with an environment of product and process innovation, labor content will decrease and any advantage of offshoring decreases. Second, innovation can foster product variety, which also fosters onshoring. Note that the total expression reinforces the impact of innovation through the impact of labor costs and the innovativeness that might be necessary for a variety strategy. The model also points out that there can be other factors such as value density.

Conclusion

The interviews at the seven companies and the analytic model developed in this chapter point out a variety of factors that shape location decisions. Companies cite the linkage to development, the importance of product and process innovation, the need to be near customers, and the impact of transportation costs. The model suggests the impact of labor content, transportation costs, the effect of value and weight, and the impact of variety and product volume also shape whether or not companies should offshore or onshore manufacturing. Thus there is no single reason to onshore or offshore and firms need to address the range of reasons. Each of these reasons has strong theoretical and empirical backing.

However, the model and interviews suggest that innovation plays a special role. Large firms think about innovation of products and processes. When companies are innovative, the impact of labor content is much smaller, and the model suggests that offshoring has a relative disadvantage. But we suggest that innovation plays an even bigger role through innovation for variety. Large firms think about product variety and its role in manufacturing and recognize that they often need to locate close to customers for this reason. Furthermore, our analytic model shows that as variety increases, the cost of inventory and hence servicing the customers becomes much more advantageous as a firm onshores. This type of innovation will play a larger role in sourcing decisions in the future.

Notes

1. http://www.businessweek.com/interactive_reports/innovative_companies_2010.html.

2. Thomson Reuters. *2012 Top 100 Global Innovators.* http://top100innovators.com.

3. CNN Money. *World's Most Admired Companies.* http://money.cnn.com/magazines/fortune/most-admired/2012/full_list/ and http://money.cnn.com/magazines/fortune/mostadmired/2011/snapshots/1057.html.

4. Technically, the forecast error is unbiased or not consistently too large or small and does not show correlation over time.

References

Amati, Michael M. 2004. *Modeling the Value to Retailers Due to Redesigning the Grocery Supply Chain.* Master's thesis, MIT.

Atkinson, Robert D., and Stehen J. Ezell. 2012. *Innovation Economics: The Race for Global Advantage*. New Haven, CT: Yale University Press.

Bowen, H. Kent., and Robert S. Huckman, 2008. *New Balance Athletic Shoe*. Harvard Business School case 606–094.

Fuchs, Erica R. H., and Randolph E.. Kirchain. 2010. Design for Location? The Impact of Manufacturing Off-Shore on Technology Competitiveness in the Optoelectronics Industry. *Management Science* 56 (12): 2323–2349.

Grove, Andy. 2010, July 1. Andy Grove: How America Can Create Jobs. *Business Week*. http://www.businessweek.com/magazine/content/10_28/b4186048358596.htm.

Helper, Susan, Krueger, Timothy, and Howard Wial, 2012, February. *Why Does Manufacturing Matter? Which Manufacturing Matters, A Policy Framework*. Washington, DC: Brookings Metropolitan Program, Brookings Institute.

Hockfield, Susan, and Andrew Liveris, chairs, Advanced Manufacturing Partnership Steering Committee, 2012. *Capturing Domestic Competitive Advantage in Advanced Manufacturing*. Executive Office of the President, Washington, DC.

Lehman, Roy J. 2011. *Allocation Strategy for Production Network Designed to Mitigate Risk*. Master's thesis, MIT.

Manyika, J., J. Sinclair, R. Dobbs, G. Strube, L. Rassey, J. Mischke, J. Remes, et al. 2012. *Manufacturing the Future: The Next Era of Global Growth and Innovation*. McKinsey Global Institute.

MIT LGO. 2012. http://lgo.mit.edu.

Pisano, Gary P., and Willy C. Shih. 2009, July/August. Restoring American Competitiveness. *Harvard Business Review*, 87 (7/8): 114–125.

Pisano, Gary P., and Willy C. Shih. 2012, March. Does America Really Need Manufacturing? *Harvard Business Review* 90 (3): 94–102.

Rosenfield, Donald, 1994. Demand Forecasting. In *The Logistics Handbook*, J. Robinson and W. Copacino, ed., 327–351. New York: The Free Press.

Tassey, Gregory. 2010. Rationales and Mechanisms for Revitalizing U.S. Manufacturing R&D Strategies. *Journal of Technology Transfer* 35 (3): 283–333.

Vega Gonzalez, Myraida Angélica. 2009. *Stock Level Optimization at the Distribution Center through Improved Supply Chain Practices*. Master's thesis, MIT.

9 Trends in Advanced Manufacturing Technology Innovation

Olivier L. de Weck and Darci Reed

The overall goal of this chapter is to explore how innovation in manufacturing process technologies and associated product design affects the prospects for manufacturing in the early twenty-first century. One of the significant interfaces between innovation and production is the invention and improvement of advanced manufacturing technologies. Innovation involves important feed-forward and feedback mechanisms with the real economy. The invention of new products and processes, as well as the improvement of existing processes, leads to higher productivity and expansion of product portfolios and associated service offerings. In turn, the experience and insights gained from manufacturing activities at scale often triggers ideas for new innovations at the front end. There is much innovation happening in manufacturing technology research. Opportunities for entirely new products and services, further productivity gains, and game-changing processes are on the horizon.

In this chapter, we inductively identify a group of twenty-four manufacturing technology areas and aggregate them into seven major categories that promise to have a positive effect on manufacturing in the early twenty-first century. We go on to explain how manufacturing has been defined traditionally and how the processes in a production plant have been viewed as a mainly stepwise linear transformation of inputs toward finished goods. We then provide a definition of *advanced manufacturing* that expands the traditional view in several ways and maps to seven key manufacturing technology categories. The seven technology categories are mapped to major trends that turn manufacturing from a traditionally linear stepwise process to a more integrated and closed-loop enterprise.

Our findings on innovation in manufacturing technologies are based on an internal scan of research at MIT, an external survey of US programs in manufacturing, and an extensive literature search. First, we conducted a scan of research taking place at MIT. We cast a wide net and examined the work of 147 MIT principal investigators (PIs). These individuals work in the broad category "manufacturing, design, and product development," which includes researchers even when they do not label their own work as *manufacturing* or *production* related (MIT Office of Institutional Research). We expanded the initial list of PIs to 199 individuals based on thirty interviews and laboratory visits carried out between July 2011 and August 2012. Second, we conducted a survey of eighty-five U.S. programs in industrial and manufacturing engineering to elicit their views on trends in advanced manufacturing technology research and development. We achieved a response rate of 34 percent and obtained interesting insights, many of them consistent with the findings from our internal scan at MIT. We also gathered important inputs on what makes manufacturing research challenging in the United States and what could be done to improve the U.S. manufacturing research enterprise. One of the key results of this effort was the grouping of advanced manufacturing research into seven distinct technology categories that complement each other. A literature search of about five hundred papers on manufacturing technology research published since 2008 showed that U.S. scholarly research in advanced manufacturing is active but quite distinct from the kind of research funded directly by industry firms.

Classifying manufacturing technologies

We used input from MIT researchers, from other manufacturing engineering programs, and from an extensive literature search to identify seven key categories of emerging and potential advanced manufacturing technologies. These seven categories emerged from an underlying list of twenty-four specific fields (see appendix 9.A). The grouping is based on the principle of life-cycle analysis (LCA) showing where in the life cycle of a manufactured product a particular technology is most likely to contribute. Figure 9.1 summarizes the position of the seven categories along the production life cycle.

The seven technology categories are summarized as follows.

Nanoengineering of materials and surfaces   This involves the synthesis and structuring of functional and multifunctional materials at the nanoscale [10^{-9} m] and microscale [10^{-6} m] from the ground up. The

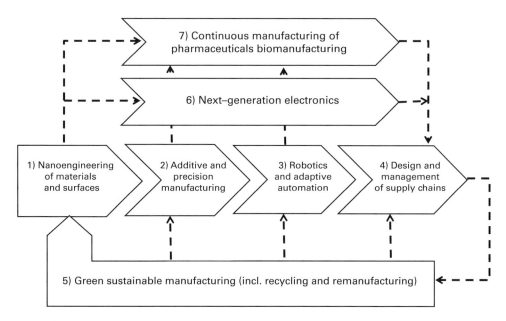

Figure 9.1
Grouping of manufacturing technologies into seven categories along the production life cycle. *Note:* Dashed arrows indicate potential linkages between technology groups.

materials include inorganic metals and composites but also increasingly biological materials and complex polymers. These technologies do not simply modify materials as they exist in nature, but rather create synthetic materials that may not have direct counterparts in the natural world.

Additive and precision manufacturing This category of technologies includes new manufacturing processes that build up macroscopic parts in fibers or layer by layer and achieve complex three-dimensional shapes starting from ingredients in powder or wire form. Often these processes are completely numerically controlled and avoid the need for expensive custom tooling. The creation of compliant actuators and sensors that can operate at a small scale also fits into this group.

Robotics and adaptive automation This group of technologies focuses on the innovative design, use, and adaptation of robots and automation equipment in manufacturing. These technologies either replace or augment human labor during manufacturing, particularly when very high precision is needed, when tasks are easily standardized and repeatable, and when large forces and torques are required. New ways of programming and reconfiguring human-robotic teams and building in adaptability are also being actively pursued in this category.

Design and management of supply chains   The fourth category of research involves planning and managing large and distributed networks of suppliers in multi-echelon supply chains. This set of technologies consists of standards, information technology, algorithms, and database management techniques for planning and tracking millions of individual items that are flowing through factories, distribution centers, and retail stores. The role of the Internet in creating real-time traceability with radio frequency identification (RFID) and other technologies is constantly growing. Besides the ability to efficiently handle the logistics of less-than-truckload shipments, one of the functions of these technologies is to prevent fraudulent imitations from reaching the end consumer. One of the drivers of innovation in this category is the increased specialization of previously highly vertically integrated firms, which requires extensive shipment of components in supplier networks.

Green sustainable manufacturing   The scarcity and potential monopolization of some materials such as rare earth elements, increases in energy and transportation costs, as well as new environmental regulations and customer perception promote more sustainability in manufacturing. These efforts primarily center on closing material loop cycles through reuse, remanufacturing, and recycling of materials, as well as the minimization of energy consumption during manufacturing.

Next-generation electronics   It has been well documented since the 1960s that electronics manufacturing has progressed according to Moore's law, roughly doubling the number of transistors per processor every eighteen months (Moore 1965). However, semiconductors constructed mainly on rigid silicon-based substrates may be reaching physical and economic limits by 2020. The next-generation electronics is currently under development including those using other materials such as Gallium-arsenide-based semiconductors, maskless lithography processes for "printing" circuits—avoiding the need for expensive masks—and the development of organic or flexible substrates.

Continuous manufacturing of pharmaceuticals and biomanufacturing   Significant efforts are underway to scale down the chemical production of small molecule drugs and provide more flexibility and real-time monitoring and control. This may not only improve the efficiency of manufacturing for "blockbuster" mainstream drugs but also enable economic manufacturing of niche or so-called orphan pharmaceuticals. Parallel research is underway to turn cells and bacteria into small programmable factories that have the ability to produce custom-designed proteins and compounds on demand. Although both pharmaceutical manufacturing and biomanufacturing are included in this group, their underlying challenges are quite different.

Taken together these seven technology categories form a complex and innovative tapestry in which new research and development of manufacturing technologies and processes are taking place. Some of these technologies are disruptive in the sense that they displace older processes, and in other cases new technologies can be inserted into existing processes. We also see game-changing technologies under development that have the potential to create entirely new niches or industries. More details and evidence of these trends is provided in the following sections.

Research in manufacturing technologies: MIT as an example

As described previously, we conducted an internal scan of manufacturing-related research at MIT. Figure 9.2 shows the distribution of manufacturing researchers at MIT by their primary affiliation. We found that manufacturing research is active and very distributed at MIT and that it covers all seven technology categories. In total we were able to identify manufacturing PIs in nineteen out of approximately thirty units at the institute.

We found that 72 percent of researchers with interests in manufacturing are affiliated with the following five academic units: Department of Mechanical Engineering (22 percent), Sloan School of Management (22 percent), Department of Electrical Engineering and Computer Science (11 percent), the Engineering Systems Division (10 percent), and the Department of Chemical Engineering (7 percent). Aside from a number of crosscutting programs such as the Laboratory for Manufacturing and Productivity (LMP) and the Leaders for Global Operations (LGO) programs, there are no central and institutionalized coordination mechanisms for manufacturing research at this time. Here, we provide one example of manufacturing-related research at MIT for each of the seven technology categories.

Nanoengineering of materials and surfaces Professor Kripa Varanasi (Department of Mechanical Engineering) has developed the capability

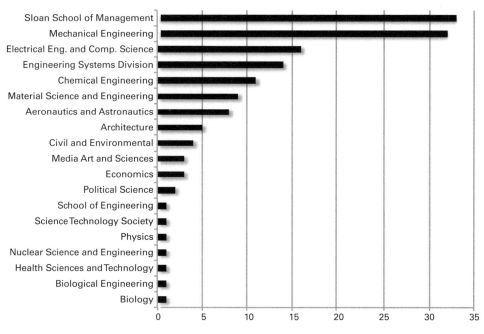

Figure 9.2
Distribution of manufacturing PIs ($N = 147$) at MIT by primary affiliation

to tailor the structure of material surfaces at the nanoscale in such a way that surfaces improve their properties such as their hydrophobicity (ability to reject water and other liquids) by significant amounts (Deng et al. 2009). This could significantly improve the efficiencies of heat exchangers and other chemical process equipment, eliminate the need for some coatings, and change the way that large-scale industrial components are manufactured in the future.

Additive and precision manufacturing   Three-dimensional printing and rapid prototyping of mechanical assemblies is the focus of Peter Schmitt's work at the Media Lab. One of the latest accomplishments is to print a functional watch movement in one single operation, rather than printing all parts individually followed by manual assembly. MIT has been a significant contributor to precision prototyping machines over the years including in the area of Waterjet cutting (OMAX Corporation) and 3D printing (Z-Corporation).

Robotics and adaptive automation   Professor Julie Shah in the Department of Aeronautics and Astronautics and the Computer Science and

Artificial Intelligence Laboratory (CSAIL), is investigating techniques and algorithms for collaborative human-robotic work (Shah and Breazeal 2010). This research shifts the paradigm from robots replacing human labor to robots complementing human labor. This requires robots to become aware of human presence and intent and the development of robust multiagent task allocation and scheduling algorithms under tight precedence constraints.

Design and management of supply chains   One of the main tenets of the lean manufacturing movement is to increase productivity by reducing work-in-progress (WIP) and inventories of materials, parts, and finished goods in the supply chain. However, as supply chains become leaner they also become more vulnerable to supply chain interruptions caused by natural disasters, acts of terrorism, or strikes. Professor Yossi Sheffi (Center for Transportation and Logistics, Engineering Systems Division) is improving our understanding of how resilience in supply chains can be achieved through the use of better modeling, planning, and visualization techniques and the intelligent use of logistics clusters (Sheffi 2012).

Green sustainable manufacturing   A part of the bigger story around sustainable manufacturing is the ability to recycle materials such as metal alloys with unknown or uncertain impurities as in the remelting of multisource aluminum. Professor Randy Kirchain and his colleagues (Department of Material Science and Engineering, Material Systems Laboratory) are working on techniques and algorithms for robust collection, alloying and pricing of aluminum, and other recycling streams under compositional uncertainty (Gregory, Atlee, and Kirchain 2006).

Next-generation electronics   Professor Karen Gleason (Department of Chemical Engineering) and her colleagues are working on so-called organic photovoltaics. This thin film technology enables the manufacturing of solar cells that can be printed onto organic materials such as sheets of cellulose (e.g., paper) or fabrics as a substrate (Barr et al. 2011). Although the efficiencies demonstrated to date are still low (a few percent) there is the prospect that we may one day have electronic components woven into or printed onto our clothes and other flexible substrates.

Continuous manufacturing of pharmaceuticals and biomanufacturing   In the area of manufacturing of small molecule pharmaceuticals Professor Bernard Trout (Department of Chemical Engineering) and his colleagues are working on shrinking the size of chemical manufacturing plants by several orders of magnitude by enabling a continuous (non-batch) process for pharmaceutical manufacturing (Radhakrishnan and Trout 2005). Firms are very interested in this approach because of its potential for transforming the flexibility and economics of the industry. One of the prerequisites for this approach is real-time in-situ sensing and control of chemical processes as well as continuous crystallization processes together with a variety of novel separations and final finishing processes. Professor Kristala Jones Prather (Department of Chemical Engineering) designs modified *E. coli* bacteria to produce biofuels with tailored chemical properties (Moon et al. 2009). This in essence turns cells and bacteria into small "programmable" biological factories. The challenges lie in ensuring consistency of biological processes and the ability to scale up processes to macroscopic quantities. Although much of biological engineering and manufacturing is geared toward medical applications, there is recent interest in producing biofuels more effectively.

There are several conclusions that come from our internal research scan at MIT. First, we found that there is critical mass in terms of faculty and researchers actively working on manufacturing-related topics. This research is distributed across the Institute and involves at least 15 percent of the active faculty at MIT. Second, the research is generally motivated by real problems in industry but tends to tackle long-term issues and out-of-the-box highly innovative concepts that may be game changers and involve significant amounts of risk and upside opportunity. The research we see tends to be nonincremental and quite distinct from the type of research happening at more applied universities that tend to cater more directly to the needs of established firms. The majority of manufacturing-related funding at MIT comes from federal sources (such as NSF, DARPA, DOE, and NIH), and a significant fraction of the research has the potential to generate new patents and start-up firms.

External survey of U.S. academic programs in manufacturing

An external survey was administered as part of this research to solicit the views of leading programs in manufacturing and industrial engineering in the United States. The list of programs was obtained from the ranking of departments in industrial and manufacturing engineering listed in *U.S. News and World Report* from PhD-granting institutions.[1] In total we achieved a response rate of 34 percent from department or program heads (N = 29 responses). The geographical distribution of respondents covers the major regions of the United States as well as leading universities in manufacturing.

The first question on the survey was open-ended and solicited ideas on manufacturing technologies and research areas that are seen as particularly promising. These responses map to the seven manufacturing technology categories without much difficulty (see box 9.1).

We then asked respondents to rate the list of twenty-four emerging technology areas (see again appendix 9.A) in terms of their promise over the next five to ten years. The responses were recorded on a scale from 1 to 5 with 1 being the least promising and 5 being the most promising. Figure 9.3 shows the results of responses regarding the

Box 9.1

Nanoengineering of materials and surfaces

Large area graphene production
Roll-to-roll manufacturing
3D-integrated circuits for semiconductors
Nanoengineered fiber-composite materials
Nanoetching of surfaces

Additive and precision manufacturing

3D printing at home (an extension of current inkjet printers to physical objects)
Rapid prototyping directly integrated into computer-aided design (CAD)
Next-generation injection molding
Advanced electrical discharge machining (EDM)
MOSIS-like foundries (http://www.mosis.com) for prototyping of physical parts
Laser-based manufacturing (fast control, short pulse)
Aluminum-, titanium-, and nickel-based sintering and forming of custom parts

Robotics and adaptive automation

Intelligent smart automation
Embedded sensors in products and processes
Reconfigurable robotics
Human-robot collaboration
Wireless real-time sensing
Networked control for telerobotics and remote operations

Box 9.1
(continued)

Design and management of supply chains

Community-based design
Open-source design of complex cyber-physical products and systems (e.g., AVM)
Decentralized supply chain management
Cloud computing for CAD/CAE/CAM

Green sustainable manufacturing

New energy sources: low-cost high-efficiency photovoltaics (PV)
Concentrated solar power (CSP) for manufacturing
Impact of availability of U.S. natural gas on energy-intensive manufacturing
Waste-to-energy conversion
New battery storage technologies
Super-capacitors for energy storage
Waste power/energy capture within plants
Remanufacturing and recycling at larger scale

Next-generation electronics

Ultraviolet (UV) nanolithography
Multifunctional devices with integrated sensing and control
Computer interfaces (touch, voice, brain waves)
Wireless revolution in manufacturing (wireless factories)
Flexible substrates for electronics

Continuous manufacturing of pharmaceutical and biomanufacturing

Stem cell–based manufacturing
Human organ engineering and manufacturing
Regenerative and personalized medicine
Tissue manufacturing

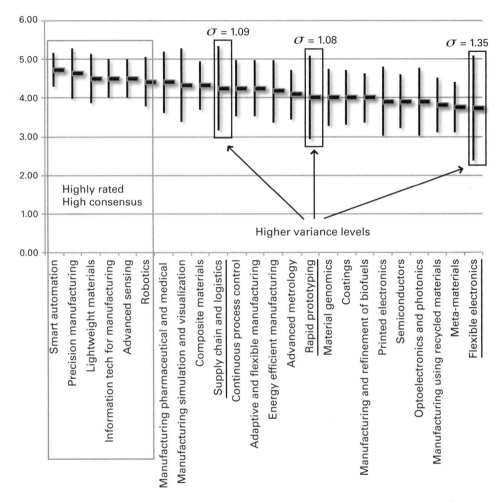

Figure 9.3
Quantitative rating of twenty-four technology research areas (in descending order)

technology areas in decreasing order of average promise. The horizontal dash shows the average score achieved by a technology area. The vertical bars mark one standard deviation (1σ) from the mean. On average all technologies were ranked at least a 3 on the 5-point scale.

The six technologies that achieved an average rating of greater than 4.4 and have a relatively small standard deviation ($\sigma < 1.0$) are as follows: smart automation, precision manufacturing, lightweight materials, information technology for manufacturing, and advanced sensing and robotics. It is noteworthy that most of the top-rated technology areas are in the robotics and adaptive automation category. These technologies all aim at increasing efficiency and precision, and decreasing the direct manual labor content of manufacturing. New kinds of robotics and automation, some acting as assistants to human workers, also fall into this category. Other areas that were highly rated are the development of lightweight materials (e.g., advanced composites) and those related to an increase in the number of advanced sensors and associated information processing during manufacturing.

Three technology areas with a standard deviation greater than 1.0 (on the 5-point scale) emerged: technologies serving to improve supply chain management and logistics, rapid prototyping, and flexible electronics. Our results confirm the large variation of opinion among respondents regarding the promise of technologies such as 3D printing. Although proponents of the technology claim that we will soon be able to manufacture many (or even most) products directly with rapid prototyping machines, perhaps even from our homes, detractors point out that parts manufactured through such techniques often do not have the necessary lifetime properties (such as hardness, durability, or fatigue life) that are required to support heavy-duty real-world use. Likewise, opinions differ about the prospects of electronic circuits printed onto flexible substrates. It is unclear whether some of the manufacturing technologies whose rating showed a large standard deviation are in fact very promising but are underappreciated by the larger community because of their novelty and lack of track record or whether there are fundamental physical or economic constraints at play that limit the future potential of these manufacturing technologies. More research will be required to examine this question more closely.

Finally, we elicited challenges faced by U.S. academics in the area of manufacturing technology research. In essence, respondents described the challenges facing U.S. university-based researchers in manufacturing as falling into two broad areas: resource limitations and collaboration with industry.

Respondents reported that the financial resources needed to create and maintain sophisticated and cutting-edge infrastructures for manufacturing research at a university are often very large (depending on the technology in question, several millions of dollars). The level of vigor in manufacturing research is mainly driven by federal funding priorities (e.g., National Science Foundation, Department of Defense, and Defense Advanced Research Projects Agency [DARPA]). When the federal government makes manufacturing research a priority and provides funding, then universities apply for grants and pursue such research. An example is the DARPA "Adaptive Vehicle Make" program that started in 2010.[2] However, when federal priorities shift and the funding goes away, so does the ability of many universities to work in these areas.

Outside of individual grant opportunities, manufacturing is often not perceived as a promising leading-edge area of research by university senior administrators and faculty search committees. Faculty members sometimes disguise or dress up their research interests in manufacturing by highlighting the connections of the research to the underlying fundamental physics or biology rather than the real-world applications of their work. Several respondents highlighted that it is difficult (but not impossible) to get U.S.-born students interested in manufacturing research and careers. At many universities only a subcritical mass of faculty members and students are interested in manufacturing. Many tend to gravitate more toward other areas perceived as more attractive, for example, energy, robotics, and so on, although some of these technology research areas themselves have direct or indirect relevance to manufacturing.

Another area that was highlighted in the external survey is related to the challenges of collaboration between universities and industry in performing manufacturing technology research. Especially when public money is unavailable or insufficient, universities partner with local or regional industry to carry out research. Universities often use industry facilities to build prototypes and test research ideas, but often give intellectual property (IP) rights mainly to the industry sponsor. It appears that a substantial number of universities are willing to trade away some, or all, of their IP rights from inventions arising out of the research in exchange for access to sophisticated facilities.

Industry tends to want quick answers, and faculty members and students tend to want to publish and do longer-term projects. There appears to be a tension between the incentives and interests of most faculty members and the need for companies to solve problems that arise in their day-to-day manufacturing operations. Academic researchers report being generally interested in working on problems motivated by industry but often feel shackled by industry legal staff when trying to reach agreement on sponsored research. Several academic respondents articulated a need to develop joint value propositions for manufacturing technology research in the United States. Respondents expressed a desire for new ways to enhance university-industry manufacturing research such as state-sponsored initiatives, industry-sponsored labs at universities, and nonprofit applied research institutes. These models would provide more long-term stability to manufacturing technology research in the United States compared to the rather short-term and volatile mechanisms in place today that appear to be very dependent on changing federal budget priorities. Taken together these comments suggest that there is room for new mechanisms and organizations that bridge between industry and academia in US manufacturing research. The nonprofit manufacturing innovation institutes that have been proposed by the American Manufacturing Partnership (AMP) are one example.[3]

Cross-comparison of technology areas across manufacturing reports
A number of important reports that have been published on manufacturing in recent years stress the importance of innovation and the role of manufacturing technology research. Five of them with particular national or international prominence, published in the early 2010s, are listed in box 9.2. In table 9.1 we map the manufacturing-relevant technologies highlighted in those reports to the seven manufacturing technology categories we identified inductively.

The rows of table 9.1 show the seven technology categories identified here and the columns correspond to the five reports published between June 2011 and November 2012. The importance of nanoengineering and new materials is discussed in all five reports. Consistently mentioned are lightweight materials (e.g., low-cost carbon-fiber composites) for application in fuel-efficient vehicles and the development of biocompatible materials for medical devices. Additive and precision manufacturing is mentioned in three out of five reports. Advances in robotics and automation are featured in four out of five reports,

Box 9.2

1. President's Council of Advisors on Science and Technology (PCAST), *Report on Ensuring American Leadership in Advanced Manufacturing*—June 2011
2. American Manufacturing Partnership (AMP), *Report on Capturing Domestic Competitive Advantage in Advanced Manufacturing*—July 2012
3. Institute for Defense Analyses (IDA), *Report on Emerging Global Trends in Advanced Manufacturing*—March 2012
4. US Manufacturing Competitiveness Initiative, *Make: An American Manufacturing Moment*—December 2011
5. McKinsey Global Institute, McKinsey Operations Practice, *Manufacturing the Future: The Next Era of Global Growth and Innovation*, November 2012

Table 9.1
Cross-Comparison of Advanced Technology Research Areas in Recent Reports

Technology Category	1 PCAST Report	2 AMP Report	3 IDA Report	4 U.S. Competitiveness Initiative	5 McKinsey Report
1 Nanoengineering of materials and surfaces	✔	✔	✔	✔	✔
2 Additive and precision manufacturing		✔	✔		✔
3 Robotics and adaptive automation	✔	✔	✔		✔
4 Design and management of supply chains	✔	✔	✔	✔	✔
5 Green sustainable manufacturing		✔	✔	✔	✔
6 Next-generation electronics	✔	✔	✔		
7 Pharmaceuticals and biomanufacturing	✔	✔	✔	✔	✔

Note: A check mark indicates that a particular technology category is discussed in the report.

particularly in the context of enabling higher degrees of flexibility. The broad category of design methodology and supply chain management is also universally mentioned. However, different reports emphasize different aspects of this category. Green and sustainable manufacturing is mentioned in four reports, focusing mainly on closing materials cycles and waste recovery. Next-generation electronics are discussed in three out of five reports, particularly with respect to optoelectronics and photonics. Pharmaceutical and/or biomanufacturing appears in every report and is perhaps viewed as one of the most innovative areas in which U.S. research is world leading and most promising.

Although the detailed examples of technologies mentioned differ from report to report, there appears to be broad agreement that the seven technology categories identified here are important and that they represents a nonoverlapping set of activities.

Literature search on advanced manufacturing technology research

Finally, we tested the relevance of our seven categories of advanced manufacturing through a literature search of papers written on advanced manufacturing research between 2008 and 2011. In total we were able to identify 558 peer-reviewed journal articles on advanced manufacturing during this three-year period. We suspect that this is only a subset of the research published because many papers on manufacturing research are presented at conferences that are not listed on the Web of Science. Regardless, we found that published research in advanced manufacturing falls mainly into the ten topics listed in box 9.3, which themselves map well into the seven technology categories.

Box 9.3

Smart automation and autonomy
Reconfigurable manufacturing systems
Process modeling, monitoring, and optimization
Machine tools and instrumentation
Design integration
Rapid prototyping and additive manufacturing
Micromachining
Sustainable manufacturing
Biomanufacturing
Medical devices

We found that a large fraction of the published manufacturing research conducted in the United States is concentrated in about a dozen universities, especially the Massachusetts Institute of Technology; Carnegie Mellon; University of California, Berkeley; University of Michigan; Georgia Institute of Technology; Pennsylvania State University; and Stanford University. Six of these seven are also the member universities of the AMP, which is a major industry-academic partnership created with encouragement from President Obama in 2010. Another set of universities is also active in applied research but tends to be less active in publishing their findings. We hypothesize that these universities are the ones that are also the ones who are more tied by IP arrangements with industry as discussed previously. In summary, we find that the United States continues to generate a steady stream of quality research on advanced manufacturing technology topics.

Definition of and implications for advanced manufacturing

Now that we have summarized important trends and categories in advanced manufacturing research, the question is, How do these manufacturing innovations affect and change manufacturing today and in the future? In order to understand this better we need to map these technology categories to the generic architecture of a typical manufacturing enterprise. Figure 9.4 shows the layout of a typical manufacturing plant. We show this to illustrate the traditional view of what manufacturing is and what its various inputs and outputs are.

Traditional manufacturing is essentially the stepwise transformation of raw materials (coming from mainly natural sources such as underground mines, forests, and so forth) into finished goods. Raw materials are provided to the manufacturing plant by the incoming supply chain and are temporarily stored in a warehouse. The main function of the warehouse is to serve as a buffer and to ensure that the production line will never be starved of upstream input materials. The next step is typically parts fabrication (PF), that is, the manufacturing of individual components that are the fundamental building blocks of the finished products. In a highly vertically integrated firm most of the parts are fabricated in-house (similar to the Ford Model T assembly line in the 1920s or Boeing aircraft in the 1970s and 1980s). More recently firms have become less vertically integrated and have increased the number of supplied or purchased parts that are coming in at some intermediate station and are then stored in an internal supplied parts buffer.

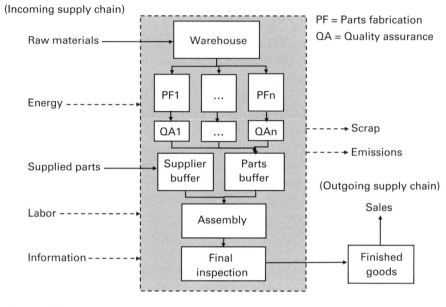

Figure 9.4
Layout of a traditional manufacturing plant

Quality assurance (QA) is critical to ensure that parts made in-house and those purchased from suppliers meet all the tolerances and other characteristics required by downstream manufacturing steps. Allowing defective parts to slip through to the next process step can be very costly, increasing scrap and rework and decreasing productivity. One of the recent trends in manufacturing has been to measure quality directly during the fabrication of parts, for example, using statistical process control rather than after fabrication is complete and errors have accumulated. This allows catching problems much earlier but requires sophisticated sensors and software and a higher level of integration and skill in the manufacturing plant.

Once parts are available, they are used for final assembly of the product. Depending on the complexity of the product, assembly may occur in multiple stages involving subassemblies, which can be put together on parallel preassembly lines that feed into the main production line. Once final assembly is complete a final inspection typically occurs, checking that the product works as intended and that it meets all requirements. Finished goods are subsequently stored for distribution to their intended markets through the outgoing supply chain.

In addition to raw materials, there are several other key inputs into the manufacturing plant. These include energy, typically in the form of fossil fuels or electricity, information from suppliers and machine vendors and customers, as well as human labor of varying levels of skill. In order to increase productivity the amount and cost of these inputs per unit of output must be minimized while maintaining the desired levels of throughput and quality. On the output side there is a need to maximize the useful outputs (finished goods) and minimize non-value-added outputs such as scrap and emissions (noise, air pollutants, residual chemicals).

In the past, the emphasis has been almost entirely on maximizing throughput and productivity of a manufacturing plant for a relatively small assortment of standard product configurations. However, since the late 1980s firms have become more aware of varying customer needs in different market segments. This has led to a larger number of variants on the production line and the challenges associated with manufacturing a larger variety of products and maintaining high levels of quality and efficiency (Hauser and de Weck 2007). Another trend is that manufacturing is increasingly using the concept of a push-pull boundary. Whereas traditionally manufacturing plants would mainly schedule their output based on sales forecasts ("push"), many plants today fabricate parts only based on forecasts, and carry out assembly based on actual orders received ("pull") on a per-shop-keeping-unit basis (Ahn and Kaminsky 2005). The Dell Computer Company was one of the early pioneers in this strategy, also known as *postponement*. This requires a sophisticated integration of production planning and scheduling with plant operations and supply chain management. Higher levels of skill and flexibility are required from production facilities, staff, and supporting information systems to deal with this dynamic complexity.

The insights we have gained in our research on advanced manufacturing technologies lead us to a much broader definition of what advanced manufacturing is in the twenty-first century. Traditional manufacturing as depicted in figure 9.4 is also shown at the top of figure 9.5 in a more abstract way, consisting mainly of fabrication and assembly and the making of finished goods in a more-or-less linear stepwise fashion. We find that this traditional linear view of manufacturing is no longer adequate. Manufacturing and production have become much broader and less linear and are changing in four fundamental ways. These are shown as shaded elements in figure 9.5 (bottom).

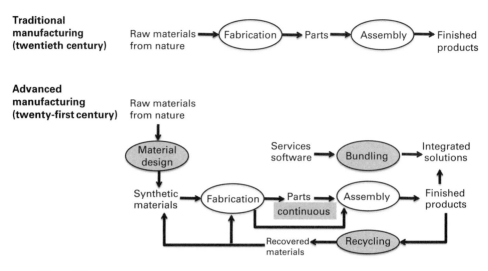

Figure 9.5
Definition of advanced manufacturing in the twenty-first century (bottom) as an expansion of traditional twentieth-century manufacturing (top)
Note: Shaded elements represent four major new trends in manufacturing that expand on the traditional linear view.

First, figure 9.5 (bottom left) shows that although fabrication and assembly are still essential and also form the core of manufacturing in the twenty-first century, our ability to synthesize new materials is now so advanced that it must be considered to be an important a step as fabrication and assembly itself. We have always processed natural materials through a combination of mechanical, chemical, and thermodynamic processes (e.g., by alloying) but the starting point was materials as they occur naturally. Material design and synthesis enables creating materials from scratch and giving them internal and surface properties that are tailored and that do not occur naturally. This has profound downstream implications, for example, the elimination of subsequent fabrication and assembly steps such as coatings that potentially become unnecessary.

Second, we observe a blurring of the boundary between fabrication and assembly in addition to the introduction of ultra-efficient processes and automation. Traditional manufacturing was very batch oriented and discretized the production process into a set of distinct steps, separated in time and space. Today, continuous manufacturing in batch sizes of "one" is increasingly practiced. This enables more synchronous monitoring, eliminates intermediate buffers, and increases process flexibility, but it also requires more sophisticated equipment, synchronization, and in-depth knowledge.

Third, the "product" is often not just a physical artifact or widget but an integrated solution that involves bundling of physical products with services and software. A number of firms we interviewed as part of the overall project highlighted how the manufacturing of a physical product is often only a means to an end, that is, the offering of an end-to-end solution to their customers. It was mentioned (by a small manufacturer of process modules for the pharmaceutical industry) that the service portion of the product-software-service bundle often contributes the majority of profits. However, the service could often not be offered on its own, without deep know-how of the physical product. This is relevant for production because products that are part of a product-software-service bundle often contain more sensors, require higher quality and reliability, and have more software content compared to traditional "inert" products.

Finally, the fourth trend is the return of recycled materials back to fabrication or even material synthesis. Here we can distinguish among reuse, remanufacturing, and recycling depending on how far upstream the material cycle reaches. Increasingly, raw material prices have become more volatile and supply for some rare elements is controlled by few nations. Hence, there is a strong incentive for material recovery that goes beyond purely ecological and environmental considerations.

The picture that twenty-first century advanced manufacturing presents is greatly expanded and more complex than in the past. Based on the framework shown in figure 9.5 we propose the following definition of advanced manufacturing: the creation of integrated solutions that require the production of physical artifacts coupled with valued-added services and software that can also exploit custom-designed and recycled materials and using ultra-efficient processes. Table 9.2 maps the seven manufacturing technology categories to this expanded view of manufacturing and the four emerging trends highlighted in figure 9.5.

For example, research in nanoengineering of materials and surfaces directly enables material design. We believe that this is not a mere enhancement of what was done previously but a fundamental new step in production that is as important as parts fabrication and assembly. Material synthesis has the potential to embed functionality directly in materials from the start (e.g., embedded sensors, functionally graded materials), may reduce the part count of products, leading to more integral and lighter-weight products in the near-term future.

Table 9.2
Mapping of Manufacturing Technology Categories to Major Trends in Advanced Manufacturing

Technology Category/Major Trends	1 Material Design	2 Continuous Processes	3 Product Service Bundling	4 Recycling
1 Nanoengineering of materials and surfaces	✔	✔	✔	✔
2 Additive and precision manufacturing	✔	✔		
3 Robotics and adaptive automation		✔	✔	
4 Design and management of supply chains			✔	✔
5 Green sustainable manufacturing	✔	✔		✔
6 Next-generation electronics	✔		✔	✔
7 Pharmaceuticals and biomanufacturing	✔	✔		✔

Note: A check mark indicates that a specific technology category directly supports the corresponding aspect of advanced manufacturing.

Advances in additive and precision manufacturing mainly benefit parts fabrication. Rather than starting with large chunks of material and removing what is not needed, additive precision manufacturing creates parts from the ground up, for example, by printing parts layer by layer. Another important objective is to reduce the need for customized and capital-intensive tooling for parts fabrication.

The technologies in the category of robotics and adaptive automation aim to replace or augment human labor. Besides providing robots and automation equipment that is easy to program and maintain, and being flexible and reliable, there is a desire to reduce capital expenditures. Robots are becoming increasingly competitive when their acquisition and operation costs are considered relative to each unit of output produced. Traditionally, robots have been used mainly during assembly but they are increasingly deployed upstream in fabrication as well as downstream in the supply chain.

Improvements in supply chain design and management affect especially the end of the value chain including the on-demand distribution of finished products, the management of information and data interfaces with customers as part of integrated solutions that bundle physical artifacts with software and services, as well as the tracking and recycling of materials at the end of life. Besides tracking the flow of items through barcodes and RFID chips, innovations in supply chain management also affect the predictive scheduling of production.

Green and sustainable manufacturing technologies help recover materials from waste streams and reduce significantly the environmental footprint and energy consumption of manufacturing. Even accurately determining the ecological footprint and the use of resources in manufacturing has given rise to innovative solutions and technologies.

The category of advanced electronics affects the manufacturing process itself through improved sensing and control and also through embedding sensors and electronics in products directly. In some cases embedded electronics are a precondition for bundling of physical products with services and software (e.g., GPS chips as a prerequisite for location-based services). For example, products that can sense their own state and alert operators when certain maintenance actions are required offer opportunities for value-added services. The role of the Internet in connecting the physical world with the virtual world is a significant aspect in this category.

Innovations in manufacturing of pharmaceuticals and biomanufacturing begin with a deep understanding of function and structure at the molecular and cellular stage (material design) and extend into the continuous processing of materials into more complex molecules and compounds such as new drugs and biofuels, among others.

Conclusion

We have observed significant amounts of innovation in advanced manufacturing technologies. MIT and other U.S. universities continue to innovate in some key technology areas related to manufacturing. Many of the innovations we found are potentially transformative and not simply evolutionary. Manufacturing technology research tends to cluster into seven manufacturing categories that are somewhat orthogonal and complementary to each other, summarized in box 9.4.

Which of these technologies are ultimately adopted by firms depends on the industry and location as well as strategic decisions by firms as they seek competitive advantages. Firms should carefully think about which manufacturing technologies they can acquire as commodities and which areas they can innovate in and pull to open new markets.

Box 9.4

Nanoengineering of materials and surfaces

Synthesis of multifunctional materials at the nanoscale from the ground up

Additive and precision manufacturing

Building up components by adding layers of material in complex 3D shapes or extrusion of fibers with customized properties

Robotics and adaptive automation

Using robotics to substitute or complement human labor in new ways

Design and management of supply chains

Enabling flexible, resilient, and increasingly decentralized distribution of components and products as well as new approaches to web-enabled manufacturing

Green sustainable manufacturing

New manufacturing and recovery processes that minimize the use of energy, recycle materials, and reduce waste and emissions

Next-generation electronics

Advanced circuits using nonsilicon materials, using maskless processes and flexible, potentially organic substrates

Continuous manufacturing of pharmaceuticals and biomanufacturing

Continuous manufacturing of small molecules as well as turning cells and organisms into programmable factories

In this context we define advanced manufacturing as being broader than traditional linear manufacturing. Instead, advanced manufacturing is the creation of integrated solutions that require the production of physical artifacts coupled with valued-added services and software. At the same time, advanced manufacturing can exploit custom-designed and recycled materials and uses ultra-efficient processes.

The technology research in this chapter leads us to three key observations about the emergence of new technologies in advanced manufacturing. First, some technologies on the horizon may enable classes of products that do not yet currently exist. Examples of these include non-silicon-based semiconductors, wearable electronics, and new drugs and fuels from biology. Many of these have the potential to create new niches that may generate substantial demand and economic activity, if not entirely new industries. A key question is whether these new products will generate sufficient value and interest over time to coexist with or partially substitute for existing products.

Second, we see the rise of "programmable" manufacturing processes that do not rely on capital-intensive tooling and fixtures. One of the trends we observe is to counteract the need for highly expensive and unique manufacturing equipment (e.g., $5 billion semiconductor fabs or $500,000 stamping dies). Examples of such technologies include 3D printing and maskless nanolithography. There are several critical questions that arise about these new flexible manufacturing processes and technologies, for example: Can they guarantee the required tolerances? Will they catalyze distributed manufacturing?

Third, there is innovation in technologies that enhance productivity and flexibility in existing large-scale manufacturing processes. As pointed out in *Made in America,* the speed of productivity gains is one critical element in a nation's competitiveness (Dertouzos et al. 1989). The technologies focused on productivity enhancement are not so much game changers as they are enhancing existing manufacturing and inserting themselves at key points along the value chain. Examples of such technologies include RFID tracking of parts during manufacturing and distribution, recycling of aluminum under compositional uncertainty, human-robotic collaboration, and flexible automation. One of the key questions is, Will there be uptake of such technologies in the U.S. industrial base?

None of these technologies is a silver bullet for the manufacturing problems in the United States—or any industrialized nation. We believe that it is the skillful combination of advanced manufacturing technologies, with innovative product designs, value-added services, and disciplined production processes, that is most likely to lead to success.

Appendix 9.1

ID-related technology

1. Flexible electronics
2. Supply chain and logistics
3. Rapid prototyping
4. Manufacturing simulation and visualization
5. Manufacturing pharmaceutical and medical
6. Printed electronics
7. Optoelectronics and photonics
8. Energy-efficient manufacturing
9. Precision manufacturing
10. Continuous process control
11. Adaptive and flexible manufacturing
12. Lightweight materials
13. Robotics
14. Material genomics
15. Coatings
16. Composite materials
17. Semiconductors
18. Manufacturing using recycled materials
19. Advanced metrology
20. Manufacturing and refinement of biofuels
21. Smart automation
22. Information technology for manufacturing
23. Advanced sensing
24. Meta-materials

Notes

1. http://grad-schools.usnews.rankingsandreviews.com/best-graduate-schools/top-engineering-schools

2. DARPA Adaptive Vehicle Make (AVM) program, http://www.darpa.mil/our_work/tto/programs/adaptive_vehicle_make__(avm).aspx

3. "Advanced Manufacturing Partnership Report" (July 2012), http://www.whitehouse.gov/sites/default/files/microsites/ostp/pcast_amp_steering_committee_report_final_july_17_2012.pdf

References

Ahn, H. S., and P. Kaminsky. 2005. "Production and distribution policy in a two-stage stochastic push-pull supply chain." *IIE Transactions* 37 (7).

Barr, Miles C., Jill A. Rowehl, Richard R. Lunt, Jingjing Xu, Annie Wang, Christopher M. Boyce, Sung Gap Im, Vladimir Bulović, and Karen K. Gleason. 2011. "Direct Monolithic Integration of Organic Photovoltaic Circuits on Unmodified Paper." *Advanced Materials* 23 (31):3500–3505.

Deng, T., K. K. Varanasi, M. Hsu, N. Bhate, C. Keimel, J. Stein, and M. Blohm. 2009. "Nonwetting of Impinging Droplets on Textured Surfaces." *Applied Physics Letters* 94 (133109).

Dertouzos, Michael L., Richard K. Lester, Robert M. Solow, and the MIT Commission on Industrial Productivity. 1989. *Made in America: Regaining the Productive Edge.* Cambridge, MA: MIT Press.

Gregory, J., J. Atlee, and R. Kirchain. "A Process-Based Model of End-of-Life Electronics Recycling Driving Eco-Efficiency-Informed Decisions." Paper presented at the 2006 IEEE International Symposium, May 8–11, 2006.

Hauser, D., and O. L. de Weck. (June 2007). "Flexibility in component manufacturing systems: evaluation framework and case study." *Journal of Intelligent Manufacturing* 18 (3):421–432.

Moon, Tae Seok, Sang-Hwal Yoon, Amanda M. Lanza, Joseph D. Roy-Mayhew, and Kristala L. Jones Prather. (2009). "Production of Glucaric Acid from a Synthetic Pathway in Recombinant Escherichia coli."*Applied and Environmental Microbiology* 75 (3):589–595.

Moore, G. E. 1965. "Cramming More Components onto Integrated Circuits." *Electronics Magazine* 38, no. 8 (April 19).

Radhakrishnan, R., and B. L. Trout. 2005. "Order parameter approach to understanding and quantifying the physico-chemical behavior of complex systems." In *Handbook of Materials Modeling,* edited by MIT-Norvatis Center on Continuous Manufacturing. Dordrecht, Netherlands: Springer.

Shah, J., and C. Breazeal. 2010. "An Empirical Analysis of Team Coordination Behaviors and Action Planning With Application to Human-Robot Teamwork." *Human Factors* 52 (2):234–245.

Sheffi, Y. 2012. *Logistics Clusters: Delivering Value and Driving Growth.* Cambridge, MA: MIT Press.

Index